THE
WEST
BANK
STORY

RAFIK HALABI

Translated from the Hebrew by Ina Friedman

HBJ

A HELEN AND KURT WOLFF BOOK
HARCOURT BRACE JOVANOVICH, PUBLISHERS
NEW YORK AND LONDON

Library of Congress Cataloging in Publication Data

Halabi, Rafik.
The West Bank story.

"A Helen and Kurt Wolff book."
German edition: Die Westbank Story.
1. Jewish-Arab relations—1949-   . 2. Jordan
(Territory under Israeli occupation, 1967-   )—
Politics and government. 3. Halabi, Rafik. 4. Druzes—
Israel—Biography. 5. Journalists—Israel—Biography.
I. Title.
DS119.7.H345613 1982   956'.046   81-47900
ISBN 0-15-195741-X   AACR2

Printed in the United States of America

C D E

*To my father and mother, who taught me tolerance,
and to my children, who will acquire it from me*

CONTENTS

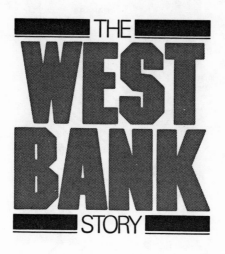

The West Bank

1
CREDENTIALS

I am an Israeli patriot, though I am not a Jew. I live in a country that remains a kaleidoscope of national cultures, in spite of untiring efforts to forge a single, unifying national ethos. Arabs consider me a Palestinian, though I have no desire to become a citizen of an independent Palestinian state —if and when such an entity comes into being. I am a Druse, a member of a minority religious sect that is only one of the sects that make up the Arab community in Israel, and I live in a country whose Jewish majority is itself but a tiny minority among the sea of Arabs in the Middle East. Little wonder, then, that both the full weight and the finer points of the national imbroglio in this region touch directly on my life every day.

Over the past few years I have been a regular on the lecture circuit that covers kibbutzim throughout the country. Since I am the correspondent who reports on the occupied territories for Israel's state-run—and so far only—television network, there is no need for a lengthy introduction of me at these affairs. Instead, the cultural chairmen who usually preside tend to open the session with a fairly uniform line that goes something like this: "We are pleased to have with us tonight a reporter from Israel Television, and we hope he won't provoke us too much. Be prepared to present your questions at the end of the lecture." When question time comes, the formula is again so uniform that I sometimes suspect the kibbutz movements have circulated a leaflet among their members listing the queries that should be posed to "the national

3

nuisance." One question that inevitably comes up is: "Who are you, Rafik Halabi? A Druse? An Israeli? A Palestinian? An Arab? Or perhaps a Zionist? The Arab students here choose to define themselves as Israeli-Palestinian Arabs. Who are you?"

In July of 1979 I was invited to speak at Kibbutz Givat Chaim, an established and prosperous collective midway between Tel Aviv and Haifa. When my lecture was over and the audience was called on for questions, I recognized the first questioner as a former Knesset member and a veteran of the Mapai party. He studied me closely, as if trying to measure the sincerity of my words, and challenged, "Why can't you speak in terms of clear-cut positions? How would you act if you were a military governor in the occupied territories?" Another member, capitalizing on the tension generated by the first question, pressed further. "We differ on basic issues," he declared, "and my Israeliness bears no resemblance to yours. I came to Givat Chaim after the Holocaust, at a time when the Arabs in this area were busy massacring Jews. You don't begin to understand the meaning of the Holocaust to the Jewish people. You don't begin to understand the significance of the Ingathering of the Exiles." Still others in the audience criticized what they took to be my philosophy and, as if they were trying to make the point that I, in particular, was shamefully ungrateful to the country in which I lived, argued that "in Egypt you wouldn't be allowed to speak freely, or in Syria or Iraq. But here, in this kibbutz, you can stand up and imply that you don't reject the notion of self-determination for the Palestinians, and no one has even attacked you!"

The demand that I come forth with clear-cut positions and definitive answers and the disregard of—or perhaps obliviousness to—the personal dilemma I face in attempting to confirm my own national identity are challenges I have faced every hour of every day since I began confronting the citizens of Israel with the hard truth about the national struggle in this region. So the question "Who are you, Rafik Halabi?" is a relevant one, and perhaps should be the first issue addressed in this book, in order to establish the somewhat out-of-the-ordinary credentials of its author.

I was born in the Druse village of Dalyat el-Carmel, on the Carmel range south of Haifa, in 1946. The village has existed since the early eighteenth century, but the Druse sect goes back much further, to the eleventh century, when it broke off from Islam during the period of Fatamid rule in Egypt. The Druse believe in one God and in the transmigration of souls, but that is about all I can say, because the Druse religion is secret and for centuries we have been scrupulous about not revealing its mysteries to outsiders. In fact, even the members of the community are divided into the *okal,* who are schooled in the religion, and the *juhal,* who are not. Today the Druse number about 300,000, who live in the mountainous regions of Syria, Lebanon, and Israel. The 33,000 Israeli Druse are concentrated in eighteen villages in the Galilee and on the Carmel and usually constitute an absolute majority in their villages.

Dalyat el-Carmel looks no different from any other Arab village. The holy books of the Druse religion are written in Arabic, and Arab customs and literature, and at times even the Arab national dream, have been common to the Druse as well. To a veteran of Givat Chaim, things may appear simple and clear-cut. He undoubtedly came to this country as a Zionist who believed that here alone the persecuted Jewish people could experience rebirth, here alone was a wellspring of hope for those who had survived the ravages of Fascist anti-Semitism. I, however, was born of a people that is groping its way through today's political realities, and it wasn't always clear to me "where I fit into it all." In time I learned the popular sociological term for the quandary my people finds itself in: the search for identity.

In Dalyat el-Carmel, I was also born into the very heart of the war zone and the struggle that preceded the founding of the State of Israel. A ring of twelve Moslem villages surrounded us, adding an important dimension to the bitter dispute that divided our village. One camp backed the Jews and the Haganah, the underground Jewish defense organization. The other camp believed that the village should support the "Arab Revolt," which had broken out in 1936 and pitted the Arabs of Palestine against both the Jews and the British. My own family sided with the Jews, and my father made no secret of his position. I can even remember him putting up a portrait of the nation's revered leader, David Ben-Gurion, on the wardrobe that dominated the one and only room of our apartment. Until 1948, however, supporting the Haganah meant provoking the wrath of the Moslems in the area, and the consequences usually were brutal; raids, looting, abuse, and the theft of entire herds of goats and sheep were daily occurrences. Abu-Dura, the leader of the armed Moslem gangs that, in the early thirties, attacked Jewish settlements and transportation arteries, cast his terror over the Druse of the area as well.

I doubt that my Jewish countrymen have any idea what goes through the mind of an Israeli Druse whenever he is reminded of Abu-Dura's marauders. Probably few are aware that the raiders desecrated Druse holy books and once kidnapped the *mukhtar* of our village (who happened to be my uncle) because of his support for the Jewish cause. The Druse living on Mount Carmel nevertheless became allies of the Jews. A prominent sheikh from the village of Usifiyeh went around the Arab village of Tira purchasing weapons from the residents and turned them over to the Jewish underground. Other courageous Druse did spying for the Haganah and established lines of contact with the leaders of the Druse community in Syria. By the time the Druse of the Carmel came to the point of refusing to contribute any funds to the insurgent Arabs, their sense of dissociation had turned into deep enmity.

Forty years have passed since then, but the issue of the Druse community's identity in Israel has still not been resolved. It has become more or less customary for the Jews to

6

divide the Arab population of this country into two camps, roughly defined as the "good guys" and the "bad guys." The Druse have oscillated between the two camps, sometimes ranked among the good Arabs, sometimes among the bad, and sometimes—when the problem of definition became too onerous—classified as just plain Druse, not Arabs at all. Perceiving the doubt and confusion among the Druse, the Israeli establishment would try to exploit it by severing them from their Arab heritage and natural environment, and there was a growing tendency to speak of the Druse as a distinct nationality. To cite one example, somewhere along the way it was "decided" that Id el-Fitr, the holiday marking the end of the period of fasting during Ramadan, was not a Druse festival, even though my ancestors had celebrated it for countless generations.

Relations between the Druse and the State of Israel entered a new stage in 1956, when, "on the recommendation of the authorities," the heads of the large Druse clans signed an appeal calling on the Israeli government to make compulsory military service binding on Druse citizens (until then, no Arabs had been drafted into the army). With the passage of a law to that effect, there was no longer any doubt that I was a "good Arab." And yet a year afterward the prime minister—who never tired of praising the Druse leaders for their "good citizenship"—turned in his identity card to the Ministry of Interior because it was printed in both Hebrew and Arabic; he objected to the use of the Arabic language in an official document of the State of Israel. Next to the word "nationality" on my identity card is the word "Druse," and that fact is recorded in both Hebrew and Arabic. "Druse" written in Hebrew must therefore be something positive, while in Arabic it is somehow unseemly. That, at any rate, was what Ben-Gurion must have thought. But the leader my father so admired evidently had overlooked one fact: Arabic is my native tongue. I fail to understand why I should be branded with that as if it were a stigma.

7

I imagine that someone coming from the outside might be tempted to describe the world of my childhood in picturesque terms. Donkeys and horses were our sole means of transportation, and it took us hours of clippety-clopping over rock-strewn paths to reach Haifa, just a few miles away. To fulfill the religious precept of an annual pilgrimage to the tomb of the prophet Shu'eib-Jethro (who is mentioned in the Bible as Moses' father-in-law), we had to embark on a full day's journey through a verdant countryside without roads. Someone else might wax nostalgic for a world and a time when things seemed so much simpler. But I don't miss it. The harsh truth is that poverty and hardship were rife in my village throughout my childhood. My elementary school was a random collection of shabby rooms barely equipped for the purpose. Our teachers presided over the dimly lit classrooms in a high-handed manner. With menacing ruler always in hand, they checked our personal hygiene every morning and imparted to us the knowledge and values printed in the curriculum dictated on high by the Ministry of Education. And I must admit that, whatever else I may have lacked as a child, the State of Israel saw to it that I got a good Jewish education. Of the history of the Druse and their heroes I was never taught a thing in school (though we did manage to pick up something about Islam and Christianity), but I can clearly remember drilling for difficult exams on the history of the Maccabean revolt. I did not know the names of any Druse writers, nor did I ever read any of their works, but I spent many hours studying the Zionist philosophy of Ahad Ha'am, learned to love modern Hebrew poetry, and dabbled in Abraham Mapu's stories of longing for Zion. The curriculum even included lessons to heighten our identification with the "Jews of Silence" in the Soviet Union. I don't know how much the members of Kibbutz Givat Chaim know about the history and aspirations of the Druse sect, but I read all the writings of the Zionist ideologue A. D. Gordon on the function of labor in the rehabilitation of the Jewish people. I also learned about the trials and tribulations of the earliest

Jewish settlers on the coastal plain and how they finally set down their roots in the soil of Givat Chaim.

In spite of the poverty and hard times, my father never lost his faith in a better future. He would look up at Ben-Gurion's portrait in admiration, purse his lips, and pronounce, "Tomorrow the Jewish experts will come here and turn our village into a paradise." He was encouraged in this faith by the sight of the thriving Jewish villages in the vicinity. In fact, some of the most memorable experiences of my childhood were the visits I made with my father to the neighboring moshav of Kfar Yehoshua. He would wake me at four in the morning, before first light, and together we would ride off to that nearby settlement. The "lords" of the Jezreel Valley had built regal chicken coops and planted flourishing vineyards. My father would buy some chickens and fruit from the Jewish settlers, return to Dalyat el-Carmel and sell the produce to his neighbors for a meager profit, and then go out to work his own plot of rocky soil. For years my father raised his primitive field crops—lentils, wheat, barley, and a few onions and tomatoes—and that plot, all of three and a half acres, was dearer to him than anything else.

A few years after the founding of the state the government began to deal with the land question, and a number of plots from our village were expropriated—some for public use, others for the benefit of the neighboring Jewish settlement. Each time we rode to Kfar Yehoshua, my father would pointedly raise the subject as his way of leading up to the real moral he wanted to instill in me. There were two rules my father considered sacrosanct, and observing them took on the proportions of a commandment: "Do not sell your land, and protect your sister's honor." At the age of eighty, my father divided his land among his sons, and he admonished us again, "Do not sell this land, which has been in our family for generations, for it is our sacred bond with this place. Do not exchange the land for tractors!"—meaning by that the trappings of modernization and technology, for which he had never concealed his distaste.

9

Kfar Yehoshua was also the scene of my first experience of Jewish society, and the well-tended settlement was an eye-opener, arousing my envy with its order and cleanliness. In those days Dalyat el-Carmel looked like the poor and neglected village it was. The villagers' clothing was tattered, the buildings were run-down, the sanitary facilities did little more than spread disease, and local medical lore was based on a selection of potions extracted from wild plants. But signs of progress and development were already on the horizon.

In 1951 a local council was instituted in Dalyat el-Carmel, and my uncle was chosen to head it. (At the time, about half of the 2,000 residents of the village were members of the extended Halabi family, whose numerous branches made it one of the most widespread families in the Middle East.) At first the advantages of democracy were not readily apparent. The Israeli political establishment did not ascribe much importance to its Druse citizens and carried on whatever dealings with them were necessary through the sheikh of each clan, who set the voting patterns of the people under his patronage. Whether or not the residents of a given village would vote for Mapai—then the country's ruling party—was essentially up to the village sheikh, and the establishment was quite satisfied with that arrangement. But it wasn't long before the people came to know their rights and to demand that those rights be honored. It was then that various government ministries began to wake up to what was happening in the countryside. We still lacked running water and electricity, but kerosene lamps and water drawn out of rain-fed wells were simply not in keeping with the spirit of the times. When day laborers began to leave the village to work in Haifa—the "big city"—slowly but surely the economic plight of the villagers improved. We adjusted very quickly to the innovations and development and soon were demanding what was rightfully our due. With other signs of progress came the first radio, bringing the village out of semi-isolation; I remember how everyone would gather around the "radio house" and thrill at the sounds emanating from the set. Still, I was thirteen years old before I ever set eyes on a transistor.

In the early decades of the new state, Israel's Arabs were under a military government, and it ruled with a heavy hand. But the state exempted the Druse villages on Mount Carmel, as a way of expressing its gratitude to their citizens, and those villages enjoyed a fully civilian administration. Then, when the compulsory draft was extended to the Druse, yet another new chapter opened in relations between the Druse community and the state. The draft set the Druse apart from the other elements of Israel's Arab minority—both Christians and Moslems—who viewed the collaboration with a jaundiced eye. In the few villages with mixed populations of Druse and Christian or Moslem Arabs, the Druse who were drafted into the army were treated like traitors to the Arab nation. It was common to sneer at the Druse for their very goodwill and readiness to share the burden as equal citizens of the state. "It won't get you anywhere," other Arabs used to taunt. "While you're serving the Zionists, we Arabs are saving our money and studying in the universities." The irony was that this assessment wasn't far from the truth. The Druse may have earned the moral right to demand equality, but in actuality their feeling that they were "Jews" when it came to obligations and "Arabs" when it came to rights has never completely been dispelled.

The draft proved to have a far-reaching impact on the Druse community. First and foremost, its effect on the "identity question" was to sharpen divisions that already existed within the community. The poet Samih el-Kasem, who opposed the draft, went on a week-long hunger strike against it, explaining that his objections were based on a refusal to bear arms against his Arab brothers. Others followed his example, especially deserters and men who had gone AWOL. While security restrictions and the arrest of deserters diminished the extent of the problem, opposition to the draft never died out completely.

The draft issue also had a religious aspect that cannot be

overlooked. One of the basic tenets of the Druse faith is the transmigration of souls. In a short story entitled "The Sheikh Murdered Me," the Druse writer Salman Natour weaves a fabulous tale of a Druse soldier in the Israel Defense Forces —the IDF—who must fight a brother from a previous incarnation who is now serving in the Syrian army. This complex work is a telling model for a Druse youth who is called to arms in the service of his country and may one day find himself pitted against an enemy soldier who is not only a member of his sect but also a blood relative from an earlier incarnation.

Nevertheless, most young Druse have accepted the draft as a fact of life, and many have even identified with it as an important achievement for their community. Army service has also changed the face of the Druse village beyond recognition, with young men of the sect, who are noted for their fondness for uniforms, strutting about the streets, weapons in hand, their chests thrust forward in pride. Most of the Druse serve in a special Minority Unit or in the Border Police, and, like every other soldier in the IDF, they must obey orders given in Hebrew and are taught to respect the symbols and customs of the army. They soon earned a reputation as daring fighters, and citations of them for acts of bravery have raised the standing of our community in the eyes of other Israeli citizens. But army service has also had less welcome consequences, mostly in the form of increased assimilation, which in any case had been making inroads in the Druse community. Its classic symptoms are intermarriage, flight from the villages, and a strong desire to melt into the urban population. Eilat, for example, supports a large community of Druse whose children speak Hebrew and study in Jewish schools, and many Druse have adopted Hebrew names. In elementary school, our teachers worked hard to drum into us the profound national message in the works of Ahad Ha'am, including his dire warning against assimilation. Can it be that the Druse citizens of Israel are experiencing a fate similar to that of the assimilated Jews of the Diaspora? As Druse soldiers have lost a sense of their unique identity, they have drifted away from their national roots. Worst of all, perhaps, the concept of "Israeli" to which they have been drawn remains fundamentally meaningless for them. They may be "good Druse citizens" of the State of Israel, but they have yet to reach the status of "Israelis of Druse extraction."

For many young Druse, the army was their first extended contact with life outside their villages. I, however, was sent out into the world at a much earlier age. Not satisfied with the education I had soaked up in elementary school, my father decided to send me to Haifa to continue my studies. High school opened the gate to a whole new world for me and became my window on Israeli society. My Jewish classmates arrived at school brimming with knowledge and sabra self-confidence. Their behavior was casual and uninhibited, and at first I had great difficulty fitting in. Coming fresh from the village and its conservative atmosphere, I considered the atmosphere of my new school sheer anarchy. For the first few days I felt as if I had been cut loose from the reality so familiar to me and cast without warning or advice into an alien, hostile world. Coeducation had been unthinkable in my village, and now suddenly I found myself seated right next to a girl my own age from Haifa. Fortunately, my teachers were patient about my discomfort and other difficulties. But often, to my dismay, I found it hard to avoid attracting unwanted attention. My less than polished Hebrew drew giggles from my classmates, and gales of laughter would sweep through the room every time I —like anyone whose native tongue is Arabic—failed to pronounce the letter p properly and instead uttered a b. Each outburst only reinforced my resolve that one day I would perfect my knowledge of Hebrew at the university in Jerusalem.

My teachers persisted in their efforts to build up my self-confidence and abet my desire to fit into the group—and that was no mean task. But slowly things improved. My classmates even gave me the Hebrew nickname "Rafi," as their way of saying they were willing to accept me into the society I was so envious of. In truth, I liked the name and didn't protest about it, though it did little to cover up the glaring social and cultural gap between us. I studied hard and had my fair share of achievements to show for it, while never quite catching up to the level of the rest of my class. It was the abyss on the social level, however, that seemed to remain unbridgeable. One visit to the home of a classmate is etched in my memory forever. His room—his very own bedroom—was furnished with a bed, a desk, shelves full of books, a stereo set, and other articles evidencing a high standard of living and the latest in technological gadgetry. All that wealth stood in stark contrast to the poverty of Dalyat el-Carmel, where my parents, my brothers, and I all lived in one room. I slept on a mattress on the floor, and the only books in our house were my school books, which took pride of place in the family wardrobe. When it was time to do my homework, I retired to a dim corner of my father's small store, and to study for exams I would take to one of the dirt paths leading out of the village. Israelis and tourists who travel through the West Bank today are puzzled by the sight of so many youngsters walking along the roadsides and reciting out of school books. I know it is not for love of nature that they have adopted these peculiar study habits. The miserable living conditions in the refugee camps, with their dark, noisy alleys, are what has driven these knowledge-starved children into the groves and byways of the countryside.

It was also in high school that I first encountered another revolutionary concept: freedom of expression. The Hebrew newspapers were nothing like the Arabic daily *Al-Yom* (*"Today"*) —published by the Arab Division of the Histadrut, the National Federation of Labor—which was the only paper distributed in our village. Simply put, the difference was that the Hebrew press didn't paper over the facts or cover up the truth. The editorials were penetrating, and in general I was astonished by the newspapers' tolerance toward "the other point of view." The only other Arab-language paper published at the time was the Communist party's *Al-Itihad* (*"The Union"*). It supposedly enjoyed freedom of the press, but one heard stories about the censorship restrictions imposed on the paper and about attacks on its editors and publishers. Before Knesset elections, for example, the heads of the Communist party would inevitably come under sharp attack, in an effort to block the inroads the party was making among the Arab electorate.

Be that as it may, the free press to which I now had access inspired me, while still in high school, to write my first journalistic piece, which I submitted to the Druse quarterly published by the Ministry of Religious Affairs. True to form, some would say, I wrote in all innocence to question why Druse notables fawned before government officials whenever they appeared in the villages. Need I add that the article was rejected?—my first piece of journalism to be quashed but, as time would show, hardly my last.

For a country boy from a poor family that had never had books in the house, this encounter with freedom was intoxicating. I read whatever I could get my hands on and developed the habit of combing every newspaper that came my way. Though I wasn't very enthusiastic about my subjects at school, when I was asked what my plans were after graduation I would reply without a second's hesitation that I wanted to be a journalist. Of course, that idea didn't go over very well at home. My father wanted me to study medicine or law, for ever since the days of the British Mandate the social hierarchy of Arab society had been static and well-defined: at the top the doctors and lawyers, below them the engineers. Journalists had never been particularly respected members of the social elite, and my father refused to be reconciled to my choice. I must say, I could hardly blame him. From *Al-Yom*, those four pages of propaganda that went by the name of a newspaper, it was hard to get the idea that journalism was a respectable career.

My father was proud of my accomplishments and made no secret of it. On the contrary, he never tired of telling his friends at Kfar Yehoshua about his boy, the son of a fellah from

Dalyat el-Carmel, who was now an "intellectual" attending a high school in Haifa. He worked hard to be sure I had the proper clothes for my "social station," and he would implore me to demonstrate my learning by making speeches before the villagers on festive occasions. I was torn between loyalty to my father and what I was learning at school, and I am still unable to resolve all the contradictions between the traditional, conservative Druse society and the free and open Jewish one. Then again, life at school wasn't always easy, either. Every so often an item would be published about the expropriation of Arab lands in the Galilee, and sometimes we would hear about the detention of Arab political activists under the provisions of the Defense (Emergency) Regulations—enacted during the British Mandate but now serving the interests of the very people against whom they had originally been promulgated. My classmates accepted the government's explanations for those policies, but I was pricked by doubts. Yet more than once, though I wanted to speak out, I kept my protests to myself, because I knew that in the hostile atmosphere surrounding us, with the constant threat of violence that seemed to be Israel's lot, sometimes the voice of justice must lie low and wait for better times.

At the end of my four years of school in Haifa, it was difficult, on the surface, to see the difference between me and my Jewish classmates. It wasn't that they had moved toward me; it was I who had taken great strides in their direction. Other youngsters from Dalyat el-Carmel soon began to stream into the secondary schools in Haifa, and a veiled struggle developed in our village between those who thirsted for progress and those who were the guardians of tradition. Only a strong desire to preserve the unity of the sect prevented an open clash and cushioned the impact of what might otherwise have been a convulsive cultural revolution. Still, one cannot miss the social and economic changes that have overtaken the Druse community. Hundreds of students have enrolled in institutions of higher learning, and even young women have recently begun to study in the universities. It is open knowledge that some advisers counseled the government that it would be best for the young people of Israel's minority groups to remain "hewers of wood and drawers of water"—in short, uneducated and unskilled manual laborers; that, they argued, would make it easier to cope with the "Arab problem." It is irrelevant to point out that such men were short on sweeping vision and imagination, for their myopic view of the future has not materialized. There are no woodcutters in Dalyat el-Carmel today, and a villager who is called on to do that kind of work undoubtedly has the aid of the most advanced technology. In fact, the technological revolution has permeated every sphere of life in the Arab villages of Israel, and its impact is evident in the economic and industrial as well as the social aspects of village life.

As my high school career drew to an end, however, I faced a more pressing question than the future character of village life. The time had come for me to resolve the question of my identity—or at least to decide where my allegiance lay. The draft notice that bore my name called on me to enlist in the service of a country in which I did not always feel like a welcome citizen. To tell the truth, if enlistment had been voluntary I don't know how I would have acted. I felt that if Israeli society failed to accord equal treatment to all its citizens, why should the deprived class have to bear an equal burden? And that sense of deprivation was not unjustified. Take, for example, the experience of the Druse village of Sajour, located directly across from Kibbutz Shazur in the northern Galilee. The Druse of Israel like to joke that their villages should be fenced off and plastered with signs like "Military Area—Photographing Prohibited" as a way of showing how "militant" they are and how many of their youth have served in the Israeli army. And yet the residents of Sajour didn't even get electricity until 1977, and its young men would return home from military service to see electric lights burning in the chicken coops of nearby Shazur, while they spent their evenings by the light of kerosene lamps. Is it any wonder the Druse have felt deprived and frustrated? Furthermore, since certain state institutions—the Jewish Agency, for one—do not deal with the Arab sector in Israel, the entire burden of development has fallen on the national budget and on the Arab population itself, with the result that many projects have been postponed indefinitely for financial reasons.

So there were legitimate reasons for my doubts, but in the end they were overcome by an even stronger desire to be an integral part of the country of which fate had decreed me a citizen. At the same time, I was driven by a need that had awakened in me during my first weeks at school in Haifa—I desperately wanted to go on to the university. I reported for the preliminary induction procedures at the appointed time and place, but I then asked to have my enlistment deferred so that I could continue my studies. The IDF granted my request, and soon afterward I moved to Jerusalem and enrolled at the Hebrew University, in the departments of Hebrew language and Semitic philology.

I was the first Druse from Dalyat el-Carmel, the largest Druse village in the country, to attend the Hebrew University. Jerusalem was a small, rather provincial city then, and on Saturdays, the Jewish Sabbath, life came to a complete standstill. Foreign students and the Arab students, far from their native villages, were practically the only souls in the dormitories during weekends, and any Arab poet or writer who happened into the city would gather us up for an evening of literature or poetry reading. In contrast to the Arab students on campus today, our political consciousness was pretty dormant back then. But that soon changed, for in June of 1967 the Middle East again became the focus of dramatic events that would decide the fate of millions and leave their mark on the entire region.

By the first days of June 1967 the streets of Jerusalem were empty of men. Fear permeated my rented room on Mamilla Street, just a few feet from the concrete wall that divided the two halves of the city, and from the window I could see the Jordanian snipers positioned on the other side of the frontier. My fellow students had been called up to join their units, but I remained idle, despite my tremendous desire to be a part of the great national effort that had united this country's citizens. I signed up for a first-aid course offered by the university, but I wasn't too happy to learn that all the other participants were young women. In the end, unable to bear the "shame," I decided to return to my village. Not that the air of tension and expectation was any less oppressive there. Those doing their regular army service in the Druse unit were anxiously waiting, like the rest of the army, for their orders to move out. Dozens of reservists who had not been called up hired a bus and went to Tel Aviv to demonstrate their disgruntlement and to demand that they be included in the war effort forthwith.

The fighting in 1967 was the first time that Druse soldiers participated in a full-scale war within the ranks of the IDF. My brother Tawfik was doing his compulsory army service then, and the rumor was tnat the Druse unit would be fighting on the Syrian-ruled Golan Heights. We knew that we had relatives there—two cousins I had never met, Rafik Halabi and Tawfik Halabi, lived in the village of Masada on the Golan—and upon hearing the rumor my mother wept, declared a fast, and remained for days absorbed in prayer. In fact, the Druse prayer houses were brimming with supplicants. I chose to close myself up at home, glued to the radio and starved for any crumb of information from the fronts. The shrill cries coming from Radio Cairo—"Kill, kill, kill! For the sake of your daughters. For the sake of your mothers. Slaughter them! Slaughter them!"—were terrifying, and the steady diet of nationalist incitement and that barbaric call to arms scared me half to death. Even worse were the hysterical shrieks emanating from the Voice of Palestine, which shook me to the core. The impassioned broadcaster, Abdul Wahad Zahada, played havoc with my insecurities, and I will never forget the sound of his voice

—and told him so when he joined the staff of the Arabic news department of Israel Television in the early 1970s. Fortunately, my ordeal was short-lived, for the IDF's blitzkrieg and awesome victory quickly changed the mood from one extreme to the other. The relief and excitement were felt even in the villages, as the young men began to return home and were greeted like victors, with hugs and slaps on the back. The IDF, instead of being pushed back by the pressure of three opposing armies, had captured the West Bank, the Gaza Strip, the Sinai desert, and the Golan Heights. What an extraordinary time!

But there was another side to the experience for me. Right in the middle of the long and subtle process that was binding me closer to the country in which I lived, along had come this stunning war and hurled me back into confusion and self-doubt. On the one hand, Israel's strength and the victory of its army reinforced my feeling of closeness to the people that had made this country their home. On the other hand, the sheer conceit, arrogant superiority, and contemptuous declarations of the victors—which soon became common throughout the country—prevented me from sharing in their victory. For example, the disparaging expressions "Arab work" and "the Arab mind" (presumably as opposed to the *Yiddische Kop*) enjoyed a great revival. My own distraught mind was an Arab one, and deep inside I could feel my resentment growing. While the country was still flushed with victory, I was already dreading its consequences.

A few days after the fighting ended, the Municipality of Jerusalem published an advertisement offering "interesting work" for Arabic-speaking students. I jumped at the opportunity to get back to work, and in June of 1967 I found myself running the first Israeli municipal office to be set up in East Jerusalem. While continuing my studies, I eventually became the deputy administrator of East Jerusalem affairs, remaining in that position until I earned my master's degree and reported for duty in the Israel Defense Forces in May of 1970.

I have never tried to disguise my pride in "having the privilege of serving in the Israel Defense Forces and adorning its uniform," as the army formula puts it. Nevertheless, at first I was anxious about what awaited me in the army. When a soldier serves in a combat unit, he does more than adorn a uniform. He is called on to bear arms, and an assault rifle "is not there for decoration," as the IDF saying goes. Its purpose is to defend human life, and sometimes to defend means to attack. In short, serving in an army like the IDF is serious business.

Just how serious was made painfully clear to me a few days before I reported for duty, when a close friend and fellow classmate from Dalyat el-Carmel, Lutfi Nasser a-Din, was killed in a clash with Palestinian terrorists on the Jordanian border. Moshe Dayan, then the defense minister, attended the funeral, and, perhaps inspired by his presence, Lutfi's father spoke of the fate shared by the Druse and the Jews of Israel and of the "blood pact" between them. I stood off to one side choking back bitter tears. How I hated that horrid way of expressing the ties between fellow citizens! I had accepted the need for an alliance of soldiers fighting side by side to defend the country they all cherished. But the words "blood pact" smacked of mindless demagoguery.

Along with the other recruits in the Druse unit, I was sent to a training base on the West Bank, where we took part in maneuvers by day and guarded the installations of an abandoned Jordanian military camp by night. Later that year my unit was sent to the Golan Heights for maneuvers, and it was then—three years after the 1967 war—that I had my first contacts with the Druse of that area in their own villages and homes. Two years earlier, a blue-eyed, fair-complexioned young man had appeared at our door in Dalyat el-Carmel asking if this was where Rafik Halabi lived. When I told him I was Rafik Halabi, he literally fell all over me and burst into tears. "I'm Rafik Halabi, too!" he finally blurted out. "From Masada on the Golan Heights." After he got hold of himself again, he went on to tell us that he had a large family in the Golan and that his brother Hamdi was studying at the University of Damascus. Rafik, the cousin I had never met, had been the principal of his village school before the war. He readily admitted that he was a supporter of the Syrian Ba'ath party and a firm opponent of the Israeli occupation. In fact, though many people in Masada had urged him to relent, he had refused to return to his school post under the occupation and had gone to work in the family's apple orchard instead. Rafik asked me what I thought he should do, but before I could answer he added, "Just remember that my brother is studying in Damascus and that I am a Syrian Arab. You know Israel. Can we trust the Israelis not to abandon us to our fate when they withdraw from the Heights?" The government had asked the Israeli Druse to do whatever they could to smooth the integration of the Druse in the Golan, or at least to temper their opposition to Israeli rule. But the blood relationship and sense of kinship between Rafik and me meant that the advice he was asking me for was more than a political assessment. In spite of the government's appeal, I was wary about becoming involved in the matter, for it was obviously a ticklish situation. Yet the full extent of the tragedy did not become clear to me until August of 1973, ten days after my release from the army.

Adib Halabi, from the village of Majdal Shams, and three other young men from the Golan Heights were standing trial before a military court in Kuneitra. I had come to know Adib through his visits to Dalyat el-Carmel, and he had always impressed me as a quiet, polite young man. Now he was being tried for having sent letter-bombs to the president of the United States, Richard Nixon, and the secretary of state, William Rogers, from the post office in the northern Israeli town of Kiryat Shmonah. Visibly shaken, Adib denied any knowledge of the acts with which he was charged, but he was convicted nevertheless. The military prosecutor asked for life sentences for all those found guilty, but the judges were satisfied with sentences of twenty years. The last time I saw Adib was in the Jenin prison, on the West Bank, and his dazed expression spoke for his condition. Our mutual cousin Rafik, from Masada, was sentenced to two years' imprisonment for not having reported the details of the incident to the authorities. The logic of "security over all" dictated that he must turn his cousin in, and he was being duly punished for having failed to do so.

It is still hard for me to comprehend the hapless fate of my people—and my family—in the Golan Heights. During the period of Syrian rule, dozens of Druse had been arrested on charges of spying for Israel, and the entire sect had suffered. Now that the Golan was in Israeli hands, other Druse were being arrested on charges of spying for Syria. There has been talk lately of making Israeli law binding throughout the Golan and of granting Israeli citizenship to the Druse there. But it seems to me that only someone who has a brother living in Syria and a cousin sitting in jail, someone who needs documents from the Red Cross and the Syrian government to visit his family on the other side of the frontier, is capable of appreciating the complexity of the problem. A person like that doesn't need an identity card—Israeli or Syrian. What he needs above all is a document assuring him of the rights of a free man.

Painful as it was to see, there was little I could do about the predicament of my relatives in the Golan. But while in the army I did find myself in a position to deal with some of the problems confronting the Druse closer to home—meaning my fellow soldiers. In 1971 I was chosen for an officers' training course, and upon completing it I was posted to a Druse unit stationed in the north, where I was delighted to learn that I would be serving temporarily as the unit's education officer. The program designed for the unit covered a broad spectrum of objectives, from the improvement of reading and writing skills in Hebrew to the forging of character in both officers and men. For many young Druses the army served as an indispensable vehicle for becoming creative and useful citizens of a

modern society. Military service bound a young Druse closer
to his country, but it also made him ever more keenly aware
of the lines of distinction that separated him from Jewish society. My work was therefore sensitive and difficult: to make the
men aware of the dangers of assimilation, which would solve
nothing for them, while being careful not to suppress their
healthy feeling that they had a right to demand equality.

The soldiers in the Druse units were acutely sensitive to
any hints of discrimination or injustice from the authorities or
society in general. Unfortunately, there have been times when
they would have had to be blind and deaf to miss the feeling
of not being wanted. Once, while I was stationed in the north,
a group of terrorists seized an apartment house in the town of
Kiryat Shmonah, near the Lebanese border, and my unit was
called in to join the rescue operation. In the subsequent exchange of fire, a Circassian soldier was killed and one of the
Druse was badly wounded and was taken to the hospital in the
city of Safed. When his parents rushed in to see him, dressed
in their traditional costume, the indignant citizens of Safed
heckled them with cries of "filthy Arabs." In Kiryat Shmonah,
a spontaneous demonstration arose under the banner "Druse
go home! We don't want Druse soldiers here!" The front
commander, Major General Mordechai Gur, who had witnessed the scene and was incensed at the insult to his men,
charged into the offices of the local council and pointedly
reminded the local leaders that Druse soldiers had risked their
lives to save the town from a terrible tragedy. Meanwhile, the
mood in the unit was grim. No one challenged the rightness
of our duty to serve the state, but I could hear the men grumbling over their coffee, resentfully summing up their situation
in these words: "When you're a member of a small sect, you
come out the loser no matter what you do. Why should we get
involved in this mess anyway?" It was as if the Druse, who for
generations had mastered the secret of "walking between the
raindrops," had recently been getting soaked through to the
skin, and the result was a chronic case of pneumonia.

I left the army only two months before the outbreak of the Yom Kippur War, and I had hardly had a chance to adjust to civilian life or think about the future when along came that earthquake, which left its mark on all of us. Suddenly, without a shadow of a doubt, I knew what I wanted to do with my life. I was no longer enthusiastic about working for the Municipality of Jerusalem (though I was offered a position and stayed with it for a while); the academic life held no charms for me; and the idea of pursuing my fortune in the business world left me cold. What I wanted was to be in a position to influence the course of events in this country. Perhaps that sounds pretentious for the son of a Druse fellah—academic degrees and officer's rank notwithstanding—and such a notion did cross my mind. But, like many others of my generation, I emerged from the Yom Kippur War with the feeling that it was incumbent on me personally to do something about the pass this country had come to.

The blunders of October 1973 could be traced directly to a process that had dulled the critical sensibilities of Israeli society. Debate on crucial national issues had been superseded by a blind faith in the country's incontestable prowess. I believed most strongly that the facts had to be brought out into the open, that covering up or reshaping the truth placed the very future of this country in jeopardy; as the war proved, public morale sagged badly when people were fed a diet of carefully distilled information. I was drawn again to my childhood dream of becoming a journalist, and this time fate interceded when an old friend happened to mention that the news department of Israel Television was looking for an Arabic-speaking reporter to cover the occupied territories. I applied for the job before any second thoughts could catch up with me.

That was in 1974, when Israel Television was still young and inexperienced—though there had been time enough for the stars of the small screen to attain the status of national heroes and become almost as familiar as the country's soccer greats. The thought of walking into that lion's den unsettled me somewhat, and not the least of the questions troubling me was my accent. Even after much hard work, there was no way that a "westernized" Hebrew accent could ever roll off this tongue. That was simply not one of the attributes I had acquired through my heritage. My spoken Hebrew was fluent, and writing it didn't pose any particular problems for me. But the thought of coping with the exposure, the glaring lights, and everything in Hebrew, before an audience glued to their sets and drinking in every syllable, made me more and more nervous. In fact, it almost overcame my resolution to go through with the job.

In the end, my adjustment and initiation went much faster and smoother than I had imagined. Everyone was extraordinarily sensitive. No one pressed me or was gruff, and, most important, the staff took great pains in teaching me the secrets of the profession. Sometimes I felt as if I were the object of "positive discrimination." I was embraced by a phenomenal group of people, who symbolized Israeli society at its best.

Many Arabs in Israel have refused to believe me when I say that Israel Television has been like a second home to me. They have put me through the third degree in trying to get me to expose the "truth" behind what they regard as suspiciously "rosy" descriptions. The fact was that working for Israel Television changed my entire outlook on this country. I had never been in doubt about my allegiance to the state or about the right of the people of Israel to an independent and creative life, but I had never particularly liked Israeli society. On the contrary, I had built up a healthy store of resentment against it for having insulted and patronized me and on occasion having stood in the way of my advancement. I was dubious about finding a place for myself in a Jewish environment, because it had been my experience that Jewish Israelis were not particularly known for their openness to "outsiders." But Israel Television's news department broke down all my prejudices on that score and dispelled my fears. One evening, when we were working especially hard and under heavy pressure, a colleague suddenly turned to me and confessed, "You know, Rafik, I feel closer to you than to any immigrant from Poland or Georgia or Iraq." That abrupt burst of feeling revealed to me a deep and fundamental truth: life in Israel has created a bond of coexistence between peoples that, if treasured and cultivated, can withstand all attempts to undermine it.

At the same time, my work as a television news correspondent has raised the matter of my identity and my allegiance to the level of a national controversy. I have never heard anyone question my duty to serve this country and fulfill the obligations incumbent upon me as a citizen like any other. But when I began to tell what my eyes had seen and my camera captured in the occupied territories, suddenly there were voices calling my "Israeliness" into question. I have tried to deal with such sniping coolly, sensibly, and professionally, and my co-workers have shored up my resolve by their unfailing support. Yet it is hard to ignore the implications of those attacks. Many people in Israel have a strong aversion to the smallest hint of social pluralism. But is the "Israeliness" of every citizen of Israel really identical? Are Boris from Kiev, Dani from Tel Aviv, and Mohammed from Jaffa really alike and equal in that sense? Obviously the answer is no. So why make an example of Rafik Halabi?

The Jewish people's struggle for national restoration over the past century is one of the most gripping tales of human valor in all of history. Here in this land the ideal of hundreds of thousands of brutally persecuted people became a reality. No wonder, then, that the founders of Israel did not look on their state as just another national entity like any other country around the globe. I appreciate the longing to be "a light unto the nations." I accept the awesome moral imperative that was laid down with the very founding of this state. History has created a reality that cannot be denied, and the dominance of Jewish culture in the State of Israel is something I do not aspire to change. As a citizen of this state, however, I see my country as a political framework within which two peoples are destined to live side by side, to build, and to strive together in peace. That was the vision of Israel's independence proclamation. That is my belief and the creed I try to instill in my children. What's more, I regard the attitude of an Israeli Arab toward "the Jewish question" and the past trials of the Jewish people as the touchstone by which to judge his morality. By the same standard, I am not afraid to judge the moral complexion of the Israeli Jew by his attitude toward "the Arab problem." And there is no denying the existence of that problem. I first learned about it when, as a boy, I saw Arab refugees who wanted to return to their destroyed villages. My father tried to play down the significance of it by telling me, "There are many countries they can live in." Finally, however, I could not restrain myself. "But the land and the honor of one's sister are sacred values!" I challenged him. "They have been driven off their land, and their daughters have been doomed to be shunted about from one place to another." My father's response was a dark scowl and a piece of advice that remained with me for years to come: "We are a small and weak sect. If we wish to survive, we must appear to resemble our surroundings. So long as you are a tender young plant, you must protect yourself against every gust of wind. But once you grow strong and strike roots in the soil, you need not fear even the gales of winter!"

I am no longer that frightened Arab boy who wandered barefoot along the dirt paths of his village, just like the children I would see so many years later in the refugee camps of the West Bank. I have put down my roots in the State of Israel, and, just as I must live by its laws and regulations, so do I feel obligated to protect and defend its security and well-being—moral as well as physical. That is why, when I come up against manifestations of insensitivity and injustice, I cannot remain silent. It is for that reason, and for my countrymen, and for my people, that this book has been written.

2
JERUSALEM

My first experience of the effects of the Six Day War on the people in the captured territories was in Jerusalem, where I went to work for the municipal government shortly after the fighting ended. I opened its first local office in East Jerusalem at a time when the frontier dividing the city was still strewn with mines and hundreds of Israeli soldiers were milling around the streets, additional testimony to the dismal events that had just racked the city. Three hundred and sixty-six people, including about a hundred civilians, had fallen during the fighting. The walled Old City was the hardest-hit area, but elsewhere shelling had caused heavy damage to electric wires and the water system, scarred buildings and burned-out cars lined the streets, and a suffocating stench filled the air. Dozens of structures, particularly the deserted buildings in the no-man's-land, had been completely destroyed. The residents of the eastern half of Jerusalem were in a state of shock and dread, and about 5,000 of them fled the city when it was captured. Clearly there was much work to be done, but the first priority was to restore life to normal.

Moshe Dayan summoned Major General Shlomo Lahat (now the mayor of Tel Aviv, and best known by his nickname of "Chich") home from a lecture tour in South America to assume the post of military governor of East Jerusalem. "If there's a pogrom in the city and Arabs are killed," Dayan told him—as usual not mincing words—"you'll have to answer for it. Jerusalem is important to me." Indeed, over the years I have seen how strongly determined Dayan was to live side by side with the Arabs. The inhabitants of the West Bank have come to respect and admire him, and Dayan has been one of the few Israeli leaders who were ever able to establish any genuine ties with Arabs in the territories.

The minister of defense was not alone in his special feeling for Jerusalem. The smoke of battle had hardly cleared when the future of the captured territories became a topic of nationwide debate in Israel. Arguments were raised both for and against trading away the territories in exchange for peace agreements—except for Jerusalem, about which a national consensus seemed to have crystallized overnight. Jerusalem was not considered "conquered territory." On the contrary, ever since the fall of the Old City it had been customary in Israel to speak of the city's "liberation." The Arabs of East Jerusalem did not grasp that nuance at first and so failed to understand that their fate was to be different from that of the rest of the West Bank. In fact, some of them didn't even know where the conquering soldiers had come from!

There was little confusion about that on the part of Jerusalem's municipal leaders, however. Salah Jarallah, the secretary of the municipality, whom I met on June 10, along with Mayor Ruhi el-Khatib, told me how Israeli soldiers had entered his home with their bayonets drawn, ordered him to come with them, and led him off—together with Sheikh Sa'id Sabru, the chief kadi, or Moslem religious judge, of Jerusalem —to the square in front of the el-Aksa Mosque. There the soldiers had frisked them, although they were later allowed to return to their homes. But the honor of an Arab notable—which Jarallah prized highly—had been trampled on, and his spirit was broken.

Another story of the first meeting between victors and vanquished was told to me long after the fact by Anwar el-Khatib, the Jordanian governor of the city. "I was summoned to a meeting with the Israeli government spokesman, Major General Chaim Herzog, and I related to that gentleman the affair of the damage caused to the el-Aksa Mosque. General

Herzog countered that the Arab Legion had stationed snipers in the minaret, and the IDF had been forced to respond." As Khatib commented to me, "I agreed he had a point," and he went on to say that he had told Herzog, "Admittedly, you are behaving like civilized people. But when your soldiers searched my home in Beit Hanina, I thought that day was my last on earth!" With that, as Khatib told it, he had burst into tears, bringing from Herzog the quick response: "You're upset because you were afraid they would do to you what you intended to do to us." Khatib, to this day a loyal supporter of King Hussein, conceded to me that Herzog had had a point there, too. Yet Khatib had contacted the king as soon as fighting broke out, so he told Herzog, and had asked for permission to surrender. Hussein's answer to his governor had been this heartening promise: "Hold out and we will save you!"

At that same meeting with Herzog, Anwar el-Khatib had asked that a few families living in the eastern sector of the city be allowed to cross over to Jordan in order to be reunited with relatives there. The Israeli representative had acceded, but for fear the gesture might be interpreted as an Israeli move to deport the families, he had insisted that the approach to him be made in writing. Once the formalities had been dealt with, on June 11 buses were hired to take the Arab families as far as the Allenby Bridge. A few hundred others also soon left the city, but only after signing statements that they were going voluntarily.

That was essentially the tone of the first contacts between representatives of the Israeli military government and leaders of the Arab population in Jerusalem—formal, civil, gentlemanly. The first task assigned to my office was to locate municipal officials and their employees and get them back to work. But when I asked the mayor, Ruhi el-Khatib, and his administrative assistant, Anton Safiye, for an up-to-date list of their employees, I came up against a wall of hostility, and it didn't take them long to raise the subject of my unusual personal status—although they did it indirectly. Safiye remarked on my fluency in Arabic, and I hesitated over what to tell him about my background. The Druse unit had not fought in the West Bank, but that had not prevented the spread of nasty rumors about "atrocities" perpetrated by its soldiers. Hoping to avoid any unpleasantness, I eased his mind by telling him that my knowledge of Arabic came from "my studies at the university." Whatever he might have thought, the subject never came up again.

Salah Jarallah, who spoke some Hebrew—he must have picked it up before 1948—was the first official courageous enough to help get the local government functioning again. He was aided by his friend Ibrahim Dajani, a scion of one of the wealthiest and most respected families in Jerusalem, and together we managed to get salaries transferred to all the municipal employees (in Israeli pounds, of course). On June 10 Ruhi el-Khatib was recruited to the cause and, accompanied by a representative of the Israeli military government, took to the streets in an effort to get local services restored. Still-wary Arab residents of the city peeked through their shuttered windows at this "integrated" group parading by. Many East Jerusalemites denounced the mayor as a traitor for daring to cooperate with the Israeli agents of the occupation. But Khatib, who admittedly was in an unenviable position, fought back in defense of his actions. Convening the members of the municipal council, he left them in no doubt about his motives: "We are living under military occupation, but we must continue to provide services to our constituents as efficiently as we did before the war." The mayor also called on all those who still possessed arms to place their weapons outside the entrances to their homes. The representative of the military government, Aharon La'ish, had assured the councilmen that no harm would come to anyone who acceded to the mayor's request, and both the appeal and the assurance were immediately broadcast over the Voice of Israel's Arabic network.

The council went on to discuss various problems resulting

from the new situation, and at the close of the meeting it released a statement to the residents of the city. The text of that initial appeal to the populace read:

1. The council calls upon all residents of the city to maintain calm and order and to refrain from any act likely to provoke the military regime to action.
2. The council calls upon all residents of Jerusalem to aid it in bringing the life of the city back to normal. The council also demands that everyone in Jerusalem with weapons or ammunition of any kind in his possession place them outside the entrance to his home while the curfew is in effect, in accordance with the order issued by the military commander of the city. Compliance with this order will obviate the need to take action against any individual or against the city as a whole.
3. The council wishes to announce that in cooperation with the Israeli administration it has made progress in restoring sanitation and the water supply to a number of sectors of the city. It is making a considerable effort to ensure that these services are extended to all parts of the city as soon as possible.
4. The council also wishes to announce that in cooperation with the Israeli administration the local electric company has resumed operations, has restored electricity to a number of sectors of the city, and continues in its efforts to supply the remaining neighborhoods.
5. The council wishes to announce that in cooperation with the military regime it is maintaining its efforts to restore all other essential services . . . and is doing everything in its power to see that life returns to normal as quickly as possible.

Battered and stunned by the magnitude of the military defeat, the mayor, the governor, and the council were in an obedient frame of mind, and the statement was accordingly moderate and to the point. Openly delighted by these signs of official cooperation, the Israeli authorities—especially Teddy Kollek, the mayor of the Jewish sector of the city, and Moshe Dayan—wanted to strike while the iron was hot and quickly get as much done as they could. Their philosophy—which continues to be a cornerstone of Israeli policy in the occupied territories—was that the most effective way to ensure continued Israeli control over captured areas that the government had no intention of forfeiting was to establish what we here call "facts on the ground"—*faits accomplis.* So it was that on June 10, before the Arab population had hardly begun to recover from its shock, the Israeli administration struck the first blow, and I can recall how stunned even I was by it. That opening blow was the decision to demolish, immediately, the Moghrabi Quarter of the Old City, adjoining the Western Wall—the Wailing Wall.

The background of that decision was a revealing story in itself. One of Teddy Kollek's first acts as mayor of a city that had doubled in size overnight was to take his venerable mentor, David Ben-Gurion, on a tour through the alleys of the Old City. The walls enclosing the Old City made a profound impression on Ben-Gurion, who feared that they would only serve to perpetuate the division between the two halves of Jerusalem and actually suggested that they be torn down. Fortunately, Kollek rejected that notion out of hand. The climax of the tour was their arrival at the Western Wall, where they stood appalled by the filth surrounding this site so sacred to Jews. Ben-Gurion wanted to remove the source of the defilement—two public toilets located next to the wall—and his request raised the whole issue of what to do about the area. Obviously the alley alongside the wall was too narrow to accommodate the crowds of worshipers and tourists expected to visit the site. After a consultation (which evidently did not take into consideration all facets of the problem), it was decided to open up a plaza facing the Western Wall. That meant tearing down the residential buildings that bordered the site.

34

On the night of June 10, an Israeli officer marched from door to door through the Moghrabi Quarter giving the residents three hours' notice to evacuate their homes. A chorus of wails rose from the quarter as whole families began to congregate by the Zion Gate carrying what meager belongings they could. As it turned out, three families defied the order and refused to leave their homes. The area was illuminated with floodlights, and a giant bulldozer moved in to commence the demolition. Two of the remaining families fled at the sight of it, but the head of the third family stood his ground, breaking only when the terrifying vehicle, moving at a menacing crawl, loomed steadily closer to his home. In spite of a search of the buildings before they were razed, one elderly woman was found among the ruins. She showed no signs of bodily injury, but nevertheless was taken to a hospital, where she died later that night. Evidently the terror of it had been too much for her.

In all, 135 families were evicted from their homes in that operation. They took refuge in empty apartments in the Old City or in nearby villages, and during 1968 I spent months trying to track them down so that they could be compensated for their destroyed property. The compensation was miserly, but it was enough to ease my own consternation somewhat.

The next step came on June 27, when we heard that Israel intended to annex East Jerusalem and make it part of the sovereign territory of the state. Ruhi el-Khatib sought verification of the rumors from officers of the military government. But the very next day, before he could get a straight answer, the government published Regularization Ordinance No. 1 (1967), which proclaimed "the application of Israeli law, jurisdiction, and administration" in the Arab portion of Jerusalem. The ordinance also defined the borders of the area being annexed as the sector under the jurisdiction of the Jordanian Municipality of Jerusalem. Two days later the army issued an order disbanding the municipal council of Arab Jerusalem and transferring its officials and employees to the staff of the Municipality of Jerusalem.

35

Those steps left no doubt about Israel's intentions, and they finally roused East Jerusalem's leaders out of the daze they had been in since the war. At the instigation of Sheikh Abdul Hamid Sa'ih, the president of the Moslem Shari'a Court, the local leaders began to organize for political action. Sa'ih's initiative caused great concern in the Israeli government, for he embodied a blend of political ardor and religious zealotry. Indeed, on July 24 a group of Arab religious and political figures met to discuss the "grave situation" and agreed to embark on a series of protests expressing their opposition to Israel's *fait accompli*. At the close of their deliberations, the group published a statement denouncing the Israeli annexation of East Jerusalem and pronouncing it "null and void, for the occupying regime has imposed it unilaterally and contrary to the will of the residents of the city, who oppose this annexation and believe in the unity of the Jordanian homeland." The participants also refused to provide the Israeli Ministry of Religious Affairs with copies of the sermons they intended to deliver at Friday prayers in the city's mosques. Further, they protested the immodest dress of Israelis visiting the mosques and the destruction of two mosques in the Moghrabi Quarter adjacent to the Western Wall. Finally, the assembled leaders vowed that they would not bow to Israel's authority and called for resistance to what they termed "Israeli attempts to take over the holy places." It was also at that meeting that a Higher Moslem Council was elected. Abdul Hamid Sa'ih was chosen "Moslem chief justice" of the West Bank, functioning under the authority vested in him by Jordanian law, and Sheikh Hilmi Muhtasib was elected "director of Moslem legal affairs." The local mufti (the chief religious functionary) and kadi both had their areas of jurisdiction broadened.

That manifesto, published a month and a half after the war, emphasized the desire to preserve ties with the Hashemite Kingdom of Jordan. In spite of—or perhaps because of —the strains between the Hashemite government in Amman and the Palestinian population of the West Bank, King Hussein had made a point of cultivating the local leadership of the West Bank, and now the leadership was reciprocating by flaunting its loyalty to the king. Yet none of those who took part in that meeting fourteen years ago will openly identify with Jordan today. While continuing to maintain a political dialogue and social and economic ties with the Hashemite Kingdom, they have not been able to deny the "Palestinization" of the West Bank and East Jerusalem. In their public statements today, they are careful not to deviate from the consensus of support for the Palestine Liberation Organization—the PLO—or to contradict the goal of an independent Palestinian state. As for the role Israel has played in the process of Palestinization, the subject deserves serious consideration, and I will return to it later in these pages.

The July 24 meeting of religious dignitaries and political figures signaled the start of civil disobedience, and the same officials who had graciously cooperated with the Israeli military administration immediately after the war now adopted a much more intractable attitude. They stopped conducting themselves as "honorable gentlemen" in their contacts with representatives of the occupation and refused to comply with the demands of its officers. Sensitive to the change in mood, the government of Israel tried to come to grips with the problem of what to do about the deteriorating situation. At one meeting called by Prime Minister Levi Eshkol, a number of advisers, including some Orientalists, were solicited for their opinions. One of those present was Yitzhak Navon, today the president of the State of Israel, and he counseled that the answer lay in setting off a train of events that would climax in the deposal of King Hussein, so that a Palestinian state could be established in his former kingdom and the Arab refugees of 1948 could be resettled there. That scenario, or variations of it, has attracted quite a following in Israel over the years. But this was an earlier time, and Navon's opinion did not carry much weight then. The majority followed Moshe Dayan in believing that Israel should continue to sit patiently at home and wait for the famous "telephone call" from the Arab rulers.

As for the day-to-day conduct of affairs in the occupied territories, the defense minister recommended following the advice of an Arab proverb, "Extract the tooth and you extract the pain with it." If local leaders in the territories were going to flaunt their opposition to Israeli rule, there was no choice but to remove them from the scene. That was the genesis of the deportation policy, and once the policy was arrived at, the military government moved to implement it immediately. On July 30, four members of the Higher Moslem Council were removed to Safed, Hadera, Tiberias (in Israel proper), and Jericho. That left the four deportees—Anwar el-Khatib, Dr. Da'ud Husseini, and the lawyers Abdul Muhsin Abu-Meizar and Ibrahim Baker—still in areas under Israeli jurisdiction. But it was not long before that policy, too, was changed. The next group of deportees was led to the bridges over the Jordan and expelled into the Hashemite Kingdom.

Whatever they achieved from Israel's point of view, on the Arab side the deportations only served to harden the positions of the local leaders. Abdul Hamid Sa'ih quickly convened an emergency meeting that resulted in the formation of a National Guidance Committee to coordinate protest activities and lead the public struggle. The new committee lost no time getting down to business. On the same day it was established it proclaimed a general strike and called on all residents of East Jerusalem to take part. Twenty-four lawyers responded at once with a statement that they would not collaborate with the Israeli authorities. The Chamber of Commerce urged its members to refuse to pay their taxes, and eighty-four public figures issued a manifesto protesting the annexation. More important, Abdul Hamid Sa'ih finally succeeded in spreading the spirit of rebellion from Jerusalem to other cities in the West Bank. In the eyes of the Israeli government, there was no doubt about the role he was playing in charging up the atmosphere, and Moshe Dayan asked the Cabinet's approval to deport him. On

38

September 22, 1967, Abdul Hamid Sa'ih was sent across the Jordan to the East Bank, and the deportation policy was at its peak.

Its effectiveness was open to question, however. When Sa'ih was expelled, Ruhi el-Khatib, the deposed mayor of Jerusalem, simply picked up where Sa'ih had left off, chairing meetings of the National Guidance Committee and faithfully reporting on its activities to his patrons in Amman. Today, fourteen years after the issuance of the order disbanding the municipal council of East Jerusalem, a forum known as the "Municipal Council of Arab Jerusalem" still exists, and in May of 1980 its members came to pay their respects to Anwar Nusseibah, a former Jordanian defense minister and one of the best known and most respected of the moderates living in Jerusalem. Nusseibah is now the chairman of East Jerusalem's electric company, and the purpose of the council's visit was to honor him for the company's achievements and for his valiant stand against the Israeli government's declared intention to take over the company. The delegation took the occasion to remind Nusseibah that Ruhi el-Khatib was a former occupant of his chair, and Nusseibah, always the perfect gentleman, smiled as a sign that he understood the nationalist message his visitors had come to deliver. Within a few months, Khatib, who sometimes appeared diffident in the role of national hero—as if it had been imposed on him against his will—also earned himself a visit by Israeli soldiers, on March 7, 1968. He was transported to Jericho, interrogated there, and summarily deported to Jordan.

Still the Arabs of Jerusalem did not yield. Ruhi el-Khatib's place as chairman of the National Guidance Committee was filled by the trio of kadi Sa'ad a-Din Alalmi, Abdul Muhsin Abu-Meizar—who had returned to Jerusalem after promising to refrain from any political activity—and the lawyer Kamal Dajani, who escalated the protests by encouraging women to march in the streets and by calling again for a general strike. It was soon clear that the local women's organizations were a leading element in the civil disobedience movement. They even made one appeal to King Hussein to come out in support of the terrorist activities against Israel. As for the general strike, the business community hesitated at first, but slowly merchants began to close their shops in solidarity with the Arab cause. The response from the authorities was swift and sharp: the leaders of the women's groups were placed in administrative detention, and fifteen shops were seized and closed, with Israeli police stationed outside them. Inevitably, the three new leaders of the National Guidance Committee, along with Mrs. Zuleikha Shihabi, the president of the Union of Arab Women, were deported to Jordan.

Apparently the Arab community was now starting to appreciate the Israelis' determination to keep a lid on the national ferment, for gradually such gestures of civil rebellion began to die down. Long before that happened, though, they were being replaced by something far more radical and more ominous: the opponents of Israeli rule were going underground and turning to terrorism. The first sign of the shift came in the form of an explosive device planted near an installation of the Israeli electric company in the residential Kiryat Moshe Quarter of West Jerusalem. That device was discovered and dismantled in time, but on September 19, 1967, the first terrorist blast reverberated through united Jerusalem. A bomb had been planted in the Fast Hotel, a large, ramshackle building not far from the Jaffa Gate, in an area that had formerly been a no-man's-land. The blast injured seven people and destroyed a printing press operating on the premises.

A few weeks later the infant terrorist movement in the city set its sights on a far more spectacular statement of its intentions. On October 8, Fatmeh Barnawi and three other members of a local el-Fatah cell deposited a bomb in the Zion Theater, a movie house in the very heart of downtown Jerusalem. An alert moviegoer noticed the suspicious package and called an attendant, who was able to have it removed from the theater. The police took the bomb to an empty lot next to the

Jerusalem Central Police Station, and it exploded a few moments later. Once again the reaction was swift, but this time it came from certain elements of the Israeli populace. A mob composed mostly of young men in a rage decided to teach the perpetrators of the abortive crime a lesson; taking the law into their own hands, they set out for the Arab quarters to punish the bombers. Their "victims," of course, were innocent Arabs who not only had had nothing to do with the incident but had hardly a clue as to what was provoking the rampage. The rioters vented their wrath on Arab property and by beating anyone who crossed their path, and only the vigorous intervention of the police prevented the outburst from burgeoning into a pogrom. I myself was collared at the Jaffa Gate by a gang of hooligans set on revenge. Evidently what saved me was that I could protest my innocence in fluent Hebrew. Even so, I didn't get off scot-free; later that night a Jewish policeman expressed the depths of his feeling by spewing out at me the epithet "filthy Arab!" The only decent thing that came out of the episode was a fierce denunciation of the Israeli mob's behavior by Teddy Kollek and a spokesman for the police, who called it a grave affront to every resident of the city.

The civil unrest, terror, and deportations, as well as the reckless fury of the Jewish mob, had seriously unnerved me, and there were days when I was almost paralyzed by despair. For some time I toyed with the idea of turning my back on the turbulent city altogether and returning to my village, and I'm sure that if it had not been for the liberal approach taken by Teddy Kollek and his aides I might well have done just that. Kollek had his own, quite original methods for assuaging the anger and rebellion, and he once gave us this explanation of his secret: "I am a disciple of the pragmatic approach. Another school, another apartment house, another hospital—that's how we'll strengthen Jerusalem. That will be our reply to resistance."

I managed to get a grip on my state of dejection, but no sooner did things seem under control again than a new issue arose, in all its grim complexity. On April 14, 1968, Israel's minister of finance issued a decree expropriating the entire Jewish Quarter of the Old City, and the hundreds of Arabs living there were forced to abandon their homes. Already, in January of that year, thousands of acres registered as the property of the Hashemite Kingdom of Jordan had been transferred to the ownership of the State of Israel and close to a thousand acres of privately owned land had been expropriated, for the express purpose of creating a Jewish-populated buffer zone between Arab Jerusalem and the West Bank. Again the motive was to create "facts on the ground," and again the effect was shattering.

Though the Druse tradition does not hold any city as sacred, I appreciated the tremendous import of the claim to Jerusalem as a holy city by both Moslems and Jews—including self-professed secularists. I had never held with the belief that historical claims should be the decisive factor in determining political facts in the present, but I knew that whoever ignored the mystique of such claims would fail to see the subtleties and intricacies in a situation. I also understood that neither the Jews nor the Arabs of Jerusalem wanted the city divided again; once it was reunited, both sides had perceived how right and natural that unity was, and both now had a vested interest in preserving it. When Moshe Dayan declared that he did not necessarily object to the prospect of the Arab flag's flying over the city's great mosques, I viewed the statement as a show of wisdom that gave great cause for hope. But time and again those hopes were dashed by actions of the government and the municipality, whose policies proved to be an erratic mixture of humane gestures and rash, inexplicable blows.

I don't yet understand why it was necessary to evict the Arab residents of the Jewish Quarter, and when I was asked to help persuade them to leave voluntarily I categorically refused. I could not help remembering stories of the hundreds of families who were expelled or were induced to leave their homes during the 1948 war and who are still refugees today.

I don't mean to say that the two situations were necessarily comparable. For one thing, the families being dispossessed this time were offered compensation for their property. Then again, it was not wartime, and no security considerations were involved in the decision to transform the demographic character of the Jewish Quarter by government fiat. Finally, who could presume to say which attachment to the Jewish Quarter was deeper, the ties of the Jews who had been turned out in 1948 or those of the Arabs who were being ordered to leave now? The powers that be were not going to stop at restoring synagogues to Jewish ownership or even at integrating the population in the district. Their order spoke of purging the quarter of its Arab residents, and that was a decision I could not come to terms with. The operation dragged on for years, ending only in 1980 with the departure of the last Arab resident, Mohammed Tutanji, who tried to get the courts to reverse the edict but lost. Teddy Kollek and his aides may have aspired to create a mood of fruitful coexistence, but the political realities and a series of ill-considered decisions caused things to turn out otherwise. Today's inhabitants of Jerusalem —Jewish and Arab—live parallel to and occasionally at odds with one another.

The men and women who have done the actual work in the field deserve recognition for their attempts to forge a policy of understanding and reconciliation. Certain persons in public service have been known for the great sensitivity they have displayed toward the touchy situation of the residents of East Jerusalem. Unfortunately, the same cannot be said of the Israeli public as a whole, and some rather unpleasant findings about the attitudes of Jewish residents of Jerusalem toward their Arab neighbors came out of a survey we took in February of 1968, in which the participants were asked to name the characteristic features of Arabs. Among the replies we received were these: "a nation of many hypocrites," "a nation mostly of poor people," "a nation of cowards," "a primitive people." Only a handful suggested that the Arab nation "wants to live in peace with the Jews." In reply to the question "Do you think that Arabs should be allowed to live in the western sector of the city?," 57.8 percent of those polled answered firmly in the negative, while 38.4 percent supported the idea. Most of the people questioned—89 percent—were emphatic in their belief that the Jews had every right to settle in the eastern part of the city and should exercise that right.

Interestingly, the Israelis who had faced and fought the soldiers of the Arab Legion on the battlefield were among those who displayed the noblest and most humane attitudes. One of the bloodiest battles of the Six Day War had been fought between Israeli paratroopers and legionnaires holed up in the concrete strongholds of a heavily fortified area known as Ammunition Hill. After a long and costly battle, the victorious Israeli fighters had inscribed this tribute to their adversaries: "Brave Jordanian soldiers fought and fell with valor here."

That simple sentence from the pages of Jerusalem's long, blood-stained history is one of the most telling and moving lines I have ever read, and it should have been an augury of future relationships of mutual respect. But to establish peaceful coexistence requires a plentiful share of consideration for the feelings of others, and that was not always in adequate supply. A case in point was the issue of monuments to the war dead. Twelve Arab families who had lost loved ones in the fighting wanted to erect a monument in memory of the Jerusalemites who had perished in the war. The first response of the Israeli military government was not encouraging. But after negotiations with the Moslem dignitaries responsible for the *wakf* (religious trust), an agreement was reached for the erection of a monument opposite the Rockefeller Museum. Teddy Kollek asked the *wakf* to contribute a share of the cost and insisted that it remove all the small, improvised memorials that had appeared in the eastern part of the city without official approval. He also insisted that the *wakf* issue a public declaration confirming that no bodies were buried under the memori-

44

als due to be removed. Nevertheless, feeling against the decision ran high in the city's all-Jewish municipal council, even after it was announced that a special government committee had approved the erection of three monuments. I accompanied my superior, Meron Benvenisti, who was then the administrator of East Jerusalem affairs for the municipality, to meetings with the secretary of the *wakf*, Hassan Tahbub, and in the end we had to work all night to be sure the monument was up and in place before the pressure of hostile public opinion could cause the decision to be rescinded.

The policies championed by Kollek and Benvenisti won them admiration and support among the Arabs in Jerusalem. In the municipal election of 1969, in which about twelve thousand residents of East Jerusalem voted, the overwhelming majority of Arab ballots went to Kollek. We in the Office for East Jerusalem Affairs placed great hopes on the outcome of the election, believing that a heavy turnout in the eastern half of the city would signal the desire of its residents to share in decisions that would shape the character of the united city. Unfortunately, our actual contacts with the voting public were quite limited and therefore not very effective. We had to conduct our dialogue with the populace through its only representatives who were willing to cooperate with the municipal government—the *mukhtars*. These appointed public officials were paid a modest wage for their trouble, but they never genuinely represented the public for whom they spoke. After the election, the municipality began to set up local committees, and naturally it was interested in having local Arab leaders serve on them. Some public figures expressed their readiness to do so, but as soon as this became known they would quickly deny any intention of collaborating with us. The pressures on them were evidently more than they could bear. Even then, terrorism in the occupied territories worked in both directions; those who resorted to violence as a political instrument appeared to have no qualms about using it against their own people as a way of neutralizing internal opposition.

By the summer of 1969, as the election approached, the mood of civil unrest in Jerusalem seemed to have peaked. Although there had been some strikes in the spring, they had not generated the excitement and banner headlines of previous years. But August brought one of the most dramatic and traumatic events to occur in Jerusalem since the war itself, and again it galvanized the Arab leadership into speaking out against Israeli rule. On August 21, 1969, fire broke out in the el-Aksa Mosque. As word of the conflagration spread, so did a wave of anguish sweep over the Arabs in the city and throughout the entire West Bank. The members of the Higher Moslem Council (now headed by Sheikh Hilmi Muhtasib), along with people from all over East Jerusalem, rushed to the scene and watched the flames in horror. Whether in grief or anger, the council members approached foreign press correspondents and charged Israel with being responsible for the fire. Their reason was that if the Israelis had not been in control of the approaches to the mosque, the fire would never have broken out. What made the fire all the more sinister in their eyes was that—as they told the journalists—Israel wanted to rebuild its Temple on the site of the mosque, where it used to be. At a subsequent press conference, Muhtasib declared, "The Moslems must sound the battle cry that will generate action and put an end to the oppression, wickedness, and anguish." He called for a general strike and demanded that the authority for guarding the entrances to the Haram e-sharif— Temple Mount—be taken out of Israeli hands.

Prime Minister Golda Meir, who was on her way to Tel Aviv when she heard about the fire, ordered the Ministerial Committee for the Occupied Territories to look into the matter at once. Teddy Kollek, the only prominent Israeli on the scene, pronounced it a "catastrophe," while trying to balance out the impression of willful negligence suggested by Muhtasib with praise for the efforts of the Israeli fire-fighting team. But nothing the mayor or any other Israeli could say was enough to alleviate the grief into which the Arab community plunged. As if intimidated by the sheer outpouring of feeling, the government responded by imposing a curfew on East Jerusalem.

Israeli police detectives paid a visit that day to the Rivol Hotel in East Jerusalem looking for Dennis Michael Rohan, a twenty-eight-year-old Australian sheepshearer and a member of the Bethel church. Rohan wasn't in, but the police gained entry to his room and found there cans of gasoline and other flammable materials. When Rohan later returned to the hotel, he was arrested and charged with arson. The deft police work and Rohan's neutral background helped to calm the atmosphere somewhat, but the fire had exposed the true nature of relations between the two communities in Jerusalem and the gaping credibility gap that separated them. Arab Jerusalem believed that the fire had been an Israeli plot to destroy the mosque; and, though Rohan's swift arrest did much to save face for Israel, Muhtasib's call for demonstrations and a strike brought a sharp reaction—the curfew. The Higher Moslem Council tried to exploit the incident for propaganda purposes and also closed mosques to visitors for a time. But on October 19, 1969, the Haram e-sharif was reopened to visitors, and in a conciliatory gesture the council was allowed to station its own guards there.

During this period Jerusalem continued to be the center of the pro-Jordanian faction in the West Bank's local leadership. Among those known to be Hussein loyalists were religious dignitaries associated with the *wakf*, directors of the electric company, administrators of charitable institutions, and former members of the Jordanian parliament. In the first years after the war, this group made no secret of its support for the element within the Israeli government that believed the solution to the problem of the occupied West Bank lay in negotiations with the Hashemite Kingdom. Yet the steady Palestinization of the West Bank, coupled with the government's rigidity on the political formula for uniting Jerusalem and its hollow or merely symbolic gestures that did nothing to change the actual situation in Jerusalem or affect the city's character—such as the legislation passed by the Knesset in 1980 making Israeli law binding on all of Jerusalem, when in fact that had been so since 1967, or the talk of moving the prime minister's office to the eastern half of the city—all that has only made things more difficult for the pro-Jordanian camp. Over the years many of these moderates have been forced into the arms of the PLO, and even those who have stopped short of openly identifying with the Palestinian organizations will not issue any public statements without clearing them first with the PLO leadership.

In the fever of establishing irreversible "facts," in the fervency of the desire to unify Jerusalem and change the face of the city, many things were done that only deepened and widened the division. What most aroused the fury of the Arab population was the extensive expropriation of land for new Jewish developments. In some areas, Jewish building contractors built luxurious villas for themselves on the plots that were parceled out to them. Such "facts on the ground" are morally grotesque, and to one who believes in Martin Buber's dictum that "we must not do unto others any more than we are forced to for the sake of our own existence," they are nothing short of monstrous.

Over the past decade, life in this divided-united city has settled into a routine. But it is still punctuated by events proclaiming the fact that, fourteen years after Israel's annexation of East Jerusalem, the city's Arabs are not yet reconciled to that unilateral determination of their fate. Strikes are still called (usually in response to a specific initiative by the government), the city is still a major target of terrorist activity, and recently the fashion of stoning vehicles has spread into Jerusalem proper from other parts of the West Bank (though on that score the number of stonings by Jerusalem's ultra-Orthodox Jews, in their war against traffic on the Sabbath, far surpasses the isolated instances attributed to Arabs). Most telling, however, is a certain sullen quality to the atmosphere in East

48

Jerusalem, despite the many signs of the city's commercial prosperity.

In 1967, I saw in Jerusalem a reflection of the Dalyat el-Carmel of the early 1950s, and I believed that just as the development and prosperity of my native village had nurtured moderation and allowed for a reconciliation between peoples, so would Jerusalem grow together—in all the meanings of those words. When I went to work for the Jerusalem city government I was full of optimism and hope, and I drew support for those feelings from the positive things that were happening in the city—such as the time, a year after the war, when dozens of *mukhtars* and representatives of the city's Christian churches came to pay their respects to Teddy Kollek on Israel's Independence Day. Today, fourteen years after the war, there are precious few optimists left. Some have visions of harrowing flare-ups in the future, and others have dubbed Jerusalem the "Belfast of the Middle East." But even these Jeremiahs deceive themselves about the difficulties of the problems here. With all due respect for the obduracy of the Irish problem, Belfast does not contain the Western Wall, the el-Aksa Mosque, and the Church of the Holy Sepulchre all within its city limits.

I still believe that Jerusalem must never again be divided, and I still hope that a solution to the city's difficult problems will be found. But it will not be found through force and "facts" and the like. Those who care about Jerusalem must show their concern by moderation and by sensitivity to the needs and desires of others. And what seems to be needed most of all now is the political maturity and magnanimity of spirit to admit past mistakes and break loose from outdated modes of thought and beliefs that are being demolished every day by here-and-now realities.

Whoever hopes to preserve the unity of Jerusalem must avoid the empty gestures that only heighten animosities. I feel less comfortable walking the streets of the Old City today than I did in 1967. An Arab resident of united Jerusalem feels his "Israeliness" less now than he did before passage of the latest law declaring the city the united capital of the country. When I think back to 1967 and try to sum up the achievements since then, I am dismayed by the thought of what a great opportunity we had to make Jerusalem into a showcase of mutual tolerance and respect, and how we lacked the vision to see it. Nevertheless, the physical unification of Jerusalem is a fact that cannot be denied and must not be undone. Now it remains for the city's leaders and its peoples to pour real substance into that bare fact by resolving their differences in a way that satisfies the interests of both sides in this torn city.

3
THE WEST BANK,
1967

When the fighting ended on June 10, 1967, a great sense of release, relief, and, ultimately, euphoria swept through the population—particularly the Jewish population—of Israel. Those feelings might have been tempered, though, if the celebrants had realized what had actually happened—not in terms of dazzling military victories but in the hard facts of the outcome. With the capture of the West Bank and the Gaza Strip, 1,100,000 Palestinian Arabs had come under Israeli control in the course of a few days. Tens of thousands from the West Bank fled across the Jordan and, willingly or otherwise, became refugees—a condition all too common in the bleak history of the Palestinian people. About 40 percent of the West Bank's population was engaged in agriculture—50,000 families working an area of about 500,-000 acres. The farmers I saw in the Dotan and Jezreel valleys, near Jenin, reminded me of my father in the early 1950s, with their primitive tools and their ragged clothes—although they lacked my father's faith in the future. They did not grasp the full meaning of what had happened or appreciate the magnitude of the debacle, but believed it was the Americans who had defeated their army. It was inconceivable to these fellahin that Jews could have given their soldiers such a drubbing.

Once again, as in 1948, whole villages were destroyed by the war (mostly in Samaria, the northern half of the West Bank). The press gave wide coverage to three in particular—Beit Nuba, Emmaus, and Yalu, in the Latrun salient—that were deliberately razed for reasons of "strategic necessity." In the 1948 war Latrun had been the scene of bitter fighting over a section of the road from Tel Aviv to Jerusalem. The Israel Defense Forces had failed to gain control of a crossroads there (which became a no-man's-land for the next nineteen years), forcing Israel to construct an alternate, and less convenient, route to the capital. When Latrun fell in 1967, the military authorities decided to settle the problem of the salient once and for all and literally wiped the three settlements off the face of the earth. Even the carefully hewn stones of demolished buildings were carted off by private building contractors.

The troops charged with executing that distasteful mission distributed water to the terrified villagers and candy to their children, but the orders were harsh: none of the dispossessed families were to be allowed to return. Amos Kenan, an Israeli writer who witnessed the operation while serving in a reserve unit stationed nearby, sent a detailed report on it to Prime Minister Levi Eshkol and Defense Minister Moshe Dayan. In his letter of protest, which was published in the press, Kenan gave this description of the incident:

> The battalion grumbled and the villagers gritted their teeth as they watched the bulldozers flattening trees. That night we stayed on to guard the bulldozers, but the entire battalion was incensed, and most of the men didn't want to carry out the orders. In the morning we were transferred out. Not one of us could understand how Jews could do such a thing. Even those who defended the action conceded that [the authorities] could have put up temporary accommodations for the villagers until a final decision was reached on where they were to go, and then they could have taken their belongings along. It was impossible to fathom why those fellahin should not have been allowed to take their kerosene stoves, blankets, and provisions with them. Chickens and pigeons were buried under the rubble. The fields were laid waste before our very eyes. And the children straggling along the roads

wailing and crying bitter tears will be the fedayeen of the next round in another nineteen years. That's how we bungled the victory that day.

There were other, more influential voices calling for an enlightened approach to the occupation. As the late Yigal Allon noted, in warning that the aim must be to live in harmony with the Arabs of the occupied territories, "This is the first time that the subjects of the real problem—the Palestinians—have been under Israel's direct control, without any intermediaries from the Arab world." To exercise that control, Israel quickly set up a military government, whose brief was to administer the occupied territories and provide services to the local population. The military government comprised special staff officers and experts in various fields, assisted by local Arab officials who were holdovers from the Jordanian bureaucracy. In the absence of other takers, Moshe Dayan concentrated the administration of the territories in his own ministry, and so the military government was structured to operate in two spheres, under the jurisdiction of two authorities. Current security and the war against terrorism fell under the military command, while civil and political affairs were assigned to the coordinator of activities in the territories, who answered to the Ministry of Defense. The territories were divided into districts, with a local headquarters in each of the larger cities. Eventually, the seat of the West Bank area commander was established in Beit El, north of Jerusalem.

Paralleling the divisions of a civil administration, the military government was broken down into various branches: security, health, transportation, agriculture, education, and other units that provided services to the people of the territories. Because of those benefits, the public attitude toward the military government was ambivalent. Respect and cooperation prevailed in such fields as agriculture, education, and transport, but there was strong resistance to the whole idea of being ruled by a military government.

The soldiers who staffed the security arm of the military government came from standing and reserve units of the IDF. This meant that paratroopers who had been trained to be frontline fighters in times of war might be equipped with police clubs and sent out to patrol the cities of the West Bank, or that tank crews might be transferred from army maneuvers or operational duty to maintain order in the streets. Only those who served in the Border Police had special training to deal with a civilian population. The worst of the situation was the pernicious effect it had on the prospects of rapprochement between the two peoples. Too many citizens of Israel and inhabitants of the territories came to know each other under circumstances of physical confrontation—as soldiers and a hostile population, or as oppressors and troublemakers—and that left ugly scars in both camps.

On the administrative side, the military government launched its operations with a zeal that left the beneficiaries bewildered. A cascade of orders descended on the inhabitants of the territories, with one branch alone—the Justice Ministry —issuing no fewer than 259 ordinances. Out of the columns of figures and statistics and the piles of orders emerged the basic outlook that would guide the IDF in organizing its rule in the West Bank. The objectives of that rule came to be defined as follows:

1. To maintain security and assure the maximum participation of the local population and its institutions in the conduct of their administrative, municipal, and judicial affairs.
2. To create a framework for the institution of stable economic relations between the State of Israel and the occupied territories.
3. To open the bridges spanning the Jordan River and allow the population to maintain its cultural, social, economic, and familial ties with the Arab world.

One of the questions prompted by all the activity was how long the Israeli rule in the territories was likely to last. It soon became clear to the Israeli side that the occupation would

54

probably go on for a long time, but the local inhabitants refused to come to terms with that possibility. On my first visit to Ramallah, when I tried to pay a merchant by check, the man merely smiled and asked—whether in all innocence or rhetorically—"How long do you people intend to remain here?" Ironically, that question is still topical today, and the answer has become the subject of sharp debate in Israel.

Another point that became clear very early in the game was that the occupation was not going to be a pleasant experience for either side. During the initial postwar phase, relations between Jews and Arabs were like a drama that shifted its tone at a dizzying pace. At first the roles were of arrogant victor and battered loser, but gradually the stupefaction in the territories was replaced by a spirit of resistance and acts of violence. The first terrorist groups to organize were in the northern sector of the West Bank. Although some groups also began to form in the Hebron mountains, the Hebronites were more wary than their compatriots to the north. Unlike the people of Nablus, Ramallah, and other northern centers, they sensed that if they pushed matters too far the Israelis would clamp down hard and perhaps have their vengeance on Hebron. People in Israel had not forgotten the bloody events of 1929, when rioting Arabs in Hebron killed sixty-seven members of the city's Jewish community, wounded many others, and caused extensive damage to Jewish property. Doubtful that the wounds of 1929 had healed, Hebron's local leaders kept a tight rein on their people—and with good reason.

In its panicked flight from the West Bank, the routed Jordanian army had left behind large stocks of weapons and ammunition. The populace was quick to seize the abandoned rifles and bullets and stash them in makeshift caches dug in gardens and courtyards, in nearby caves, and in the fields. But the IDF was equally aware of the hoards and instituted a campaign to purge the region of arms. The operation turned up hundreds of rifles and thousands of bullets, but the bayonets had vanished and have never been found. While the army's searches did not get rid of all illegal weapons, they did make it more difficult for insurgents to arm themselves. Terrorist cells were forced to smuggle in weapons via the Jordan bridges, where the watchful guards of the IDF thoroughly searched every person and vehicle entering or leaving the West Bank.

Inevitably, the military aspects of the occupation came to dominate whatever weak lines of communication existed between the people of Israel and the people of the territories. As soon as they were allowed, curious Israelis began to stream into the occupied areas to sightsee, shop, and perhaps enjoy a heady sense of breathing room. But almost from the start a silk curtain descended between the two populations on the person-to-person level. Whether due to the language barrier or to a traditional difficulty in establishing new relationships, Israelis were reduced to gaining any information about the territories from the media. The press supplied little that was concrete, and most of what it did publish dealt with military affairs, if only because journalists had easy access to the military and could cultivate their own sources of information. Predictably, distortions resulted. Indeed, the questionable authenticity of the material being passed on to the Israeli reading public was obvious from the briefest glance at the newspapers. Most reporters had trouble even deciding on an appropriate term for the inhabitants of the territories (few used the word "Palestinians," the majority preferring "the Arabs of the West Bank" or "the Arabs of Gaza"), and when reporting on civil unrest or strikes they often fell back on such words as "incitement," "unruliness," and "hostility" to explain the reasons behind an incident. An Israeli television reporter once referred to women in Gaza who had sheltered terrorists as *sharmutot,* which means "whores" in Arabic. Obviously he didn't know that to an Arab that word is, hands down, the most offensive insult in the language. Fortunately for us, the inhabitants of the Gaza Strip were not then in the habit of watching the news on Israeli television.

Television coverage of the territories probably had the most insidious effects, because of the graphic message conveyed by the small screen. In its infancy, Israel Television had given us close-ups of Arab men sitting in cafés passing their time in idle talk, strings of worry beads in their hands and hand-rolled cigarettes dangling from their lips. Little wonder that before long the lumpy woman carrying bundles on her head and the angry young men came to symbolize the West Bank for Israelis. It wasn't for nothing that the military governor of Ramallah once found it necessary to chide Israeli journalists for their condescending attitude toward the residents of that city.

When the IDF entered the cities of the West Bank, it encountered a traditional local leadership that proved adept at carrying on a dialogue with the new rulers. Most of the mayors were members of the Palestinian aristocracy, wealthy merchants who had maintained close relations with the Hashemite regime for the nineteen years of Jordanian rule. "The pro-Jordan camp," as they have come to be known in the territories, displayed great wisdom, courage, and civility in their dealings with the Israeli administration; it must also be said that most of the military governors had been chosen with care and that some of them won respect and admiration from the local population. The Palestinian poetess Fadwa Toukan, for example, once spoke of the military governor of Nablus, Colonel Shaul Givoli, as a "gentleman, not a military governor."

The character of the West Bank's local leadership is best exemplified in the dramatic stories of the surrender of Nablus and of Hebron—after Jerusalem, the two largest cities in the West Bank. On June 7, 1967, snipers were still firing on Israeli troops from the rooftops, and the IDF was systematically tracking them down, in an effort to clean out the last pockets of resistance, when the mayor of Nablus, Hamdi Kenan, decked out in an official-looking suit and with a white flag in his hand, made his way resolutely toward the command vehicle of the armored brigade that had captured the city. He knew that further resistance was futile, and by his offer of surrender he hoped to avoid unnecessary bloodshed. The initial meeting between the proud, polished, self-possessed mayor and a Colonel Uri, the commander of the armored brigade, opened on a jarring note. The brigade commander, in dust-covered uniform, refused to shake the hand the mayor was extending toward him in peace. Uri made it clear to Kenan that the IDF intended no harm to the civilian population, but he said that as long as his soldiers were being harassed and fired on they would not lay down their arms. Kenan protested that in the prevailing chaos he had no control over the population, but he did express his willingness to help the IDF restore order. At that, the mayor was bundled into a military jeep and given a loudspeaker so that he could inform the residents of Nablus that the city was being placed under a curfew. His conduct recalls the attitude adopted by the municipal leaders in Jerusalem after the fall of that city.

On that same June 7, Lieutenant Colonel Zvi Ofer's armored battalion was rolling toward Hebron, where he and his men expected to meet heavy resistance from the local population. Since the days of the British Mandate, relations between Hebronites and Jews had been marked by enmity. The undisputed leader in the city and the surrounding area was the mayor, Sheikh Mohammed Ali Ja'abri, and Ofer knew that his first task must be to find the mayor and get him to sign a declaration of surrender. When Ofer and his men reached the sheikh's home, they found a dignified elderly gentleman capped, as always, in his famous tarboosh (as if he would forfeit his elegance and authority without it). Ja'abri's wife stood beside him, clutching his arm tightly and trembling with fear. Ja'abri told me a few months later that he, too, was terrified over the summary vengeance he expected from the Israeli soldiers in retaliation for the 1929 slaughter of Jews in Hebron. The people of the city looked up to the elderly sheikh for the active part he supposedly had played in instigating the assault on the Jews, and, although there has never been any firm evidence for their belief, Ja'abri knew what the Jews thought about him. But Colonel Ofer had other ideas. Without a moment's ado—without even heeding the oriental requirement of sheer good manners—he turned to Ja'abri and snapped, "You are the mayor and I am the officer who has assumed control of your city. I hereby demand that you tender your unconditional surrender to the Israel Defense Forces by signing the declaration of surrender." Ja'abri instantly assented, but he asked that the signing ceremony take place in the municipal building and that the secretary of the municipality and the kadi of the city be invited to attend. From then on, Ofer, who set up his headquarters in the Park Hotel, received the full cooperation of Ja'abri and his staff in bringing the city's life back to normal.

Hamdi Kenan and Sheikh Mohammed Ali Ja'abri were typical of the Palestinian leadership that had emerged in the cities of the West Bank during the period of Jordanian rule. Israel's defense minister, Moshe Dayan, who had a keen understanding of their character and traditional outlook, set about establishing a modus vivendi with them. On June 17, for example, Dayan met with the leading public figures of Nablus and subsequently ordered the military government to shorten the hours of the curfew and allow the local population a greater say in running their own affairs. He also ordered the military to remove all barricades in the city and stop demolishing the homes of known terrorists' families. Dayan was attentive to the complaints raised by the city's notables, and his meeting with them was generously peppered with smiles. Indeed, he capped it off by promising that if things in the city did not go smoothly he would hang the military commander in the main square. The local gentry grinned with delight as the commander did a slow burn. But Dayan, by establishing rapport with the municipal leadership, got what he wanted.

The open-bridges policy was another facet of Dayan's desire to institute a viable working arrangement in the occupied territories. He knew the harm that could result from leaving the local population cut off from its culture and from its family and economic ties with the rest of the Arab world. As a side benefit, the policy helped accelerate the restoration of essential services by bringing a sense of calm to the area. Having the option of crossing over to the East Bank seemed to alleviate anxiety in the territories and mitigate the hardship of the occupation. By the same token, it boosted Jordan's chances of maintaining its influence in the West Bank.

The humiliating defeat had caused Jordan's stock with the people of the conquered territories to hit an all-time low. On the streets of West Bank cities, Hussein was openly mocked as "the little king" and vilified as "the grandson of the traitor Abdullah." In a bid to polish his tarnished image, the king began to pump in funds, using truck drivers who made regular runs across the bridges as couriers. The open-bridges policy remained in force even after the annexation of Jerusalem brought the "honeymoon" between the military government and the local populace to an abrupt end, and the local leaders, who by now had become very circumspect in their associations with the military government, began to refurbish their ties with Amman. Striking lawyers, school principals, and other members of the civil service continued to receive their salaries from Jordan. And when municipal services in Nablus approached the brink of collapse, because of financial difficulties, Moshe Dayan agreed to let Hamdi Kenan cross over to Amman and collect a "back debt" Jordan owed the city.

Kenan, a successful businessman, is the owner of a soap factory in Nablus. Two years ago, in a long talk I had with him in his modest shop in the city's commercial district, he spoke of the motives behind his actions then. "I had no choice," he protested. "I had to walk a thin line, for I was convinced that pursuing a solution to the Palestinian problem through Jordan was the best option open to my people." As to whether it had been a good idea to accept money from the Jordanian government, Kenan had no doubts: "I told the Jordanian prime minister that the money would serve our national interests, for it would be beyond the reach of the military government." As Kenan told it, the prime minister had accepted this reasoning and encouraged him "to pour dinars on the flames of civil disobedience and rebellion."

The connection between Jordan's guaranteeing the salaries of civil servants in the territories and the spread of civil disobedience is readily apparent. The Union of Palestinian Teachers, for example, called on its members not to return to the classroom after the summer recess. Merchants, who did not even benefit directly from any support coming from across the river, were warned against selling goods to Israelis. But although the traditional leadership fanned the first flames of rebellion, it was soon charged with failure by the younger generation. They, in their impatience, wanted to channel the popular insurgency in other directions and opted for terror.

As the first terrorist cells began to form in the West Bank, the work of building them into a network was taken on by a rotund little man who shuttled between Nablus and Jenin on a motorbike, and soon he began to harvest the fruits of his labors. In time he would become world famous as the head of the Palestine Liberation Organization, but back then Yasir Arafat slipped through the net of the military government, determined though it was to quash any hint of insurgency. In the first year of the occupation Israeli troops arrested hundreds and conducted some 1,100 trials. Among those detained were members of the Communist party (which had been outlawed by the Jordanian government), activists of the Arab Nationalist party, followers of George Habash's Popular Front for the Liberation of Palestine, and defiant public figures. The arrests were made under provisions of the Defense (Emergency) Regulations that had been promulgated by the British in 1945.

Just as the deportations in Jerusalem had had a dubious effect, this latest crackdown in the West Bank seemed to be of limited value. The first auto tire to be set aflame in the territories by terrorists burned in Nablus, and ever since billows of

black smoke and the smell of burning rubber have been like
a clarion call to rebellion against Israeli rule. In response to
the growing resistance, the military government decided to
punish Nablus's mayor, Hamdi Kenan—"the man with his
nose in the air," as the military governor described him—and
closed down his two shops. Moreover, Kenan was ordered to
return the money he had obtained from the Jordanian prime
minister. Striking back, on August 17 Kenan informed the
military government that he was resigning and was also disbanding the Nablus municipal council. The same man who had
formerly been denounced as a traitor for cooperating with the
military government became overnight a national hero and a
paragon of the nationalist leadership in the territories. In this
way, too, the course of events in Nablus paralleled that in
Jerusalem.

Moshe Dayan's barometer for registering tension in the
air sent him rushing to Nablus in an attempt to halt the rapid
deterioration in the situation. A special meeting of the municipal council was convened, and a tense silence filled the hall as
Dayan took the measure of the grim-visaged councilmen. This
time he dispensed with superfluous pleasantries and got right
down to business. "If you wish to resign, Mr. Kenan, then by
all means do so," he began, in the inimitable Dayan style. "But
I hope you realize that the people who will suffer most from
your move are the residents of your city. You are deserting the
ship in its most critical hour." Kenan complained about his
treatment at the hands of the military governor and demanded
to know why his shops had been shut. In an apparent gesture
of conciliation, Dayan ordered the measures against the mayor
rescinded immediately. Then the two men turned to the real
source of friction between them, and the basis of their power
struggle: the Jordanian funds being distributed in Nablus. At
one point in the subsequent discussion Kenan even argued
that money to pay the local police had come out of his own
pocket because his "heart broke at the sight of guardians of the
law suffering from hunger." Kenan's resignation maneuver

ended as a victory for Dayan. The mayor ultimately backed down and, under the watchful gaze of a military government officer, repaired to the Dayma Bridge and returned 62,000 dinars to a senior Jordanian official waiting for him there.

Formally, the matter was closed. But the leaders and inhabitants of the territories both drew a clear lesson from it. The full significance of the open-bridges policy was plain to them now, and they drew encouragement from the incident as telling them that in an hour of need they would always have a broad shoulder to lean on: the Kingdom of Jordan.

Meanwhile, senior military government officials continued to take a cold view of the acts of civil disobedience, endorsing a slogan then making the rounds of the administration: "The Arabs are intimidated by force, and a firm hand will settle them down." That is a briefly put and somewhat simplified version of the "firm-hand policy" that was adopted in the occupied territories. In fairness, advocates of that approach should not be accused of a secret desire to incite unrest or churn up discontent. Rather than indicating maliciousness or lack of sensitivity, the firm-hand policy was symptomatic of a chronic shortsightedness and a strain of simplemindedness that prefers to ignore realities. Take, for example, an incident that occurred on August 20, 1967, when shots were fired at some Israelis traveling near the village of Abu Dis, on the road from Jerusalem to Jericho, injuring three security officers. In retaliation, the IDF blew up a number of houses in the village, and three other structures collapsed from the shock waves. The form and force of the punishment only served the interests of the original assailants by igniting tempers throughout the occupied territories. The policy might have deterred property owners, but it infuriated the young people—so much so that there was doubt whether the new school year could open on schedule. Moshe Dayan's response to that possibility was a shrug of the shoulders, as if to say, "If they want to learn, they'll go to school. If they don't, they won't." Right or wrong, he started from the assumption that the Arabs of the West

63

Bank needed a strong government and an atmosphere of calm as much as the military governors did.

One hand would be extended in aid, but the other could beat down mercilessly. That appeared to be the point Dayan was trying to make when he reminded the Arabs of the moral of their own proverb, "If you can see the lion's teeth, don't be tempted into believing that he's smiling." When Dayan feigned indifference, the press dubbed his attitude the "kid-glove policy"; when he came down hard on the territories, the phrasemakers were quick to come up with "firm-hand policy." Sheikh Ja'abri summed it up in this graphic metaphor: "Dayan slaps you across the face and then immediately retrieves your hat for you and places it perfectly on your head." I, for one, have never understood either the psychology or the efficacy of the carrot-and-stick approach. Even God Almighty has some-times faltered when pursuing such a course, so why should Moshe Dayan have expected to be any better at it? Far more important, I was concerned about the moral implications of such a policy. A people that resorted to carrots and sticks to bend another people to its will was doomed to become a nation of overseers. And a nation that attempted to subjugate another could hardly expect its own liberty to be secure.

Within a few months after the war that had touched off such a storm of emotion in me, a war that my country had fought in self-defense against those who wished to destroy it, I had come to see that our victory was not "sharp, smooth, and elegant," as the popular saying had it. The IDF had defeated three Arab armies and overrun some of their territories, but it had not liberated the people living there. The real struggle had only begun, and the first question to be faced now was: Who rules the West Bank?

The military government could point to some impressive achievements in its work with the local population, especially in agriculture and industry. It had a few unsung heroes, such as the staff officer in charge of the agricultural desk, Eitan Yisraeli, whose enormous efforts had saved the harvest, threat-

ened with ruin because of the war. Nevertheless, the unrest
continued to simmer. Once the Jordanians recovered their
wits, they began using their broadcasting station to raise the
pitch of civil disobedience in the West Bank by relentlessly
calling for a general strike. While it was not clear what effect
the broadcasts had, they certainly were not conducive to a
climate of calm. In any event, when on September 19 the
National Guidance Committee in Jerusalem distributed handbills calling for a general strike, the rise in its standing and
influence was hard to miss. The strike was a failure in Jerusalem—undoubtedly because of the deportation of the committee's chairman, Sheikh Abdul Sa'ih—but the same could not
be said about the West Bank. Shops in Nablus locked their
doors and many merchants remained at home. Mayor Hamdi
Kenan was in something of a bind. He wanted to remain in the
good graces of his constituents, but he was wary of the
likely response from the Israeli authorities. He therefore told
the military governor, "We shall strike but not demonstrate.
The residents of Nablus wish to express their opposition to the
Israeli occupation and to rouse public opinion around the
world and at the United Nations."

Before long, however, events slipped out of the mayor's
control. In September of 1967, Nablus took over from East
Jerusalem as the standard-bearer for the entire West Bank. A
local constable who had joined the Israeli police was shot to
death on the main street, causing a mantle of fear to settle over
the city and sending residents scurrying for shelter behind
locked doors—in essence, the people were declaring a curfew
of their own volition. The first shot of internecine terror had
been fired in Nablus—a deed justified by the ordinary citizen
as "a traitor's just desert."

Regardless, the Ministry of Defense and certain circles
within the military government continued to believe it was
possible to "educate a nation." The only question was what
punishments or other steps would be the most effective means
of doing so. Suggestions ranged from the imposition of collec-

tive punishment and deportations to closing the bridges and prohibiting travel to Jordan. At one point Moshe Dayan ordered the military government to close twenty shops in Nablus (including Kenan's), take five buses out of operation, and rescind the business licenses of strike activists. By then, though, a pattern of action and reaction had already emerged. Open animosity between the military government and the local leaders had only grown sharper, and a mayor—unless he wanted to earn the stigma of "traitor"—had to do what his constituents expected him to. When Kenan was summoned to appear before the military governor, he refused to go and bluntly told the deputy military governor, who had brought him the summons, "If he wants to see me, let him come here!" The military governor countered with a common tactic: he called in Kenan's political rival, the deputy mayor, Haj Mazuz el-Masri, and informed *him* of the punitive measures to be taken against the city.

It should not have surprised the Israeli authorities that Nablus was the site of recurrent showdowns with the military government. The city had become an important social and political center during the period of Jordanian rule. It was the headquarters of a number of political parties and prided itself on a thriving local intelligentsia. Moreover, a few months before the Six Day War, Nablus had been the scene of a mass demonstration against King Hussein. The entire city had erupted in turmoil, and twenty residents were killed in the ensuing melee. The king responded by imposing a twenty-day curfew, but Hussein was not able to break the city's defiant spirit, and the spark lighted there had threatened to ignite the whole West Bank. Now Israel believed that its military government could succeed where Hussein had failed. Yet the situation had already escalated beyond the worst scenario of Hussein's day, for along with political protest came the first signs of underground activity. The military government knew that groups of young people were being trained in sabotage, and in flushing them out it only raised tensions in the city another notch. What saved the situation—temporarily, at least —was one more meeting between Moshe Dayan and Mayor Hamdi Kenan. Both men, astute politicians, knew there was little point in continuing to pursue their course of brinksmanship, and as his way of stepping back from the edge Kenan announced the opening of the school year. His reward was a severe tongue-lashing from Jordan and a chorus of jeers from the youth of Nablus, who refused to accept his "capitulation" and turned their anger against their own people by terrorizing local merchants who trafficked with Israelis.

To a large extent, Israel's approach in dealing with the problem of organized terrorism in the West Bank forged the character of its relations with the whole population there. Terrorism became a two-way street; every time an attack was perpetrated against the civilian population in Israel, the military government retaliated with a severe blow to the people of the occupied areas—and the punishments it dispensed were dire. Acting under the Defense (Emergency) Regulations issued during the Mandate, the military government believed it could calm the turbulence by blowing up the homes of captured terrorists and their families. It was against this background that Dayan and Kenan carried on their covert struggle. Dayan was backed by the full weight of the government's power, but Kenan controlled the people of Nablus. In the end both lost, and their mutual defeat set the pattern for subsequent relations between the Israeli government and the Palestinian leadership. In embracing the punitive strategies recommended by his officers, the defense minister lost his influence with Kenan. The mayor, for his part, failed in his desperate effort to "walk between the raindrops." He wanted to remain in favor with his constituents and declared his support for their struggle, but he was forced to yield to the dictates of the military government and thereby lost their confidence. Kenan emerged from his dilemma a loser on both counts, and present-day mayors have learned a cardinal lesson from his experience. They have become doubly wary of being seduced into performing the will of the occupying regime for fear that they, too, will lose the respect of their constituents.

Kenan appears to have been sincere in his desire to establish a pattern of peaceful coexistence with the new rulers of the West Bank. He held Moshe Dayan in great esteem, and in September of 1968 he became the first public figure in the West Bank to entertain the defense minister in his home, for lunch—using the occasion to talk about the oppression of the Palestinians. In the end, however, the mayor found himself in a blind alley. In a year and a half he had brandished the threat of resignation about ten times, indicating both how weary he was and how little power he actually wielded. He had called press conferences to warn of the violent convulsions that would rack the territories if the military government did not retreat from its strong-arm policy. And the government might have been more attentive to his admonitions had it not been for the relentless tide of terror against civilian targets. As matters stood, each additional attack only strengthened the government's resolve to quash every last sign of rebellion. Kenan's constituents began to avoid him and to reject his moderate line, though they continued to look to him as an intermediary with the authorities. In short, he was useful for sending cables to the defense minister and protesting acts of repression and brutality. But Hamdi Kenan was never able to ease the plight of the people of Nablus or to reverse the oppressive measures taken against them, and so it seems quite logical for him to have concluded that his only way out was to resign.

The IDF high command may indeed have had tucked away in its files detailed military plans for the capture of enemy territory in the event of all-out war. But I doubt that any authority in Israel had given thought to the parallel question of how to manage those territories after they were conquered. The 1967 war was as much of a surprise to Israel as it was to the people of the captured areas. Within a few days the map of the Middle East was changed beyond recognition, and Israel's political leadership never got the chance to develop an overall strategy for utilizing the military victory to lay the foundations of a secure and comprehensive peace. On the contrary, a sense of bewilderment, which seemed to extend from the highest political level down to the commanders in the field, was all too evident in many of the decisions of the military government. Israel assumed that once the army had triumphed on the battlefield the ball was in the other court. Furthermore, for the first few months after the war the Israeli government gave the distinct impression that its only interest in the territories was as a bargaining chip when the redeeming telephone call from the Arab capitals finally came. Rafael Vardi, a major general in the reserve and the first commander in the West Bank, has conceded that neither the senior officers of the military government nor those responsible for political decisions were aware of trends that had been evolving in the occupied territories prior to the war. As a consequence, the Israeli government missed a golden opportunity to take advantage of the prevailing mood in furthering its own interests in the area.

King Hussein had played a double game in his rule of the West Bank. He had courted the Palestinian aristocracy while simultaneously spurning it by showing his preference for his own capital, Amman, over Jerusalem. Likewise, while cultivating his West Bank followers, he had made no secret of his desire to transform the Palestinians into Jordanians—a purpose he was abetting by bringing many Palestinians into his government and the ranks of his civil service. Christian Arabs from the Bethlehem area were appointed consuls in some of the major cities of Latin America. Distinguished personalities like Anwar Nusseibah were made government ministers. More and more Palestinians began to call themselves "Jordanians of Palestinian origin"—though there was also opposition to that trend and a determination to protect the Palestinian people's right to maintain a distinct identity.

Today, fourteen years after the war, a number of Middle

East experts believe that the capture of the West Bank arrested a very welcome process—welcome from Israel's point of view —just as it was developing momentum. Under Hussein's tutelage, the Palestinian problem was moving swiftly toward a resolution, but then the war intervened and reawakened the Palestinians' nationalist sentiments and their craving for political independence. As the occupation wore on, Israel hinted to Hussein that if he failed to move toward some sort of accommodation, it might seek out other solutions to the West Bank problem. The notion of instituting a form of self-rule in the West Bank and linking it to Israel in some sort of federation was never entirely ruled out. Local self-rule implied a spirit of cooperation between the Israeli authorities and the local inhabitants, who would be expected to manage their own affairs, and the very fact that it was even considered suggests that, despite the unrest, there were encouraging signs that the idea might have worked. One reason for such optimism could well have been the example of the mayor of Hebron, Sheikh Mohammed Ali Ja'abri.

From 1967 through the mid-1970s, two mayors symbolized the wide disparity of views that prevailed in the West Bank. At one end of the spectrum stood Hamdi Kenan, governing a city whose residents were seething with rebellion. At the other end was Mohammed Ali Ja'abri, whose twenty years of rule in Hebron had consolidated his and his family's position in and around the city. Ja'abri had been one of King Hussein's most devoted loyalists in the West Bank and had been entrusted with ministerial duties since the 1950s. In the following decade, when the influence of the pro-Nasserite camp led by the Kawasmeh family began to grow, Ja'abri succeeded in toppling his political rivals—who were also Hussein's rivals—and further enhanced his own standing. In 1972 Ja'abri supported the idea of reconstituting a united Jordanian Arab kingdom, which meant uniting the two banks of the Jordan. But after the Yom Kippur War he changed his mind, no longer believing, as Kenan did, that the occupied territories should be returned to Jordan immediately. Moshe Dayan found in Ja'abri a trustworthy ally in his campaign to extend a degree of self-rule in the territories. Later Dayan would speak of him as "one of the most scrupulous and wisest leaders the Arabs ever had."

In his great wisdom, the mayor of Hebron knew that he couldn't promote his policies without first gaining some allies. He therefore solicited the support of the president of the Ramallah Chamber òf Commerce, Aziz Shihadeh, and his son-in-law, the former governor of Jerusalem, Anwar el-Khatib. Having broadened his base, Ja'abri was no longer reluctant to denounce the spread of terrorism, and in January of 1968 he called on the people of Hebron to "rid ourselves of those who do us harm and whose deeds bring no benefit." Kenan's response to Ja'abri was to proclaim from Nablus, "If I were a young man, I would join the Fatah!" As the dialectic continued, it became apparent that two contradictory trends were emerging in the territories. Every so often a mayor or some other public figure would stand up and announce his support for self-rule in the territories. Political commentators and officers of the military government would quickly tag that person a "moderate"—which hardly made life any easier for him. At the same time, King Hussein was certainly not interested in nurturing this group. In fact, he repeatedly told envoys sent on behalf of the Israeli government that he would not discuss any solution to the Palestinian question until Israel withdrew from the occupied territories. Rashad a-Shawa, the mayor of Gaza, once proposed to the king that a deep-water port serving Jordan could be built in his city with Israeli aid, and even that was met with the same rebuff.

One of the more painful ironies of the period was that just when some circles in Israel were talking about the need to encourage self-rule in the territories, decisions were being made in the field that sabotaged any move in the direction of increased autonomy. Even those who argued in favor of a more liberal occupation policy seemed to be baffled by the everyday problems in the territories. How could one reconcile a desire to broaden the scope of self-rule with the antinationalist censorship of textbooks in the West Bank? Or with the cancellation of standing arrangements applying to historical sites and antiquities and the transfer of responsibility for those sites to the military government? If Israel truly wanted to create a basis for independent economic activity in the West Bank, why weren't the major banks allowed to reopen their doors? Finally, a question that continues to haunt many Israelis to this day: Why wouldn't the government permit independent political activity in the territories? Such a move, many now argue, would have spurred the emergence of a local leadership willing and able to reach an accommodation with Israel; instead, the prohibition on free and open political activity only opened the way for Palestinian organizations based outside the territories—meaning the PLO—to tighten their grip.

As the Israeli elections of 1973 approached, the volume of public debate on these issues rose considerably, and voices from both ends of the political spectrum began to demand that some hard thought be devoted to the future of the territories. From the right came a call for their unilateral annexation, based on historical rights and the contention that security considerations made it unthinkable to relinquish the lands to a country or regime inimical to Israel. Opposing them was the element scoffed at as "bleeding hearts." These "prophets of doom," who saw the corrupting effect of the occupation on the moral and social fiber of Israeli society, spoke of the occupied territories as "a cancer gnawing away at the moral strength of the State of Israel" and drew on an arsenal of arguments to show that Israel's hold on the territories was doing nothing to improve its security. To the contrary, they warned that grave dangers lurked ahead for a society that became accustomed to lording it over a foreign population—or, less euphemistically, to suppressing another people.

Whatever their worth in such a debate, the press reports coming out of the territories supported the proponents of withdrawal. It may have the best of intentions, but a "liberal military government" is an obvious contradiction in terms. Though defeated on the battlefield, the Arabs had refused to bow down and sign a declaration of surrender. And as their expressions of defiance grew sharper, so did the military government's responses and its choice of punitive measures. In short, the Palestinian problem—which many had believed was about to become a "fossil of history"—had reemerged in all its stridency, and the entire world was beginning to follow events in the area. What's more, the unrest in the territories was having a direct effect on the surrounding Arab countries, and some Palestinians were speaking about a "great mission" to rouse the entire Arab world from its languor. The Palestinian writer Anis el-Kasem prophesied, "The day will come when history tells of the impact of the Palestinian dispersion on the modern Arab revival. History will yet declare that the Palestinians led many Arab countries out of the Middle Ages and into the twentieth century."

History may yet tell of many prodigious effects of the Middle East conflict, but for the present one thing is certain. A situation that was at first considered temporary has dragged on and on, and every additional day of Israeli rule in the territories only contributes to the general dismay and drives the hawkish elements on both sides to ever greater extremes. Those are facts that history is not likely to judge kindly.

4
THE HORNETS' NEST OF GAZA

The tension that had been building in the occupied territories since the summer of 1967 reached a height in 1970, a year of turbulence for the Palestinian people in the occupied areas and beyond. For all the ferment in the West Bank, however, it was in the Gaza Strip that events seemed to outstrip Israel's ability even to assimilate them, much less control them. More important, perhaps, it was what happened in Gaza that gave the Israelis their most frightening glimpse of what might lie in store for both sides.

In sharp contrast to the West Bank, with its firmly rooted urban and rural population, the Gaza Strip is inhabited mostly by refugees who have never known what it is to live in peace or happiness. The entire Strip is less than five miles wide and only thirty miles from north to south, yet in 1948 it had absorbed up to 150,000 people, most of whom had fled the fighting in the lower coastal region of Palestine expecting to return to their homes before long. When things turned out otherwise, the refugees settled into makeshift camps and for the next eighteen years lived there under Egyptian administration. Unlike Jordan, which unilaterally annexed the West Bank in 1950, Egypt never incorporated the Gaza Strip into its sovereign borders, but administered the area along the lines of a trusteeship. It did nothing at all to ease the suffering of the refugees by clearing slums or alleviating the abysmal poverty in the camps. The mazes of narrow alleyways turned to rivers of mud in winter and gave off a suffocating stench in the burning days of summer. Little wonder that long before the

Six Day War the camps had become hornets' nests of simmering resentment. But the Egyptians brutally quashed any sign of insurgency and kept a tight rein on the refugee population.

When Israeli troops occupied the area in 1967, they found that the population had swelled from approximately 200,000 in 1948 to almost 350,000—presumably from natural causes alone—giving Gaza one of the highest population densities in the world. The overwhelming majority of the people were still housed in camps. Under the Israeli occupation, their physical distress was augmented by a feeling of national oppression, and the combination boded an eruption of frightening proportions. By 1970, hundreds of youths had armed themselves with Karl Gustav and Kalachnikov rifles and were pouring fire on any Israelis who crossed their path. Ahmad Shukeiri's Palestine Liberation Organization had gained dominance in the area, and it found an eager response to its recruiting drives among the embittered young people of the Strip. Before long Gaza was swarming with terrorists.

I had heard and read a good deal about the situation in the defiant city of Gaza, but until 1970 I had avoided going anywhere near the Strip for lack of the courage to confront the unspeakable misery. And the violence was, if anything, even more daunting. In June of that year, four Israeli soldiers were shot to death by terrorist assailants. Stonings of buses and the hurling of grenades at Israeli visitors were commonplace. Determined to restore its rule in the Strip, the Israel Defense Forces made exhaustive searches to trap the terrorist bands and their leaders. One of those operations turned up Dr. Fayek Abdul-Hai Husseini, the leader of the Arab nationalist organization Kawmiyoun el-Arab. Husseini, who was related to Yasir Arafat, had been politically active in the Gaza Strip since the mid-1960s, and he was considered quite a catch. In spite of the heightened vigilance, however, political activity continued, under the leadership of Ibrahim Abu-Sita, a refugee from Beersheba, who had once been Ahmad Shukeiri's political secretary.

75

Abu-Sita was not a man noted for his political finesse. In 1967 he had been permitted to return from Egypt to the Gaza Strip, after pledging to the Israeli military governor that he would not engage in political activity. Three years later, in his first meeting with Mordechai Gur, the commander of the Israeli forces in the Strip, he showed no qualms about pouring out his indignation. "The country must be divided between Jews and Arabs," he lectured the future chief of staff. "So I fail to understand how you can speak of a liberal policy or enlightened rule when you go around demolishing the homes in which Arab freedom fighters have lived. Why is a father guilty? How is a mother at fault?" So Abu-Sita was banished again— this time to a military camp in the heart of the Sinai desert. The first time I met him, in 1974, it came out that my brother Sa'id had been the Israeli soldier who guarded him at that camp. "I was charged with inciting the people to strike. And it's true. I did," he told me. "How would you act under the yoke of occupation?"

Once again Abu-Sita promised his Israeli wardens to avoid political activity, and once again he was allowed to return to his lovely home on the Gaza coast. But he was highly conscious of the fateful historical processes going on around him, and sometimes he was unable to check his tongue. He once told me, with his characteristic candor, "If I don't speak out, I will be betraying my people. If I do speak, the government will punish me. Since my people are more important to me than the government, and since I can get around the area commander by a little politicking, I'm better off taking the punishment of the military government than facing the punishment of my people."

That outlook seemed to be shared by many in Gaza, for by 1970 the lawlessness had reached intolerable proportions. Israelis employed by the civil service or serving in the army could not travel the roads of the Gaza Strip or walk through the refugee camps unmolested. Moshe Dayan once suggested simply abandoning the local population to its own devices.

"Let them turn their lives into hell," was his advice. But his fellow ministers in the government found it unthinkable for the Gaza Strip to be beyond the pale for Israelis. The longer Israel delayed in dealing with the Gaza problem, the more audacious the network of terrorists and their supporters would become. As it was, the young people of the Strip thought nothing of offering aid or a night's shelter to wanted men.

That was the atmosphere throughout the occupied territories when I began my army service in 1970. The goal of the terrorist organizations was to paralyze the military government, and in Gaza they almost succeeded; in 1970 life in that teeming region bordered on anarchy. When the terrorist cells in the northern part of the West Bank were exposed and neutralized, the people of Gaza had taken up the baton. Soon hair-raising shoot-outs were erupting in the narrow alleyways of the refugee camps. In 1970 alone, about 1,100 young people were trapped by the IDF in the Gaza Strip. Some 370 confessed to engaging in guerrilla activities, and 125 others admitted having aided terrorists. More than half of those arrested—633—were classified as "suspects" and released. The precise legal meaning of that term has never been clear to me. Sometime later, when I saw arrests being made at a demonstration, I innocently asked the military government officers why so many people were being taken into custody. To them, the answer was simple: suspects were interrogated, and then were released if they were found not guilty of any untoward behavior. By that kind of reasoning, every Arab in the Gaza Strip was a "suspect" until he passed the test of interrogation.

Perhaps the most harrowing aspect of the violence in the camps was the heavy toll it took of the local population. No fewer than 106 residents of the area were killed in 1970, 94 by terrorist fire and 12 by Israeli soldiers. Finally the government decided it must put an end to the havoc, and on January 3, 1971, the commander of the Gaza Strip and northern Sinai, Brigadier General Menachem Aviram, received the signal to act. His first move was to dismiss the mayor of Gaza, Rageb

77

el-Alami, for harboring a hostile attitude toward the authorities and failing to cooperate with the IDF. The two main counts against the mayor were his refusal to denounce terrorist activities in the city and his opposition to having Gaza linked to Israel's nationwide electric power system. He also had made a practice of protesting the "persecution of the Arabs of Gaza." Thus his dismissal was meant to be seen as a political show of strength. But the authorities did not stop there. The real point of no return came with steps to intensify the IDF's presence in the area. On January 11, the Border Police—Israel's "Green Berets"—moved in to restore order in Gaza.

Their first target was the Shati refugee camp, which was notorious as a hotbed of terrorist activity. A total curfew was imposed on the camp, and heavy machinery was brought in to raze buildings and widen the alleys into roads that could accommodate motor vehicles. When the passages were clear, troops arrived and began house-to-house searches. Needless to say, dozens of arrests followed. The media in Israel did not report on the action at the time (though if they had, public opinion would doubtless have supported the need to "punish the Strip"), but journalists who toured the area afterward came away with the impression that the residents of Shati were sitting on a smoking volcano of rage. Women charged that soldiers had beaten their men, damaged their property, and committed other acts of brutality.

When the commander of the Strip was asked to reply to those harsh allegations, all he could say was, "It would take hundreds of investigators an entire year to get at the truth— and even then it's doubtful that the real story would come out." The flood of complaints reaching the General Staff did not abate, and victims were not the only ones registering protests. Four soldiers sent a letter to the General Staff detailing the excesses committed by their units, and none other than the chief of staff himself, Lieutenant General Chaim Bar-Lev, summoned them to a private meeting to hear their version of the events. On February 19, the daily *Ha'aretz* reported that as a result of the outcry two senior officers had been rebuked for their conduct in the Gaza Strip. Subsequent trials of Israeli soldiers revealed that instances of robbery and brutality had indeed accompanied the police action in Shati, and two members of the Border Police were dismissed for unjustified use of force.

Gaza was still smarting from its bruises when some of the armed youths still at large decided to stage a series of spectacular actions to prove they had not lost their clout. In their most ambitious action, they blew up the main post office in the city of Gaza. Sixty-one people were wounded in the blast, four of them fatally; and to add insult to injury, innocent people were again punished in the IDF's intensified effort to close in on the terrorists. In the recurrent tests of strength between the two armed camps, many innocent lives were lost as both sides tried to cow the people into submission. The terrorists relied on summary justice. A taxi driver from the Nutzeyrat camp was shot to death for refusing to aid a wounded terrorist. A woman from the same camp was murdered at the door of her home, in broad daylight, for having "collaborated" with the military authorities. (One of her neighbors summed up his opinion of the affair with the comment "the fate of a traitor.") In another incident, two youths from Gaza who were suspected of passing secrets to the Jews were summarily executed. In April 1971, a paramedic was gunned down in the a-Shifa government hospital for refusing to join the Popular Front for the Liberation of Palestine to tend its wounded who were hiding out in the citrus groves. Dozens of people witnessed the shooting, but not one of them dared stop the killer from making his escape. The inhabitants of the Gaza Strip felt themselves being crushed between the hammer of repression and the anvil of terror. Each day the IDF's spokesmen issued fresh bulletins on armed clashes between Israeli troops and Gazan terrorists. The mounting bloodshed and ruthless acts of murder had made life in the Gaza Strip unbearable.

I was undergoing special training in an officers' course during those dreadful days of 1971, and my unit was sent to the Gaza Strip on operational maneuvers. When the education officer called us together for a briefing on how to deal with the local population, he pointedly stressed that "not all Gazans are terrorists" and warned us to be scrupulous about observing the IDF code of ethics. Naturally, we had heard about the violence in Gaza and the "excesses" perpetrated by Israeli soldiers, so we knew what he was getting at. After dark we climbed into trucks weighed down by weapons and ammunition and were taken through dim alleys and past dense orchards to the outskirts of the Mugazi refugee camp. Our force encircled the camp and waited for dawn, when a crier made his way through the alleys announcing the start of a curfew. He warned that no one was to enter or leave the camp and that "anyone disobeying this order will be shot on the spot."

Then we entered Mugazi and systematically searched house after house, following a standard formula. The soldiers would kick in the rickety door and burst into the hut. All the men were frisked and interrogated; closets were thoroughly searched; any place that could possibly serve as a hideout got close scrutiny. In one house we were met by an old woman who kept muttering, "May Allah have vengeance on you." The commander of my squad asked me to translate. "Allah have pity," I told him, afraid that if he knew what she was really saying he would harm her. Instead, he just chuckled, and I could feel the revulsion rising in me over what we had to do. During the daylight hours we combed the orchards, under explicit orders to "shoot at any suspicious movement after 6:00 P.M." An old fellah whose legs were not dependable enough to get him home in time might have to pay for that weakness with his life.

The fact that I was a soldier on active service prescribed that I keep my feelings to myself, and neither within the unit nor back at camp did I ever speak about what the experience had been like for me. But back home on leave, I confided to

80

my father that I wanted to drop out of the officers' course. He talked me out of it by showing me that, either way, I couldn't get out of facing up to the duties an army must perform. Even so, I never was able to forget that behind the narcotic clichés —"subduing the population," "collective punishment"—was a cruel, painful reality. In August of 1972, four thousand families were turned out of the Jebalya refugee camp in the Gaza Strip. A detention camp was set up at Abu-Zneima, in the Sinai desert, for a hundred families whose sons had been captured as terrorists. Dozens of prisoners were held in administrative detention in the Gaza prison and never brought to trial. In Israel itself, more and more people were ready to defend the policy of force against force and in agreement that the military government must have a free hand to "overpower a population that shelters murderers."

"Security considerations" were elevated to the status of a sacred cow and were well on the way to becoming the sole criterion against which everything else was measured. Even members of Israel's intellectual community lent themselves to the national consensus by affirming that a country in a state of siege should not be judged by conventional standards. Few had the inner strength to step back and take a hard look at the true state of affairs, to admit the malignant, brutalizing effect the occupation was having on Israeli society. Who was to say what the limits of "security considerations" were? Could we justify assaulting innocent civilians as the price of trapping sworn enemies of the state who had taken shelter in the refugee camps? Did the security requirements of the State of Israel really require massive action on Lebanese soil? I struggled with such questions endlessly, and they gave me no rest. But I did complete the officers' course and, mercifully, was then posted to a station in the north.

Gaza's rebellion went on for eighteen months, and day in and day out the IDF kept up its searches and patrols. Eventually, the tug-of-war completely paralyzed life in the area. When unemployment reached insupportable proportions, the gov-

ernment relented and allowed the Gazan leadership to recon-
stitute a local council. Rashad a-Shawa was appointed to head
the Gaza municipal council, and slowly but surely things returned to normal. What remained of that harrowing year and
a half of violence was the festering resentment of the people
of Gaza. One can still see it in their eyes today. When I visited
the Shati refugee camp with a television crew in 1975, I could
read the implacable rancor in the looks directed at us. The
military governor insisted on a troop escort for us at night, for
our own safety. I wasn't afraid that we would come to any harm
in Shati, but we were constantly showered with abuse. As we
walked through the dim, stinking alleys, dozens of the women
sitting in the doorways of their tumbledown mud houses
would spit stinging remarks at us. Not one resident of the
camp saw fit to ask us into his home. I assume that the memory
of so many people being cut down for collaborating with the
Israelis was still fresh—and so, too, the memory of all those
killed in the cross fire between presumed assassins and pursuing Israeli soldiers.

The residents of Shati and the other camps have not been
particularly welcomed in the city of Gaza or in the West Bank
—or by Israeli Arabs, either—since they are considered a
lower class of Palestinian. When Ibrahim Abu-Sita stood for
election as mayor of Gaza, the native-born leadership sounded
a great hue and cry: "He is a refugee from Beersheba, and he
should aspire to return to his own city, not set down roots in
Gaza." As a citizen of a country that has consistently tried to
rehabilitate the weaker elements of its population, I was appalled by the attitude of the Palestinian aristocracy toward the
refugees. Since 1967 Israel has made an effort to improve the
lot of these wretched people by constructing new quarters for
them beyond the confines of the camps. But funds for that
mammoth job are limited, and at any rate are insufficient to
keep up with the high birth rate of the refugee population.

There is, of course, another Gaza, distinct from the camps
and their brooding misery, and it is symbolized by the figure

of Rashad a-Shawa, who has been mayor of the city of Gaza for close to a decade. Tall, broad-shouldered, and suave, he has something about him that recalls Egypt's President Gamal Abdel Nasser. A-Shawa is an astute and seasoned politician, whose practical experience dates back to the days of the British Mandate, when he served as a district officer. In the 1930s he was quite candid about his admiration for Mussolini, and many of his associates openly sympathized with the Nazis. What he did conceal from his employers—the administrators of the British Mandate—was that he was also serving as a liaison for the chief of the Arab gangs, Sheikh Az-a-Din Kasem, who was operating around Jenin. After the 1948 war, a-Shawa was known to be a supporter of the Moslem Brotherhood, which opposed the Egyptian regime, and he adopted a pro-Hashemite stance. A leader of the fedayeen who used the Gaza Strip as a base from which to sow panic and destruction through the southern part of Israel, he was arrested by the Israeli troops who entered the Strip in 1956, during the Sinai campaign, and was held for the duration of that occupation. Various parties in Gaza—including the terrorist bands scattered throughout the city—had backed him as their candidate for mayor. He was believed to be so influential that as the IDF tightened its cordon around the terrorist groups, their commander, Ziyad Husseini, asked a-Shawa to intercede with the military authorities and see if they would "open a channel to Jordan for the Palestinian guerrillas hiding out in the orchards." Hundreds of respected local figures signed a petition urging him to accept the position of mayor. He keeps that document in a special case in his plush villa in the center of Gaza, not far from Abdul Nasser Square.

One night in October of 1971, Ziyad Husseini—who was a relative of both Fayek Husseini, the commander of the Kawmiyoun el-Arab, and Yasir Arafat, the head of the PLO—ran into a troop of Israeli soldiers in Gaza. He managed to evade his pursuers and with his last ounce of strength reached a-Shawa's doorstep. His beard grown wild, his clothes in tatters, and a Kalachnikov rifle in his hand, Husseini looked larger and more menacing than he actually was, and he made the mayor swear to protect him until the danger had passed. A-Shawa let the terrorist leader in and bundled him off to the basement.

Ziyad Husseini was born in Gaza in 1943, completed his secondary education there, and then applied for admission to the police officers' school in Cairo but was turned down. Reluctantly, he was recruited into Ahmad Shukeiri's Palestinian Liberation Army, and after he returned to the Strip, as a lieutenant in Shukeiri's ranks, he became addicted to alcohol and hashish. Husseini's acquaintances in Gaza remember him as a prodigal and unstable man. When the terrorist bands were being organized in the region, he assumed the rank of *nakib* (lieutenant colonel) and soon became a commander of unquestioned authority. It is hard to see why Husseini's men looked up to him, especially since he was careful not to take an active part in military operations. However, the shrewd a-Shawa knew how to exploit his association with Husseini for all it was worth. Whenever the radical West Bank mayors accused a-Shawa of excessive moderation, he would pointedly remind them that the commanders of the terrorist groups in the Strip—including Husseini—had backed him for mayor.

Husseini hid out in Rashad a-Shawa's cellar for thirty-five days, and then he took his own life. When the story came out, the Gazans were frankly skeptical of the mayor's version, suspecting a-Shawa and his son of having murdered a fugitive who had asked for sanctuary in their home. Ariel Sharon, then the commanding officer of the IDF's Southern Command, also thought a-Shawa was guilty, but of sheltering a wanted man. Sharon called for the mayor's ouster from office and the destruction of his villa. Pale and shaken, a-Shawa appeared before the local military governor and asked to give his version of the affair directly to the minister of defense. He evidently knew what he was doing, for Dayan heard him out and, after consulting with the prime minister, decided to spare a-Shawa and his home.

With Ziyad Husseini's death, the last of the terrorist bands in Gaza scattered and gradually were wiped out. Five of Husseini's comrades fled from the Jebalya refugee camp and hid in the Faluja girls' school, not far from a-Shawa's home, but all of them were killed when an IDF force infiltrated the building at dawn on June 26, 1972. Twenty others laid down their arms. The citrus groves emptied of their temporary residents, and no new recruits joined the terrorist cells. For a while, dry statistics about the number of dead and wounded, the dimensions of the internal struggle, and the fate of the thousands of refugees who had emigrated from the Gaza Strip since 1967 piled up silently in the offices of the military government—though the calm turned out to be short-lived.

In the meantime, a-Shawa resumed his duties and tried to revitalize the economic and social life of his wounded city. But the energetic mayor did not confine himself to municipal affairs alone. He met regularly with Israeli leaders and traveled to Amman and Beirut to report to King Hussein and Yasir Arafat on those meetings. In fact, he became the unofficial envoy for this implausible triangle. It is hard to imagine anyone more suited to the role, and in the course of my work I, too, have come to appreciate his irresistible charm. A steaming cup of strong coffee always awaits a visitor to his villa, along with revealing conversation on the ins and outs of the Palestinian problem. In the bookshelves in the living room, the curious browser will find Ben-Gurion's volume on the restoration of the Jewish state casually placed alongside the works of Hitler and Mussolini. Our talks on topical issues are always peppered with his fascinating impressions of people he has met and events in which he has played a part. Time and again a-Shawa returns to his assertion that the United Nations' 1947 plan for the partition of Palestine must be the basis for future negotiations between the Jews and the Palestinians. When he addresses Israelis, he makes unequivocal pronouncements that are meant to show his great self-assurance, but he has often spoken to me in terms that reveal a far more complex view of the situation: "From Arafat's point of view, an independent Palestinian state is a temporary plateau. In the eyes of the Arab states, it's a volley-ball. But for us it is a matter of our very existence."

A-Shawa's political finesse has not always been enough to protect him from harm. With great emotion, he told me how assassins had made an attempt on his life in September of 1972. It seems that reports of his contacts with Jordanian officials, published in the Israeli press, had infuriated local extremists. "I returned home at 2:15 with three companions, and a grenade was thrown at the car. God be praised, it didn't explode, but then the assassins began firing handguns and shattered the front windshield. Fortunately, I came out of it without a scratch."

Rashad a-Shawa has been trying for the past decade to pick his way among four formidable factors: Jordan, Israel, Egypt, and the PLO. When the military government ordered him to provide municipal services to the Shati refugee camp, he took it as a political act altering the status quo, and he refused. I pressed him on why he was unwilling to help his brothers in need, but a-Shawa merely smiled at me like an indulgent father and carefully explained, "We must keep the camps the way they are as a reminder to the world, a reminder to Israel, and a reminder to the Arab countries. The refugees must understand that their one and only goal is to return to their homes in Israel." On that occasion, even a-Shawa's political opponents, such as Abu-Sita, supported the defiant mayor. But the area commander was not so receptive to a-Shawa's explanations, and the outcome of that confrontation was the mayor's dismissal and the appointment of an Israeli officer to manage the city's affairs.

It was not a very smart move, for a-Shawa's dismissal served as a signal for renewed acts of violence in the Strip. Again the military government and the Border Police poured in forces to trap the terrorist gangs. Again the contest between terror and force paralyzed the city's economic life. Again Gaza was subdued and chastened. And when things settled down Rashad a-Shawa again resumed his post as mayor and turned to his task of rehabilitation.

To this day, internal disorders and the settling of accounts are common occurrences in the Gaza Strip, but the threat of total anarchy no longer hovers in the air. In an IDF raid on terrorist targets in the spring of 1973, a trove of documents was seized from the Beirut headquarters of the Democratic Front for the Liberation of Palestine. Among the documents were detailed lists of the organization's members in the Gaza Strip, which led the IDF to the remaining cells in the area. One of the last acts of murder perpetrated by young insurgents was the assassination of Dib Horbidi, the chairman of the local council at the Shati refugee camp. His crime had been to cooperate with the IDF in its attempt to ease the plight of the Shati residents by rebuilding the camp after the severe damage inflicted on it during police actions. Horbidi had even been so bold as to criticize a-Shawa for his negative attitude toward the Israeli authorities. He paid for that daring with his life, although the group that executed him was apprehended about a month later.

A-Shawa, resuming his duties as mayor, tried to bring the shambles of Gaza back to some state of order. I asked him why he had agreed to return to the post after being dismissed so unceremoniously, and he replied, "To save the Arab character of Gaza and not let some crass Jewish officer run our affairs." That statement says a lot about one essential quality of the attitude toward Israel in the territories. The people of the West Bank and Gaza tend to use the words "Jews," "Israelis," and "Zionists" interchangeably (the Arabic word for "Zionists" has taken on extremely negative connotations). When I comment on this, they deny that there *is* any difference between the three, maintaining that "every Jew is an Israeli." It is hard to miss the anti-Semitic overtones in such statements. Then, to illustrate the real complexity of the problem, I go on to ask them how they feel about me. Some Palestinians dismiss my association with the State of Israel as sheer toadying and a lack of basic self-respect. But most of them understand that the question does not yield to any simplistic or doctrinaire explanations—though they admit to being baffled by the status and feelings of an Israeli Arab.

After the brutal experience of the early 1970s, the military government finally saw that its first priority must go to improving the economic welfare of the inhabitants of Gaza, and the process of integrating workers from the Strip into the economy of the State of Israel moved ahead at full speed. I encountered the "new Gaza" about three years ago, when I was sent to do a feature on the economic situation in the Strip. In an interview with Mayor a-Shawa, I asked him where the workers of his city were employed. As his answer, he invited me to accompany him on a tour of the city at five o'clock the following morning. I led my crew to Palestine Square at dawn, and the scene that unfolded before us was incredible. Thousands of laborers crowding into the square had created a true carnival atmosphere as they busied themselves preparing their breakfasts—soft doughnut-shaped rolls sprinkled with sesame seeds, hollow pita overflowing with a paste of cooked chickpeas known as *humous,* spicy fried calf's liver, steaming coffee, and glasses of the aromatic drink called *sahlab,* made of ground almonds, milk, and mastic, an evergreen resin. It was the labor market run by the *ra'isin* (local labor contractors), who supplied hands for Israeli farms and other enterprises.

Such a scene would have been inconceivable five years earlier. But once the grenades stopped wreaking their destruction and Israeli troops no longer stalked the Gaza Strip with bayonets drawn, the laws of economics began to exert their influence on the fabric of relations between the State of Israel and the occupied region. Now each side has become dependent on the other, and any abrupt upheaval in the relationship would likely have grave consequences for employers and employees alike. For Gaza—for the tens of thousands still housed in the refugee camps, with little hope of a brighter future for their children—all this remains only a palliative, not a cure. The terror has abated but not disappeared. Poverty and despair seem to breed in the camps like the invincible mosquitoes. And, given the camps' history of violence—a strategy that might well be dubbed the "politics of desperation"—there is ample cause to fear that the next outburst is only a matter of time.

5
EXIT HUSSEIN,
ENTER THE PLO

The West Bank I encountered in 1970, as a soldier, was in a state of turmoil, with the Palestinians drifting on a collision course with Jordan and Lebanon, as well as with Israel, and toward a crisis that threatened to cripple their national movement. New winds had begun to blow in the occupied territories. By hindsight, it was clear that for all their political skill, the traditional leaders in the West Bank had failed in the eyes of their people, and they were gradually being replaced by younger men much less disposed to compromise with the occupying authorities. Neither were the new leaders particularly squeamish about resorting to radical means of action, including terror.

Symptomatic of the shift in mood was the rise of a group of mayors who had not previously been ranked among the more outstanding political figures in the region. The spotlight had moved away from Nablus and Hebron, and Abdul Jawad Saleh of el-Bireh and Nadim Zaro of Ramallah had begun to set the tone of relations between the military government and the people of the West Bank. Saleh threw his energies into a campaign on behalf of the villagers who had been evicted from the Latrun area. Unlike his colleagues in the West Bank's larger cities, he had little use for the so-called benefits of a modus vivendi or the winning ways of traditional Arab courtesy. In one conversation, he bluntly told Moshe Dayan, "I am not a religious man and I do not pray in a mosque. But if I did pray, I would do so seventeen times a day, rather than the five commanded by Islam, and each time I would entreat Allah to throw you out of here!" Zaro was a pugnacious man whose loathing for Israel seemed to know no bounds. One newspaper interview quoted him as saying the IDF "resembled the Nazis." To illustrate the extent of his forbearance and of the Palestinians' determination to rid themselves of their "captors," he used to cite an ancient Bedouin adage, "A Bedouin waited forty years for his revenge, and when the opportunity came he felt he had acted in haste." For the generation represented by men like Saleh and Zaro, it apparently was not enough to solve the Palestinian problem; they also wanted revenge. The mayor of Ramallah, for one, may have judged the fortitude of his people accurately, but he was far less adept at assessing the patience of the military government. In October of 1969, he and seven other activists, including the mufti of Ramallah, were deported to Jordan.

Another sign that men like Kenan and Ja'abri were losing ground was the widening base of the opposition to Israeli rule. Educators, religious leaders, and even merchants began to join the ranks of the resistance movement. When the first Palestinian youth died in an Israeli prison, feeling ran high on the streets of the West Bank, and the women's organizations again proved the swiftest and most energetic in their response. But what really sounded the death knell for the traditional leadership was a series of developments outside the occupied territories that revolutionized political thinking and patterns of allegiance within the West Bank.

The two key dates in that process were September of 1970 and October of 1973. The first, remembered as "Black September" in Palestinian lore, marked the violent rupture of a tacit alliance between King Hussein and the Palestinian organizations based outside the occupied territories. After the IDF's dragnet left those organizations powerless in the West Bank, they began to establish bases in the refugee camps of neighboring Arab countries—particularly Jordan and Lebanon— and from there waged a three-year war of attrition against the IDF. Their campaign of sabotage actually opened just nine days after the 1967 cease-fire and was centered mainly along the Jordan valley. Official Israeli statistics cite 5,840 incidents of aggressive actions originating in Jordan between June of 1967 and September of 1970. The two sides laid ambushes for each other, and the IDF poured funds into improved methods for detecting infiltrators the minute they crossed the frontier. Nevertheless, fire fights and attacks on civilians living in border areas claimed 141 Israeli lives and left 800 others wounded. It was a stubborn and costly confrontation.

Initially, King Hussein was only a passive factor in this "war after the war," going no further than to permit the Palestinians to operate from Jordanian soil. But soon his army was drawn into the fighting, regularly engaging the IDF in artillery duels in the Beit Shean and Jordan valleys. The Palestinian organizations in Jordan flourished in this benevolent climate —so much so that by the summer of 1970 their strength had become a source of alarm to the king, and with good reason. Especially after three commercial airliners were skyjacked and forced to land in Jordan early in September, seasoned observers began to wonder aloud whether Hussein was still master in his own kingdom. In any case, by then the king had undergone a radical change in his attitude toward both the Palestinian organizations and the prospects of reaching a Middle East settlement. In July of 1970 he accepted an American peace initiative known as the Rogers plan, which the Palestinians took as a slap in the face. He also told Joseph Kraft, in an interview in the *New York Times,* that he would be willing to accept certain changes in the 1967 borders in return for a full Israeli withdrawal. As for Jerusalem, he could hardly relinquish his claim to sovereignty over the Arab sector, but he said he was prepared to consider such an option as placing the city under international supervision.

To Palestinian ears, those words smacked of treachery. Hussein further reinforced that feeling by dismissing his prime minister, Bahjat Talhouni, and replacing him with Abdul Munem Rifai, who proceeded to crack down on the Palestinian guerrillas. The showdown came in September, when Jordanian army units pitted their strength and prestige against the forces of the Syrian-backed a-Sa'ika and Yasir Arafat's el-Fatah. While the fighting lasted—at one point it threatened to draw in Syria on the side of the Palestinians and Israel to shore up Hussein!—the king's supporters in the occupied territories kept a very low profile, because of the tales of horror about the persecution of Palestinians being brought back by travelers from Jordan. In Israel, people openly expressed satisfaction at the spectacle of Hussein slaughtering Palestinians. But one could hardly say they were blessed with political acumen. For King Hussein may have lost the West Bank, but it wasn't Israel that got it—it was the PLO.

The bitter civil war of September 1970 had a deeper effect than the damage to Hussein's standing in the West Bank. It gave a powerful impetus to a shift in the thinking and self-image of the populace there. After the bloodletting, Jordan could no longer continue to be the symbolic "broad shoulder" it had once represented for the people in the territories. Most of the Palestinians who had left the West Bank after the Six Day War now fled on to Lebanon for sanctuary. The Beirut regime was not happy about that, but it was too weak to do much about checking the growth of the Palestinian organizations on its soil (which ultimately led to a second, a longer, and a far bloodier civil war in the region). Moreover, the events of "Black September" lent added credence to el-Fatah's claim that the Palestinians had nowhere to go. Lebanon was trying to push them out. Jordan was massacring them. Though the entire Arab world was crying out in indignant protest, no one would lift a finger on their behalf. The Arab establishment, particularly in the wealthy oil-producing states, felt threatened by the spirit of rebellion that the Palestinians brought with them everywhere they went. Hussein had held back from clamping down on the Palestinian insurgency as long as he could control and channel it for his own ends. But in 1970 he lost control; and Yasir Arafat, who had once been considered a dangerous rival by the Palestinian aristocracy, now emerged as the candidate to lead the insurgency—a "compromise" candidate, the candidate of "no other choice."

In the long run, this latest wave of despair among the Palestinians only strengthened el-Fatah by increasing the appeal of its two-pronged philosophy of armed struggle and political action. In Israel, however, the government continued to misread the meaning of "Black September." In the army I heard lecturers speak about "the death throes of the Palestinian struggle," and for a while I believed that I might have been wrong, that maybe a firm and forceful policy really could crush the spirit of an entire people. Then the earthquake came, and it was a very rude awakening indeed for all of us.

I had been discharged from the army only a few months before the Yom Kippur War, and I was at home in Dalyat el-Carmel when the fighting broke out on October 6, 1973. There was no panic in the village; the women did not rush to the Cave of Elijah to offer prayers. But, like the rest of Israel, Dalyat el-Carmel was stunned by the news, even though there had been subtle signs that something was afoot. For example, my neighbor Mu'in, who was my brother Walid's closest friend, had been called back to his unit the previous night. Mu'in's mother later told us that her husband had answered the phone call summoning him back to his base and had tried to get around it by saying his son was out. Mu'in—who was taking a section leaders' course at the time—had reproached his father for the lie. He was preparing himself to become an officer in the Israel Defense Forces, he said, and if the army was calling him it must be because he was needed. Gathering up his things, he had left immediately. That was a characteristic attitude in our village. Anger against the government for its neglect of the Druse vanished completely, and all were united in their sense of identification with the state in its time of trial.

Until the afternoon of October 6, 1973, everyone in Israel had seemed to believe that because of the IDF's awesome strength no Arab leader would dare to provoke it into action.

Ministers and senior officers alike were supremely confident—and liberally shared their confidence with the public. That attitude carried over into the first reports we heard from the fronts. The Israel Television correspondent in the Golan, for one, said emphatically, "Our armor—the IDF's steel fist—will teach Syria the price of impudence!" The coming days would show how very wrong our leaders had been in their assessments. On the northern front, for one example, the IDF was pushed back by the Syrian onslaught and was fighting for the state's very existence.

My unit was sent to the northern border, with orders to seal it against any armed infiltrators who might try to exploit the situation by attacking civilian centers nearby. Another Druse unit fought on the Golan Heights, and hundreds of Druse were scattered through the IDF's combat arms. On the fifth day of the war, my unit came across evidence that a group of saboteurs had penetrated our sector. We located them after a brief search and engaged them in fire, killing two and taking a third prisoner. Under interrogation he identified himself as an Iraqi soldier who had enlisted in el-Fatah. Asked why he had come to fight on this front, he answered, without a moment's hesitation, "To die for Palestine!"

Even before the fighting ended, word reached the Druse villages of a heavy toll in casualties. The politicians were quick to remind the Druse that that was the price of the "blood pact" between them and the Jews, their contribution to the defense of the homeland. But the women derived little consolation from the rhetoric. Dressed in black, they went into mourning. The grief was particularly heavy in our neighbor's house, for Mu'in had fallen in battle in front of a captured Israeli outpost on top of Mount Hermon. He had been cut down while providing covering fire for a demolition man laying explosives for an attempt to retake the position. He had volunteered for the mission.

Thinking back on those days, I cannot help comparing the postwar moods of 1967 and 1973. In June of 1967, Israel was

95

swept away on a wave of euphoria, singing songs of the return to Sharm a-Sheikh and the capture of the Mitla Pass as if those were places Jews had carried in their hearts for two thousand years. In 1973, the IDF strained to stave off the attacking Egyptian and Syrian armies and won the decision on the battlefield. But the cost was enormous, and there were no hymns of joy this time. On the contrary, the country was steeped in depression for months afterward. For all that, we obviously hadn't won in 1967, and we might have gained something more important in 1973. I recently talked with a senior IDF officer who believed that the Yom Kippur War probably saved the State of Israel and the Jewish people. He put it this way: "The war restored us to a state of sanity. In fact, Egypt and Syria attacked just in time. Another quarter of an hour and Israel's political and military complacency would have been so gross that we would have become downright catatonic! The people of Israel may be divided over the best way to solve the Middle East problem, but after 1973 few of them can deny the existence of the Palestinian problem, and fewer still are unaware of just how serious it is."

There was no doubt that the war upset a number of applecarts. For one thing, the harrowing battle for the Golan, coupled with the Egyptian army's boldness and sheer grit in the first days of the war, put to rest some tenacious myths about the Arabs' fighting abilities. Soon after the war I talked with my former boss, Meron Benvenisti, who was then a deputy mayor of Jerusalem, and he believed that some good would come of it. "The Arabs have their pride restored," he said, "the arrogant Israeli has been taken down a few notches, and we'll be able to talk as equals—rather than from positions of strength and inferiority." Others, less sanguine, drew very different conclusions. They believed that the chance of achieving a settlement was more remote now than ever. If the Egyptians could build such a strong army, they reasoned, Sadat would probably try to exploit the slightest opportunity to destroy Israel. For them, the real lesson of the war was that, in a world permeated by cynicism and power games, Israel must remain strong and uncompromising.

As Israel brooded through the long, freezing winter of 1973–74, with much of the IDF still mobilized on the cease-fire lines and the economy limping, the upbeat mood in the occupied territories was hard to miss. Arab soldiers had not, after all, abandoned their boots in the dunes so they could flee faster, and the Egyptians had shattered the myth of the "invincible Israeli air force"—even Phantoms could be matched and overcome. Once again the prophets proclaimed the dawn of a new age of progress in the Arab world, seeing the war as the final break with the backwardness that had typified that world in the past. Those eager to prove their sophistication about global politics held forth on the decisive role played by the United States. One Haj Yusuf Kashour of Jerusalem summed it up for me in this short analysis: "The Americans arrange everything. In '56 they sent the British and the French to wallop Egypt, and in '67 they helped you beat the Egyptians and the Syrians. Today you have a very big country, and the Americans felt you should be cut down to size. So they decided to help the Egyptians beat you." The belief that Washington pulls all the strings in the Middle East is still widespread— although recent events in Iran should have finished off that farfetched theory. Instead, I am told that the American "master plan" just "hit a couple of snags" there.

For a while after the war, cracker-barrel political analysis became a fad here, and I heard enough nonsense to last me a lifetime. A journalist colleague who had left Israel to settle in France could not understand the depression I was in—and so many other Israelis, too. "Were you really glad when the IDF crossed the Suez Canal?" she asked in astonishment. "What do you care? I mean, an Egyptian victory would only strengthen your position."

Even the most superficial analysis of the war could not help but show that no one had come out of it stronger. Mutual bloodletting and bereavement do not look like "fortifying factors" to me. If anyone could be said to have benefited from the war, it was the Palestinians. From 1967 to 1973, they had suffered at the hands of both Israel and the Arab states. On the eve of the war, their organizations had seemed to be at the point of disintegrating for good. Then came the earthquake and saved them.

The PLO emerged from the 1973 war a winner by default —or, to be more precise, as a result of King Hussein's incredible misjudgment. Ezer Weizman, the former defense minister in Menachem Begin's government, once told me that over the past fourteen years the Hashemite ruler had made three irreparable mistakes. His first fateful error was in 1967, when he swallowed Egypt's optimistic reports of the situation at the front and decided to enter the war. The heavy price he paid for that error in judgment was the West Bank. In 1973 he erred again, but exactly in reverse, by deciding *not* to join as a full participant in the war against Israel. Because he was not a party to the conflict, Hussein was not offered a separation-of-forces agreement, which would have meant a partial withdrawal of the IDF from the West Bank. His third mistake was to turn down an invitation from President Anwar Sadat to join him on his historic visit to Jerusalem in November of 1977.

In 1974 the Syrians got back the city of Kuneitra as part of a separation-of-forces agreement with Israel, and a year later the Egyptians retrieved the Sinai passes as part of an interim agreement negotiated between President Sadat and Yitzhak Rabin's government. Only Hussein was left out of the game altogether. But his error of 1973 had even graver consequences for Jordan. By Hussein's failure to take an active part in the Yom Kippur War, he further diminished the moral force of his claim to represent the Palestinian people. The PLO could now make its bid for hegemony with a sure hand, for after 1973 few were prepared to challenge its right to speak on behalf of all Palestinians—those living under Israeli rule and those scattered throughout the Arab diaspora. After 1973, the PLO won many supporters even among Israeli Arabs.

It may be true, as Weizman suggested, that King Hussein had only himself to blame for losing the West Bank, physically and politically. That did not mean that Israel abandoned its attempts to involve Jordan in the quest for a solution to the problem. In January of 1974, for example, the late Yigal Allon met secretly with Hussein in Jordan's Red Sea port of Aqaba. In those talks the king demanded that Israel relinquish the West Bank and restore Jordanian sovereignty over "Arab Jerusalem," warning that if Israel refused to comply he would be forced to yield to the demands of the Palestinians. Other emissaries tried to mediate between the two sides. Rashad a-Shawa of Gaza proposed a "Jericho plan," which called for Israel to pull back to the area of Ma'aleh Adumim, placing the city of Jericho under Jordanian control again. Sheikh Mohammed Ali Ja'abri of Hebron wrote to the king expressing his full support for the plan, and Israel intimated it was willing to consider other proposals. But Hussein would not budge from his position. The result was predictable, for deadlock is always a boon to hard-liners. In October of 1974, Moshe Dayan—no longer the minister of defense, but still a member of the Knesset from the Labor party—added his signature to a petition being circulated by the opposition Likud party. The petition decried the "return of Judea and Samaria to foreign rule" and vigorously demanded that Israel make manifest the "right of the Jews to settle in the area." On the Arab side, Hussein, having achieved nothing for his kingdom or for the Palestinians, found himself being shunted to the sidelines. The way to Rabat was wide open to Yasir Arafat

The Rabat Conference of Arab Nations, held in December of 1974, passed a number of resolutions with implications crucial to the Palestinian question. The delegates to this Arab summit conference called on the entire world—but first and foremost the Arab leaders themselves—to recognize that:

1. The Palestinian people has the right to return to its homeland, to self-determination, and to invest Pales-

tinian national authority in the leadership of the PLO, which is the sole representative of the Palestinians.

2. The PLO has the right to carry out its national and international responsibilities within the framework of the Arab world's undertakings.

3. Jordan, Syria, Egypt, and the PLO will meet to prepare and confirm a formula for regularizing relations among themselves.

4. The Arab states have no right to intervene in or make decisions on questions relating to the future of the Palestinian people.

The Rabat conference was a stunning diplomatic victory for the PLO and a stinging defeat for Jordan. Buoyed by his achievements at Rabat, Arafat went on to enhance his standing still further by an act suffused with high drama. I happened to be at the home of Elias Freij, the mayor of Bethlehem, when Israel Television showed the film clips of Arafat's speech before the General Assembly of the United Nations. The sight of that gun-toting leader commanding the rapt attention of diplomats from all over the world, who applauded him long and hard, was a tremendous shot in the arm for the PLO's supporters in the territories. Even Freij, who is considered a moderate, clapped his hands in delight at Arafat's aggressive proclamation of his people's right to return to "stolen Palestine." Arafat called for the establishment of a Palestinian national entity as the basis of a "secular-democratic" state to be set up within the borders of the old Palestine mandate. Warning of a possible nuclear confrontation in the Middle East, he invited the world's governments to "liberate yourselves from Zionism."

The day after Arafat's United Nations speech I saw firsthand its effect on the comportment of moderate leaders in the West Bank. Elias Freij, in his office in the Bethlehem municipal building, seemed to be just waiting for the foreign press—especially the television correspondents—to show up. Like a man who has stumbled on buried treasure, he could hardly wait to tell viewers throughout the world what he thought. As expected, the television reporters arrived and asked the proper questions. Freij paused, as if hesitant to answer, shot a meaningful glance in the direction of the building housing the military government, and pondered the likely Jordanian response to his comments (which was so important to him). His reply reflected due consideration for each of those factors. "Jordan and the Arab world have recognized Arafat's right to represent us," he said. "The entire world applauded him. It is a very important day for the Palestinian cause." I, for one, could not allow him simply to bask in the glow of Arafat's victory and pressed him: "What, as you understand it, is a democratic state à la Arafat?" Freij parried the question with an impish grin. "I can only hope that a democratic state will arise. After all, you [Israeli Arabs] want it, too."

Freij was well aware that Arafat's ideas could never be acceptable to Israel, if only because that "secular-democratic state" would have to be built on the ruins of the Jewish one. The return to Israel of hundreds of thousands of Arab refugees implied the displacement of the hundreds of thousands of Jews who had come there since 1948. Did anyone really think there was any chance of holding a dialogue with Israel on those terms? Could anyone blame Israel for rejecting the notion out of hand?

The problem was that such questions implied a willingness to reason, and reason seemed to have become obsolete in the post-Rabat era. In those circumstances, one cannot overestimate the impact Arafat's UN debut had on the political climate in the territories. The younger generation turned its back on anyone calling for moderation or a realistic approach. Meeting the "firm hand" of the military government with an implacable nationalist spirit, it opted for terror in countering the settlement moves of the Israeli religious faction called Gush Emunim. Radical pronouncements won the hearts of many Palestinian youths for the simple reason that their longing for a sovereign and independent country was mixed with a thirst for savage revenge. As passions mounted, so did the wall of alienation between the two peoples. Indeed, who could expect Jews to react with equanimity to feelings such as those expressed by the Beirut-based Palestinian writer Nasser a-Din Nashashibi? I was introduced to Nashashibi about two years ago, in the offices of the Jerusalem daily *El-Kuds*, by Mahmud Abu-Zuluf, its editor. Our meeting brought to my mind the lyrical tone of certain passages in his book *Calling Card*, published in Beirut in 1967:

> Each year our young hearts murmured: we shall return again. We two will return to our country, kick off our shoes, and fondle its holy earth with our toes. We will fill our souls with its air and its soil; stroll through the orange groves, sand, and water. We will kiss the seeds and the fruit, doze in the shade of the first tree we reach, bless the grave of the first to fall in the holy war, search out our existence. Where are our lives? In the village square, in the minaret, the lovely date palm, the broken wall, the building razed without a trace—our lives are there. Ask any grain of sand. Surely you recall Jaffa, Haifa, Beisan, the fields of luscious fruits and vegetables, Nazareth and the peal of the bells, Acre in the shadow of al-Jazar, Ibrahim Pasha, Napoleon, and the fortress, Jerusalem and its alleyways—my beloved Jerusalem—Tiberias and her shoreline with its gold-tipped waves, Majdal and my family there.

Nashashibi's longing for those lost and fading landscapes is easy to understand. But his vision of return ends on another note entirely, as he drums into his son the doctrine of vengeance:

> Let the holocaust of 1948 drown in a torrent of blood those who stopped them from entering their country. The homeland is dear, but vengeance is dearer still. We will

enter their houses in Tel Aviv, hack them to pieces with hatchets, rifles, hands, nails, teeth. As we hum the strains of Kibyeh, Dir Yasin, and Nasser a-Din, we shall sing the anthem of the victorious and vengeful return!

The young people raised on literature of that sort drank in its message well, and by 1974 terrorist activity was on the rise again. The same week I began working for Israel Television, terrorists infiltrated the town of Kiryat Shmonah, near the Lebanese border, and seized schoolchildren as hostages. The IDF rescued them and then took retaliatory action, demolishing twenty-two houses in southern Lebanon and taking thirteen young people prisoner. To no avail, it seemed, for a short time later terrorists mounted a suicide mission in a Tel Aviv movie theater. A young man and woman hurled grenades into the audience, injuring fifty-one but losing their own lives in the process. And so it went: blow and counterblow, strike and counterstrike—as if it were possible for the Palestinians to blast Israel out of the territories with homemade explosives or for the IDF to bomb the Palestinians into submission!

Sometimes I think the roar of exploding grenades made us deaf to the cry of despair coming from the territories. The cry echoed through the mountains and the wadis of this land, but we closed our ears to it and, perhaps out of desperation, abused our power by wielding it with force. During those grim days of 1974, Yigal Allon's voice again rang out in the name of sanity and reason. Then the foreign minister, he recommended that Israel return to the "Jordanian option" as the best way of resolving the conflict, and he warned his countrymen to recognize the gravity of the Palestinian problem. But Allon's voice went unheard—one more cry in the wilderness. His offer to negotiate with the Palestinian organizations on condition that they recognize Israel's sovereign right to exist did not even receive the courtesy of a reply. And the occupied territories—those smoldering coals in Israel's backyard—flared up anew at each lightest touch of a breeze.

I have seen it happen again and again since 1974: thousands of young people take to the streets to demonstrate against the endless occupation. Fired up by nationalist slogans, they unfurl the flag of Palestine and march down the boulevards of Ramallah roaring, "My land, my land, my land! For you, my love, my heart. Palestine, you are the soil of self-sacrifice." I have seen women and children in the Amari refugee camp turn tires into flaming barricades. I have seen girls building roadblocks out of stones as other girls, masking their faces with their kaffiyehs, have rained rocks on Israeli soldiers. Again and again I have seen the main street of Ramallah blocked by dozens of burning tires. The black smoke billowing skyward has summoned the young to come and swell the ranks, while women watched from their balconies to warn the demonstrators of approaching Israeli patrols.

The military government has standing orders for dealing with such situations. Journalists are told that the army has no intention of dispersing the demonstrators as long as they do not block the main arteries and do not prevent other citizens from going about their business. But policy is one thing, and the reality on the streets is another. At some point patience gives out, and soldiers charge the crowd and make their arrests, with the aid of tear gas and clubs. Others scour the streets in half-tracks and jeeps, hauling in anyone who gets in their way. Shuttered shops are marked for special squads of welders, who force open the locks. In Nablus I once saw a group of soldiers dragging a child of about eight or nine by the hair. "Why?" I shouted at them, and their answer shocked me even more than the act itself—"So that his friends will see and beware!"

Recently the demonstrators seem to have become more eager for violent confrontations with the IDF—or, at least, less afraid of them. I particularly recall the day I accompanied the coordinator of activities in the occupied territories, Major General Dani Matt, on a visit to the a-Tira high school in Ramallah. When we arrived, the street leading to the school was blocked by improvised stone barricades. Girls whose faces were masked by scarves lined the road and threw stones at Matt and his entourage. An officer raised his gun and sent a warning shot into the air, hoping to scatter them, but the girls were not deterred. Then the officer aimed his rifle straight at them menacingly, and one of the students shrieked, "Go on, make me a Muntaha Hourani!"—a reference to a girl killed during a demonstration in Jenin in 1974. General Matt, who cuts an impressive figure, kept walking on under the shower of stones, straight-backed and determined. Afterward he confessed, "An officer cannot cringe or back down, but the truth is that all the time I was glancing sideways at the girls for fear one of them would hit me." The principal of the school, who saw it as her duty only to provide instruction, did not seem particularly intimidated by the area commander's threat to make her responsible for holding down the nationalist fervor.

Hundreds of work days have been lost in the West Bank due to strikes and demonstrations. Most people prefer the curfews imposed by the authorities over strikes called by their compatriots, for when it is a curfew they don't have to face the dilemma of whether to stay at home and risk being punished by the Israelis or go to work and expose themselves to their neighbors' wrath. The moment a curfew is announced, people scurry home to bar their doors and shutter their windows against the Israeli soldiers combing the streets in search of suspects. Then they can all pride themselves on being patriots groaning under the burden of the occupation.

A city or town is automatically closed to journalists whenever a curfew is in effect. Nevertheless, in the intractable city of Nablus, I was once allowed to accompany the IDF during a curfew and saw for myself how the house-to-house searches were conducted. The soldiers were not always meticulous about their conduct in these actions, and they certainly were not above insulting or manhandling people. Only someone who understood Arabic could appreciate the scathing abuse the women poured out as their husbands, sons, and brothers were taken away by the Israeli troops. I went about my work silently; words were superfluous. I filmed and recorded, and that evening citizens throughout Israel, from the comfort of their living rooms, watched what was happening in Nablus. I am sure it wasn't pleasant for them, but I am equally sure my report told them things they were obliged to face up to.

It has been painful for any Israeli to watch the deterioration in relations between the two peoples that begrudgingly share this land, but I often think that my own position makes me more vulnerable than most. In November of 1974, when five leaders of the Palestine National Front—including Hana Nasser, the dean of Bir Zeit College—were deported from the West Bank, I made for the college to record the reaction there. Feelings were at a high pitch by the time I arrived. In fact, the students wouldn't even let our crew through the gates. Among the demonstrators was a Jewish "fellow traveler" from the New Left–style Matzpen (Compass) Movement, who turned on me and screamed, "Fascist Arab! You've sold out! The revolution will deal with you." For a moment I felt myself losing control and was afraid I might beat him senseless. That self-righteous demagogue who condoned violence against his own people was calling *me* a Judas!

I turned my back on Bir Zeit and walked away, cursing Jews and Arabs alike for forcing me to cope with their simplistic, inane absolutes in my search for the meaning of my own identity. My frustrations seemed to follow me everywhere that day. On the way back to Jerusalem, I came across the military governor of the West Bank, touring the area with an escort of Border Police whose commander happened to be a cousin of mine, Halil, from Dalyat el-Carmel. I was obviously in a black mood, and when I told them what had happened at Bir Zeit their responses were typical. "Forget it, Rafik," was Halil's advice. "You mustn't let yourself get involved." At which the governor quickly added, "Those friends of yours will be taught a lesson today"—my so-called friends clearly being the Palestinian demonstrators.

If I listened closely to the message being carried by such students, I could recognize the words issuing from their mouths as those of the terrorist leaders and ideologues Na'if Hawatmeh, George Habash, and Ahmad Jabril. Revolution, the popular struggle, and the rehabilitation of Arab pride were the main motifs that informed their chants. Unlike those less educated, they insisted on drawing a distinction between Judaism and Zionism, asserting that in its generous attitude toward Jews the Arab nation has a record unrivaled in history, but that Zionism is a racist, imperialist movement whose declared aim is to establish an empire extending from the Euphrates to the Nile.

For some reason, I had the feeling that it would be easier to deal with these youths, whose views were so ingenuous, than with their elders. There was undoubtedly an element of healthy adolescent rebellion in their behavior, as shown by the way they boasted about being arrested. The real pillars of implacable opposition were the older leaders, who didn't throw stones or chant slogans in the streets and who sometimes even negotiated with the authorities, but who nonetheless fanned the flames of insurgency. They were men like Abdul Jawad Saleh, Dr. Walid Kamhawi of Nablus, and Abdul Muhsin Abu-Meizar of Jerusalem, who never made any bones about their animosity toward Israel.

One day in 1976 I was sitting in the Café Zatara, near Jerusalem's Damascus Gate, playing backgammon with one of the regulars and keeping my ears open for tips, when Abu-Meizar happened in. I had known Abu-Meizar for years and had always thought of him as a proud man of great personal integrity. I well remember the talks we used to have about the future of the region in the days when I worked for the city government. Back then, he had believed that Israel would withdraw from the territories before long, but evidently his patience had worn thin by 1976. Striding past me, he suddenly stopped and scolded, "Tell your bosses that we won't rest until the last of the Zionists have left the territories." I was offended by his sheer rudeness, more than anything else, and demanded an apology. In the end it took a *sulha*—a formal reconciliation ceremony—arranged by one of the Arab newspaper editors in Jerusalem, to patch up our rift. The military government knew that people like Abdul Jawad Saleh and Abu-Meizar had a hand in organizing demonstrations, and, true to the "firm-hand policy," they ultimately deported the two from the West Bank. Abu-Meizar, a sharp-witted politician as well as a fascinating conversationalist, joined the ranks of the PLO and soon became one of its leading ideologues.

The cumulative effect of such encounters as these with the students and public leaders of the West Bank sobered me. I had started my television career believing that if I presented the harsh truth about life in the territories, I could make the Israelis see that their blind devotion to the conventional wisdom was actually undermining the security of the State of Israel. I wanted desperately to believe that the faithful reporting of events could somehow bridge the yawning chasm between the two peoples and revive hope in the prospect of attaining peace through mutual respect and recognition. After a year on the job, I stopped believing in facile solutions—though not in the need to find some solution to the problem of the territories quickly, before extremism swamped the last vestiges of reason on both sides of the barricades.

6
A NEW GENERATION
OF LEADERS

B y 1975, relations between the military government and the people of the occupied territories were on the brink of total collapse. Most channels of communication had been disrupted, and violence was fast becoming the leading avenue of contact between the two sides. It was inevitable that the growing strength of the PLO and the stormy mood in the streets would leave their mark on the power structure in the West Bank. Indeed, by 1976 there had been nothing less than a revolution in the local political leadership.

The emergence and consolidation of the new class of mayors in the West Bank was a classic lesson in the subtle dynamics of occupation, in how a supposedly powerless and oppressed group could override the supposedly omnipotent authority ruling it. A population living under occupation tends to adjust quickly to new conditions and develops a high degree of resourcefulness, while their rulers, in this case the military government—like public opinion throughout Israel—hold fast to outdated ideas and modes of action. To a large degree, the failure of Israel's policy in the West Bank can be traced to such an inertia. If the Israeli government had been more imaginative and politically nimble, it might have managed the situation more adroitly. As things were, the government in effect paved the way for the advent of a fiercely nationalist leadership in the West Bank.

Eight years into the occupation, the military government faced a very complex situation. Most of the residents of the territories had ties of one kind or another with the terrorist organizations. Even a man like Sheikh Ja'abri, a firm opponent of the PLO, had a son associated with el-Fatah. Whether or not as a direct result of such ties, the demonstrations had begun to escalate from small gatherings of radicals to mass outpourings. The military government found it was unable to maintain its indifference to the sight of burning tires. After one outburst of defiance in Nablus, Israeli troops entered the classrooms of the Kadri Toukan high school and began beating students. The Nablus municipal council resigned in protest and councils in other towns followed suit, setting off a chain reaction, as the two sides warmed to the fray. Each resignation seemed to incite a new wave of disorders, and soon the unrest spread to Hebron, where soldiers chasing demonstrators broke into the municipal building and damaged some property. Ja'abri, who took the incident as an affront to his honor, now joined the list of recalcitrant mayors—though the elderly sheikh was careful to cover his line of retreat. He summoned a meeting of local notables and tearfully announced he would defer to the will of the people. In Hebron, at least, the outcome of that kind of drama was predictable: "the people" clamored for their mayor to come back, and Ja'abri returned to his post.

At first the favored assumption in military government circles was that the Communists were behind the wave of national ferment. Following that logic, Bashir Bargouthi, one of the party's leaders in the territories and a high officer in the Palestine National Front, was brought to trial before a military court in Ramallah. Needless to say, the unrest did not abate. On the contrary, the political front now blanketed almost the entire region, and the younger generation of activists proved most adept at using the communications media, and particularly the press, to their best advantage. If the Israeli government was alarmed by these developments, it must be said that the PLO was no less concerned over what was happening in the territories and tried to exploit the situation for its own purposes. From the organization's Beirut headquarters came a decision to assign a "mentor" to every prominent personality in the territories and thus ensure the orthodoxy of his actions. The message behind that move was not so much a fear of incompetence as a healthy, and justified, suspicion that, given half a chance, the new leaders in the territories might become too independent and overshadow the PLO's own influence within the occupied borders.

Curiously enough, it was right in the midst of this period of mounting agitation that the government of Israel decided to hold mayoral elections in the territories, and the date was set for April of 1976. As election day neared, it became increasingly apparent that a single united front was coalescing throughout the cities of the West Bank. Young activists and members of existing nationalist bodies had managed to form what they called national blocs. In the 1972 mayoral elections, the PLO had opposed such activity and had even ordered its own followers to boycott the polls. This time the organization reversed itself and went out of the way to make it known that it supported the new blocs.

Heading the ballot of the national bloc in Nablus, the largest and most influential city in the West Bank, was Bassam Shaka, a newcomer to the political scene and something of an unknown quantity. I wanted to talk with Shaka, to find out more about him, but when I phoned him to ask for an interview he turned me down flat. "I don't understand journalism," he demurred. "Besides, I have had bitter experiences with the Israeli press." However, I am not paid to give in easily, and, since I couldn't interview him in person, I continued to question him over the phone. Our talk was brief, and Shaka showed little promise of being more loquacious in the future.

"People say that you support Arafat," I began.

"Let them say it."

"And that you'll win the election because the el-Masri family supports you."

"Let them say it."

"Why do you attack the military government so vehemently?"

111

His reply to that was to the point and presumably exhaustive: "Give me just one reason why I should love the military government!"

"Why aren't you willing to be interviewed on Israel Television?"

At that, my reticent interviewee evidently felt I had gone too far and slammed down the receiver.

Shaka's evasions only whetted my curiosity, so I made for Nablus and caught up with him in the open vegetable market, where he and some other candidates were campaigning. He appeared to be a modest, soft-spoken, genial man, but as soon as he discovered who I was he gave me the cold shoulder. I turned to Dr. Hatim Abu-Gazala, a candidate on Shaka's slate, who was known to be a personal friend of George Habash, and struck up a conversation; but Shaka soon came over to us and asked the doctor to refrain from making any statements to the press.

Bassam Shaka had been a businessman before the election. He was from a wealthy family that owned a soap factory in Nablus and had extensive real estate holdings, as well as wide commercial ties in the West Bank and beyond. For a decade, beginning in 1952, he had been a member of the Syrian Ba'ath party, but since then he had consistently held independent views. Drawn by his admiration for the Egyptian revolution and its leader, Gamal Abdel Nasser, he had visited Egypt in 1953. After the Egyptian-Syrian union—the United Arab Republic—Shaka had returned to the West Bank, but in 1959 he had moved again—this time to Syria, where he lived until 1962. He has a secondary-school education but cannot converse well in any language except Arabic.

Because of my dogged persistence, Shaka finally agreed to meet with me, on condition that I not quote him on the air. That agreed to, he spoke frankly about his feelings as a Palestinian: "We own land in the Netanya area—orchards we tended before 1948—and I long to return to it." Even in this first conversation, he seemed to be hinting at the course he would pursue in the future. "Until now the local leaders have been 'walking between the raindrops'—between Jordan and Israel, the PLO and the military government. I am not a virtuoso acrobat, and I shall express my views without fear," he assured me. "Before 1967 and for a while after the war, many people in the area refused to accept the State of Israel as a fact of life. I doubt they still hold to that view today." I sensed that a token of something new had come out of this conversation with the man likely to become the new mayor of Nablus. Shaka had been forthright about his identification with the Palestinian national ideology, yet when it came to solutions for the Palestinian problem he had quite pragmatically spoken in terms of dividing the old Palestine mandate into two states.

Hebron underwent a period of great turbulence prior to the 1976 elections. In fact, that city known for its patently religious and traditional nature did a complete about-face and withdrew its incontestable support from Sheikh Ja'abri. Concern had mounted within the military government when the name of Dr. Ahmad Hamzi Natshe, a fervent Marxist, who lived in Bethlehem, was advanced as a possible candidate for mayor. Defense Minister Shimon Peres and senior officers of the military government had implored Ja'abri to declare his candidacy, but the old man saw the handwriting on the wall and was not prepared to risk the humiliation of defeat. Then Dr. Natshe was conveniently eliminated from the race when, on March 27, 1976, the authorities decided to deport him and Dr. Abdul Aziz Haj, a candidate for mayor of el-Bireh, on charges of inciting and organizing strikes. Now there was no doubt among Hebronites that the military government was doing everything in its power to guarantee the election of Ja'abri. Perhaps for that very reason, the deportation tactic backfired. After Natshe's removal, Ja'abri's stand-ins lost any chance they might have had of winning. Professor Amnon Cohen, an adviser on Arab affairs to the commander of the area, made one last effort to persuade the old man himself to run, but Ja'abri stood fast. Cohen knew when he was beaten and finally turned his attention to other candidates, with Nazieh Hijazi, an employee of Israel Television and a resident of Hebron, making the necessary contacts for him.

The candidate with the best chance of winning—by virtue of his association with the national bloc—was Fahed Kawasmeh, a diminutive man who radiated an aura of poise and confidence. Kawasmeh's ancestors had migrated to Palestine from Iraq about seven hundred years ago, and in the Hebron area today the Kawasmeh family is second in size and influence only to the Ja'abris. Inevitably the rivalry between the two large clans had taken on political overtones. Sheikh Mohammed Ali Ja'abri had searched his heart, made his calculations, and decided to back the Jordanian court, while the Kawasmeh family's enthusiastic support of Egypt was well known. In 1948 Kawasmeh had gone to Cairo to study agronomy, and after that he was never in particular favor at the court in Amman. He returned to Cairo a second time, twenty years later, to complete his master's degree in agronomy and arrived back in Hebron in 1972. Those two extended stays in Egypt had left a distinctive mark on his personal manner, his tastes, and even the dialect of Arabic he spoke.

A man of tact and easy grace, with a flair for finessing his ideological and political opponents, Kawasmeh met with me right after announcing his candidacy. Since his return to Hebron, he had been employed by the military government as the director of the Agricultural Research and Development Division in the West Bank, and his close familiarity with the military government was immediately evident. He also revealed a keen understanding of the idiosyncrasies of public life in Israel, and he often drew comparisons with the Israeli political scene to illustrate his points. When I asked his reaction to Dr. Natshe's deportation, for example, he replied, "There are thousands of people in Israel who oppose the policies of Prime Minister Rabin. Would anyone dream of deporting them from the country?" Kawasmeh's approach to the subject of Jewish settlement in the territories was just as disarming: "By all means, let them come here and settle alongside us. But we also have thousands of apartments, orchards, and plots of land in Israel—in Jaffa and Haifa. We are prepared to return your property to you on condition that you return our property to us." That irresistible brand of common sense extended to his reply to a question about his attitude toward the PLO: "The whole world recognizes the PLO. Even in Israel there are many people who do. Why, then, should I be expected to oppose it?"

Kawasmeh and Shaka did not know each other. They met for the first time, purely by chance, in March of 1976 on a street corner in Jerusalem. Yet there was a close similarity in their views. Kawasmeh was a proponent of the 1947 United Nations partition plan as a plausible solution to the conflict. Although he had a decidedly negative opinion of the settlers in Kiryat Arba—a new Jewish development just outside Hebron—he explained that "had you sent other Israelis here— not fanatics—you might have succeeded in winning us over. We are thirsty for progress, but you have sent us people with whom we cannot establish any lines of communication." When I reminded him of his own "transgression" in giving the first residents of Kiryat Arba temporary quarters in the Park Hotel (which is owned by the Kawasmeh family), he rapped his head with his knuckles and confessed, *"Mea culpa.* Believe me, they treat us like retardates. In 1975 the settlers broke up one of our demonstrations with dogs. They beat us with whips and strutted around the open market with guns in their hands. They even forced our kadi, Rajab Tamimi, at gunpoint, to dismantle stone roadblocks." That conversation left me in little doubt that Fahed Kawasmeh's election would inaugurate a new era in the annals of Israeli-ruled Hebron.

The rising star in the neighboring town of Halhul was Mohammed Milhem, a handsome, American-educated young man, who promised to take a new tack in his relations with the military government. In Ramallah, the elections boosted the standing of the incumbent, Karim Halaf, who was atypical of the gallery of new mayors in other ways as well. Halaf, a lawyer, had once served as a district prosecutor. Ideologically, his views were close to those of the Palestine National Front and the Communist party, though he belonged to neither. An irascible, impulsive man, he was a fastidious dresser with a taste for games of chance, which had won him a reputation as a playboy. In delivering himself of frequent and trenchant criticisms of Israel, Halaf was not always meticulous about his facts. But none of those drawbacks seemed to detract from his influence. He played a key role in the election of Ibrahim Tawil in the nearby town of el-Bireh and of Bishara Da'ud in Beit Jalla.

The 1976 mayoral elections capped a trend that had been obvious in the territories for years. Most of the candidates were younger men sporting a new political style and forthright in their support for the PLO. The significance of the shift in emphasis did not escape the attention of well-informed Israelis. The press had been warning for years of the PLO's creeping take-over in the territories, yet the government had seemed at a loss to arrest it. Once, when Defense Minister Peres was on a tour of Gaza, I asked him if the military government would allow PLO supporters to stand for election. "There are PLO supporters, Hussein supporters, and Communists in the territories," he said. "The elections will be fully democratic, and unless they come to the ballot boxes with guns in hand we won't interfere."

The 1976 election campaign was an all-out one, waged in a manner that would have been unimaginable before then. The military government tried to keep it within manageable bounds by issuing warnings to local leaders, prohibiting posters bearing the Palestinian flag or conveying messages of incitement, and breaking up mass demonstrations in support of known PLO supporters. But the battle was a losing one. Every available inch of wall space was papered with posters in support of the PLO and its candidates. Not a word was said about the need to improve municipal services in Nablus, Ramallah, or Hebron; the election propaganda dealt solely with broader political issues. The PLO's representatives pulled out all the stops in their struggle to achieve a sweeping victory over the supporters of the Hashemite regime. In Nablus, hundreds of youths ran wild through the casbah in demonstrating their allegiance to the PLO. A mob of students took to the streets in Hebron, and pupils at the Tark Ben-Ziyad school painted the walls with slogans in support of Kawasmeh. Literally, now, the handwriting was on the wall, for all the members of the veteran leadership to read, and they got the message loud and clear. Hikmat el-Masri of Nablus, who had once been the speaker of the Jordanian Parliament, lamented to me, "If Ja'abri has fallen in Hebron, it's best not to say the word 'Jordan' at all today. Even I support the PLO. After all, Bassam Shaka is my son-in-law."

Off the record, the pro-Jordan camp spoke bitterly of Israel's negligence in allowing the PLO to galvanize the masses. Some critics went so far as to claim that the Israeli government had deliberately allowed the new leadership to emerge, in order to justify its claim that "we have no one to talk to." Hussein's supporters were convinced that only the king knew how to handle the young hotheads. To the conservatives who had flourished under Hussein's patronage, Bassam Shaka was apparently more of a radical than Arafat was!

Whatever mistakes had been made, however, they could not be rectified now. The national blocs swept municipal councils throughout the West Bank, leaving the military government to call a frantic series of discussions on what to do. The new formula adopted by the Ministry of Defense, which was soon leaked to the press, made up in subtlety for what it lacked in realism: representatives of the people in the territories should be included in any negotiations toward peace, and the mayors might be considered as surrogates for the PLO. In principle, that is, there was no objection to having representatives of the local population openly identify themselves as PLO supporters, but they could not come to the negotiating table as official representatives of that organization.

When the stunning impact of the elections wore off, however, the Israeli government came to see that the new mayors were not all of a piece, and the military government tried to exploit their differences by stoking the traditional rivalry between Nablus and Hebron. On closer examination, Kawasmeh appeared to be relatively moderate and not quite ready to burn all his bridges with Jordan. He paid a visit to Amman immediately after his election and received promises of substantial aid toward the development of Hebron. Thus, in the military government's scenario, Fahed Kawasmeh of Hebron, Elias Freij of Bethlehem, and Rashad a-Shawa of Gaza might serve as counterweights to the more radical mayors of Samaria.

Kawasmeh grasped the role envisioned for him by the Israeli authorities and did not seem to object to it. One time in August of 1976, when he was entertaining me at dinner, he went out of his way to shower praise on the military governor, Lieutenant Colonel Yehoshua Ben-Shahal, while implying that he, Kawasmeh, aspired to become the uncrowned leader of the West Bank. Kawasmeh believed he was a natural for the role and had all the necessary requirements: he was acceptable to the PLO; Jordan would support his bid for leadership; and Israel also had an interest in promoting him as an answer to the likes of Bassam Shaka. The new mayor sounded as if he were toying with the notion of being all things to all men.

I have developed a close personal relationship with Fahed Kawasmeh over the years, not least because I was impressed by his abilities and the sincerity of his declarations in support of peace and rapprochement. I was gratified, therefore, to learn that certain quarters in the military government had also come to admire him, and for much the same reasons. He proved adroit at juggling conflicting elements and was always careful not to close off his options. Though his loyalty to the PLO was beyond dispute, he told me more than once that he would not hesitate to sever his ties with the organization if Arafat ever stopped serving the best interests of the Palestinians. A similar message must have seeped through to the military government; although the mayor's association with the PLO was well known to the authorities, no one considered that an obstacle to the development of an intelligent working relationship with him. (In retrospect, there must have been something of a "honeymoon" syndrome in the tolerance. When Kawasmeh's relations with the military government soured and he was deported, in May of 1980, one of the reasons cited for his banishment was his association with the PLO.)

From his vantage point in Nablus, Bassam Shaka soon caught on to the military government's intention to disrupt the alliance among the new mayors. In contrast to Kawasmeh, he chose to come out punching rather than concentrating on fancy footwork. In August of 1976, when the Israeli authorities decided to extend Israel's value-added tax to the occupied territories, Nablus, the city of merchants and industrialists, declared a general strike and made it stick for fifteen days. With Shaka leading the defiant business community, the strike turned into a classic political struggle. In his speeches to his constituents, Shaka played up the sinister implications of Israel's move, declaring that "imposition of the value-added tax is even graver than the partition of Palestine." As the flames of this revolt spread to Tul Karem, Jenin, Anabta, and Ramallah, the new leadership in Samaria appeared to have made its long-expected opening move. Now it was up to the military government to react.

The military governor of Nablus was determined to break the strike and tarnish the mayor's personal prestige by humiliating him. But when an officer phoned the mayor and ordered him to present himself at military government headquarters, Shaka snapped indignantly, "If the governor wants to see me, let him come here." Unperturbed, the governor went ahead with a sure hand. Toward evening, he sent a command car filled with soldiers to the mayor's home, and this time Shaka

responded to the warrant. The staff back in the military governor's headquarters rubbed their hands in glee. "We told you
so," was the standard comment. "That's the only language he
understands."

The meeting between the mayor and the military governor of Nablus was a tense and dour one. The governor accused
Shaka of instigating the strike and demanded that he take
measures to end it at once. Shaka claimed in his defense—not
wholly ingenuously—that he had been ordered to deal exclusively with municipal affairs and had no intention of intervening in political matters. The results of the showdown were
inconclusive—except for making it clear that there would be
no cooperation between the two men responsible for running
the city. And, if Shaka's conduct was any indication, the military government could expect confrontations with others
among the new mayors.

Before long even Fahed Kawasmeh was drawn into the
radical camp, as cracks began to show in the facade of amica-
bility between him and the military government. The source
of the tension was friction with the Jewish settlers of Kiryat
Arba, just outside Hebron. The settlers were determined to
restore a permanent Jewish presence in the heart of Hebron,
and Kawasmeh was equally determined not to be the first
mayor to have Israelis settle within his sphere of jurisdiction.
Campaigning to have the mayor dismissed, the settlers portrayed him as a sworn enemy of Israel. (In accordance with
Jordanian law, which was binding in the territories, the military
commander of an area was empowered to depose a mayor.)
Lines of battle were being drawn, and the mayor of Hebron
was learning that it was not so easy to be all things to all men.

Kawasmeh, finally despairing of his attempts to pursue a
moderate line, turned northward to his more radical colleagues. But the military government was not alone in its concern over the rising tide of extremism. Both King Hussein and
Yasir Arafat were growing anxious about the demonstrable
independence of the West Bank leaders—particularly the may-

ors of Nablus and Ramallah—and they tried to stem the development of a local leadership that might come to flout the authority of the Palestinian organizations. In the Middle East, politics makes not only strange bedfellows but curious reversals in policy as well. Arafat paid a call on King Hussein in 1978, and shortly afterward Farouk Kadoumi, head of the PLO's political department, met with Mohammed Milhem of Halhul and tried to persuade him that it would be in the best interests of all concerned to calm the tempest raging in the territories.

If the PLO's leaders were worried about losing their long-distance control over events in the West Bank, they were already too late. On October 1, 1978, Mohammed Milhem phoned me with a tip that political activists from all over the West Bank would be meeting that afternoon in Beit Hanina. He would not go into any detail and asked me to keep the information secret for the time being, for fear the authorities would step in and prevent the meeting from being held. Gathering in the labor union building in Beit Hanina, the activists decided to set up a new body called the National Guidance Committee (not to be confused with the committee of the same name organized in Jerusalem in 1967). Its avowed purpose was to provide guidelines for the inhabitants of the territories in their dealings with the Israeli authorities. To ensure their new organization the broadest possible base of public support, the prime movers behind the meeting had invited representatives from all levels of society and all political parties in the territories. It was clear from the general disposition of the new committee that the aim of the assembled activists was to generate static in the dialogue between the Hashemite Kingdom and the PLO. Indeed, as soon as he received word of the development, Arafat, who was in Algeria attending the funeral of Houari Boumédienne, wound up his business there and made directly for Amman, hoping to get things under control again.

While the meeting was going on, I waited outside the

labor union building in the hope of picking up some information. I knew that the makeup of the committee would reveal
a good deal about it, and when I finally got hold of some
details about the organizational structure I could see that the
National Guidance Committee was essentially a reflection of
the new mood prevailing in the West Bank. The area was
divided into three subdistricts, with committee seats appor-
tioned on a geographical basis. The north was represented by
Bassam Shaka of Nablus, Wahid Hamdallah, the mayor of
Anabta, and Hilmi Hanoun, the mayor of Tul Karem. From the
central region came Karim Halaf of Ramallah, Ibrahim Tawil
of el-Bireh, Bishara Da'ud of Beit Jalla, and Samiha Halil,
representing the women's organizations. The delegates from
the southern district were Fahed Kawasmeh and Mohammed
Milhem, of Hebron and Halhul respectively. Also affiliated
with the committee were representatives of labor unions, student organizations, and three newspapers—*a-Shab, al-Fajr,*
and *a-Tali'ah.* Two representatives from the Gaza Strip, the
lawyer Zuheir Rayes and Dr. Haydar Abdul Shafi, the president of the Red Crescent, were also named. Though there
were pro-Hussein people among the committee's membership, they seemed to be only a token group.

The new organization's steering committee likewise reflected the spectrum of political factions in the territories. It
consisted of Karim Halaf as a representative of the Democratic
Front, Bassam Shaka speaking for the Ba'ath party and also as
a supporter of Ahmad Abdul-Rahim's Front for Arab Struggle,
Dr. Haydar Abdul Shafi as a supporter of George Habash's
Popular Front for the Liberation of Palestine, and Fahed
Kawasmeh as a supporter of Arafat's el-Fatah and not above
preserving a dialogue with King Hussein. The committee established branches in all the large cities of the West Bank,
placing local activists in charge.

In time, it became clear that two meetings held just prior
to the founding of the National Guidance Committee had
played a key role in its genesis. On September 27, 1978, a

number of academics and public figures had met in Jerusalem and reached the conclusion that "a stable peace cannot be achieved in this area without the consolidation of Palestinian-Arab sovereignty over Jerusalem, the West Bank, and the Gaza Strip under the leadership of the PLO, the sole legitimate representative of the Palestinian people." The signatories to that proclamation included several prominent figures who had never before lent their names to such unequivocal declarations —the most prestigious being Anwar Nusseibah, a former defense minister in the Jordanian government. One of the organizers of that session was Ibrahim Dakak, who was affiliated with the Communists, and who turned up again among the organizers of the October 1 meeting in Beit Hanina. Also in September of 1978, the Communist party had convened and published a position paper demanding the establishment of an independent Palestinian state in the West Bank and the Gaza Strip, along the borders of June 4, 1967.

Wary of jumping to conclusions about the new committee, the military government allowed it to function, if only to see where it would lead. Yet a close reading of the manifesto published after the founding meeting left little doubt about the committee's political cast. The document stated that "there can be no peace without a full Israeli withdrawal from the occupied Arab lands and without according the Palestinian people the right to return to their homeland, determine its future, and establish an independent state in their country and homeland, of which Jerusalem is the capital."

Curiously, in adopting that formulation the founders of the National Guidance Committee totally ignored the sensational events that had occurred in the region the year before. In November of 1977, Egypt's President Sadat had taken his historic step of visiting Jerusalem and initiating a dialogue meant to launch Egypt and Israel on the road to a formal peace treaty. Setting a tone of reconciliation and regard for sensitivities on the other side, Sadat had laid a wreath on the grave of Israel's Unknown Soldier and had paid his respects to the memory of the six million victims of the Holocaust. Peace-loving people throughout the region were filled with hope and looked on this bold act as an irreversible breakthrough. But those who later founded the National Guidance Committee evidently took a dim view of the Israeli-Egyptian peace process —though some of the West Bank leaders probably had been backed into a corner and found themselves supporting a policy about which they were not entirely happy. Fahed Kawasmeh confessed to me that "Sadat may be doing damage to the Palestinians today, but his visit will certainly be good for us in the long run."

I had covered Sadat's visit with unconcealed excitement. Filming him during prayers in the el-Aksa Mosque, I could feel my hands trembling, and I was moved by the sight of Israeli and Egyptian security men working in tandem. During those three heady days I also helped out a colleague from the Egyptian television network by arranging for him to meet with Fahed Kawasmeh at the mayor's office in Hebron. Kawasmeh agreed to talk with the Egyptian but refused to appear on camera, explaining, in his pronounced Egyptian accent, "You want to film me using an Israeli television crew and develop the film in their laboratories to show your people that I support them." Bassam Shaka and Karim Halaf were less ambivalent, denouncing Sadat's visit from the outset. That reaction made me fear that the Palestinians were going to miss the boat again. On the streets of Ramallah, people were swept up in a spontaneous outburst of joy at Sadat's arrival and openly expressed their goodwill toward the Egyptian president, but their leaders were careful to toe a line of firm opposition.

One year passed between President Sadat's visit and the establishment of the National Guidance Committee, and during that year the Camp David conference advanced Israel and Egypt well along the way toward their peace agreement. The quick response from the new committee was to undertake a series of moves designed solely to detract from that achievement and impair the chances of fulfilling the Camp David accords. The understanding reached at Camp David had addressed itself explicitly to solving the Palestinian question in three stages and within five years of achieving the first stage: the granting of "full autonomy" to the inhabitants of the West Bank and Gaza. Once that "self-governing authority (administrative council)" was established, negotiations would take place "to determine the final status of the West Bank and Gaza . . . and to conclude a peace treaty between Israel and Jordan by the end of the transitional period." The parties to those negotiations were to be "Egypt, Israel, Jordan, and representatives of the inhabitants in the West Bank and Gaza"—and that, evidently, was the rub. In addition to bringing Jordan back into the picture as a legitimate party to the negotiations, the Camp David agreements effectively squeezed out the PLO through a clause stipulating that "the delegations of Egypt and Jordan may include Palestinians from the West Bank and Gaza or other Palestinians as mutually agreed." And Israel had made it clear on countless occasions that it would never agree to sit down and negotiate with the PLO. So, regardless of the benefits the Camp David agreements might hold for the people of the occupied territories, the National Guidance Committee was having no part of them.

The new committee's popular support was demonstrated beyond dispute when, soon after its founding, 3,000 people—including such classic pro-Jordanian figures as Hikmat el-Masri—gathered in Nablus for a boisterous protest rally. Dozens of buses brought in participants from all over the West Bank, including students from Bir Zeit, Ramallah, and Bethlehem, and they put on an impressive show. The mayors were greeted with thunderous applause. As the atmosphere warmed up, PLO battle cries rose from the throats of thousands of people waving homemade Palestinian flags. Israelis on the scene felt distinctly uncomfortable, to put it mildly. I could hear my cameraman muttering, with a tinge of panic, "Where are we? Why isn't the military government out here?"

When Bassam Shaka strode to the podium, a hush came

over the crowd. With the Palestinian flag to his right and a map of Palestine, from the Jordan to the Mediterranean, to his left, he called on the Palestinians to do everything in their power to scotch the Camp David process. Each time he mentioned the PLO the crowd broke out into cheers. Fahed Kawasmeh followed with mocking words for the United States, and Karim Halaf did his bit to whip up the crowd by quoting from a poem by Kamal Nasser, who had been killed in an IDF operation in Beirut: "My brother refugee, do not despair . . . To return to our homeland is a sacred duty, the return to the hills of Jaffa and Jerusalem."

In my report on the event, I noted that, although the rally had taken place only a few hundred yards from the military governor's headquarters, the Israelis present had felt they might as well have been in Beirut or Damascus. Immediately after the report appeared on the evening news, the studio switchboard began to light up with calls from an irate citizenry. Some of the callers made threats on my life, but most merely expressed their outrage that Israel Television was carrying "that PLO propaganda." The director of broadcasting answered the calls personally, explaining that a journalist's first duty was to report on events, whether viewers found them palatable or not.

Despite the impressions of those on the scene, the military government had not been indifferent to the rally. In Ramallah, for instance, the governor called Karim Halaf into his office afterward and demanded an explanation for his inflammatory statements. Halaf denied any intent of incitement, protesting that he had actually spoken about peace but that Rafik Halabi had quoted him out of context. When I heard about that, I approached Halaf and demanded some explanations of my own. The mayor merely smiled wryly and said, laughing, "If you hadn't been there, I would have had to find someone else to blame." At least, I thought, he had the courage to be honest with me.

Inspired by the turnout in Nablus, the protests went on.

Other rallies were held in Bir Zeit and Bethlehem, and each sent out an unmistakable message: adamant opposition to the Israeli-Egyptian peace process. The residents of the territories seemed intoxicated by a newfound sense of power brought on by their series of bloodless victories. Soon they were openly mocking the military government for its weakness. Ibrahim Tawil, the mayor of el-Bireh, jumped to the conclusion that, as he boasted to me at one of our meetings, "*we're* running the territories, not Israel."

Meanwhile, the PLO was monitoring the buildup of feeling in the West Bank with growing alarm and, fearing for its own interests, continued appointing its "mentors" as watchdogs for the leadership of the National Guidance Committee. But that supervision proved ineffectual—or at least did not prevent the committee, in April of 1979, from denouncing the Jordanian-Palestinian dialogue. The committee even tried to orchestrate a coup that would have given it control of East Jerusalem's electric company and squeezed out the pro-Jordanian and pro-PLO directors of the company. The board chairman, Anwar Nusseibah, was summoned to Jordan, received the blessing of a joint Jordanian-PLO committee, and managed for the time being to outmaneuver the "rejectionist front" on the National Guidance Committee. Yet such machinations made their point. Soon afterward Arafat was making overtures to Rashad a-Shawa, Hikmat el-Masri, and Fahed Kawasmeh, in the hope of forging an alliance with them that would exclude Halaf and Shaka. The response was a backlash against Arafat from many residents of the occupied areas, who told him in no uncertain terms to stop meddling in the internal affairs of the territories and stick to representing the Palestinians to the world at large.

On the face of it, the strains within the Palestinian movement seemed to offer Israel an opportunity to play off against each other the various factions represented within the National Guidance Committee. But events in the field and the conduct of Menachem Begin's government only served to

unite the people of the West Bank. The furor over the settlement at Elon Moreh upset all the forecasts.

The Elon Moreh affair extended over a number of months
—in fact, a number of years, since its roots went back to the
period of the Yitzhak Rabin government. The climax of the
affair came in the latter half of 1979, though, after the first
group of settlers moved in above the Arab village of Rujeib,
about three and a half miles from Nablus. The settlement itself
was to be built on state-owned land, but to provide an access
road the government expropriated some cultivated land belonging to the villagers of Rujeib. In a surprise move, the
fellahin of Rujeib filed an appeal with Israel's High Court of
Justice—and ultimately they won. Before the affair was over,
its reverberations spread far beyond Rujeib and the question
of where one settlement group was to put down stakes. Elon
Moreh was a key factor in spurring radicalization throughout
the West Bank.

On June 17, 1979, ten days after the settlers arrived at
Elon Moreh, Bassam Shaka made his opening move, seeking
to lead a mass protest march from Nablus to the village of
Rujeib. He didn't get very far, however. Israeli soldiers had
erected a barrier beside the municipal building, and they
halted the long column of demonstrators there. As tension
mounted along the line separating the soldiers from the
marchers, Shaka began to fear that the demonstration would
turn into a bloodbath, and he contented himself with delivering a protest petition to the military government. Then he
deflected the crowd toward the municipal building and delivered a heated address in which he said that protest must not
stop at petitions, that everything possible must be done to get
the settlement at Rujeib dismantled. Some of the young people in the crowd, taking his words as a call to violence, made
off to confront the Israeli soldiers, to cries of *"Allah akbar"*
("Allah is great") and "Palestine is our country." Tear gas and
clubbings persuaded the youths to retreat, and the demonstration dispersed.

The immediate effect of the incident was to make Bassam Shaka the uncontested leader of the National Guidance Committee. Even the West Bank moderates supported him now, and when the mayor went to Amman to pledge his cooperation, King Hussein had little choice but to treat him as befitting a man of authority. Shaka did indeed prove to be more than a shooting star in the Palestinian firmament, and his standing was never higher than after his famous run-in with the coordinator of activities in the occupied territories, Major General Dani Matt.

In November of 1979, a few weeks after the High Court issued its judgment in favor of the appellants from Rujeib, forcing the Elon Moreh group to vacate the settlement, Matt asked Shaka to attend what he planned to be a routine working session. The commander of the West Bank, Brigadier General Benjamin Ben-Eliezer, was out of the country at the time, and his deputy had tried to dissuade Matt from meeting with the mayor precisely because Shaka seemed to be at the zenith of his power and popularity. But Matt would not be put off and summoned Shaka to his office.

As might have been expected, in light of the prevailing atmosphere, the two men engaged in a lively discussion punctuated by mutual gibes. Speaking of the vicious cycle of violence in the region, Shaka warned that "as long as Israel keeps on attacking Lebanon and the Palestinians, there will be Palestinian acts of resistance against Israel." When Matt asked the mayor whether he saw any difference between a political assassin and the men who were about to stand trial for the slaughter of twenty-nine innocent civilians in a bus on the coastal road in March of 1978, Shaka replied, "The men involved in the coastal road incident did what they did because of the occupation and because they want their independence. Even international law condones that and recognizes them as prisoners of war."

"Do you condone it?" Matt challenged.

"No, I do not condone throwing a child into a fire," Shaka

conceded. "That's taking things a bit too far. But I wasn't there, and I cannot say whether that is really what happened."

Matt countered that the terrorists had boasted about it in court, to which Shaka replied, "The way I heard it, they did that out of a sense of duty, because they wanted to free their brothers from imprisonment. If such deeds occur, they are merely in response to other actions. Look at Israel. It's a country that responds brutally—in southern Lebanon, for example. As long as the occupation and the killing go on, you can expect many actions like that."

"And you condone them?" Matt pressed, as if bent on extracting a confession through cross-examination.

"I assume there's a chance that such actions will yield results because of the situation we live in," Shaka parried. "As long as the Israeli state denies the rights of the Palestinian people and holds to a policy of force, there's no question that it will elicit responses of that sort."

Details of the conversation were leaked to the press, and the inevitable public outcry ensued. When I called Shaka to get his reaction, he told me, in a surprised tone, that he had never identified with the terrorist action on the coastal road. What's more, he suspected an ulterior motive behind the publicity about the meeting, for, as he noted, "This is the first time the army has leaked the details of a secret and private conversation between a military man and a mayor from the territories."

The following day, November 8, 1979, I called Nablus again and asked the mayor for an interview, and this time Shaka granted my request with alacrity. He could feel the storm brewing around him, and he knew he had better give his version of the meeting with General Matt—and quickly. After our interview, he convened the notables of Nablus, also inviting other West Bank mayors to attend. One indication of both the animosity hovering in the air and the undaunted defiance of the West Bank leadership was that a number of mayors showed up, in spite of the military government's explicit prohibition against such gatherings. Shaka had never denied his vehement opposition to the occupation; he had even attacked the "Zionist state." But now he did his utmost to convince everyone that, although he could understand the motives of the men who had committed the action on the coastal road, he had never expressed support for the deed.

The report I prepared for broadcast included film clips of the public meeting and segments from my interviews with Shaka and with Karim Halaf of Ramallah. To my utter amazement, the director of the Broadcasting Authority scrubbed the piece, on the ground that Israel's state television network did not exist to serve as a platform for people who condoned the murder of Jewish children. I tried to make him see that his reading was only one side of the story, that Shaka had vigorously denied the statements attributed to him in the press, and that any self-respecting journalist had an obligation to provide an outlet for a man who claimed he had been wronged—otherwise, we would be abetting the practice of "trial by leak." All the time, I knew that we were contesting something more than the handling of the Shaka issue. What was at stake was the whole character of Israel Television's coverage of the occupied territories. The Broadcasting Authority director stood his ground, and the report was never broadcast. But my news department colleagues and the TV Journalists' Committee voted unanimously to black out the screen for the length of time the piece would have run as their protest against the director's decision.

I suppose that on the narrowest, most personal plane the exercise could have been considered a victory of sorts. It had brought to the forefront questions about the role and responsibilities of broadcast journalism, and such issues are by no means trivial ones—especially in a country like Israel, whose people are addicted to the news (our nightly telecast falls right in the middle of prime time). But that was not at all what I had set out to do. As I saw it, a diversionary second front had been opened. Instead of being able to consider the implications of the "Shaka flap," the public was caught up in a debate over whether or not Israeli audiences should have Mr. Shaka brought into their living rooms via the television screen—and that was not going to do anything to change the critical situation developing in the territories.

Meanwhile, the snowball kept gathering momentum until, on the recommendation of the military, the Israeli government decided to deport the mayor of Nablus. Shaka was arrested, pending implementation of the deportation order, and the spiral continued to grow as all the mayors in the West Bank submitted their resignations in protest. Once again the military government had succeeded in creating unity where the efforts of everyone else—from the PLO, operating outside the territories, to the mayors themselves—had failed. The inevitable pilgrimage to Nablus began, this time including men like Rashad a-Shawa and even Elias Freij of Bethlehem, who was generally considered an incorruptible moderate. The National Guidance Committee was flush with victory, and the streets of the city turned into a caldron of nationalist frenzy. In condemning Israel's "arbitrary rule," the assembled mayors asked why Rabbi Meir Kahane and his followers were not being deported for their campaign of incitement and for promoting the expulsion of the Arabs from the territories.

Bassam Shaka appealed the deportation decision, and the matter was referred to the Military Board of Appeals. Meanwhile, the commander of the West Bank, back in Israel, sensed that a few people were having a change of heart over the affair. Defense Minister Ezer Weizman, who had initially supported the deportation and had even secured the prime minister's approval for it, was beginning to fear that the episode would have an adverse effect on the peace process. A-Shawa, Kawasmeh, and Freij all tried to mediate between Weizman and Shaka, without success. By then it was clear that the Ministry of Defense was looking for a way out that would not cause it to lose face, and it was decided that if the mayor made a public apology the deportation order would be canceled. But Shaka, heartened by the unanimous display of support, was in no mood to play the penitent and demanded an opportunity to explain his motives before the Military Board of Appeals. Fortunately, the law in force in the West Bank allowed the military commander of the area to nullify a deportation order, and Weizman used that provision as his escape hatch. The scenario had General Ben-Eliezer recommending that the matter be closed. Weizman, with studied formality, then placed the commander's recommendation before the Ministerial Committee for Security Affairs, which adopted it and canceled the deportation order. In a parallel decision, the Military Board of Appeals ruled that Shaka had not made the statements attributed to him in the press. It was all over but the shouting.

On November 5, 1979, Bassam Shaka reported to General Ben-Eliezer's office. The exchange between them was brief and formal.

"I wish you all the best and a fruitful return to work," Ben-Eliezer began. "I hope the events of the past few days will not have an adverse effect on you. You must restrict yourself to municipal affairs and not engage in political matters."

"Thank you, sir. I am aware of your role in this affair, and I again thank you for it."

And so, his eyes misted over with emotion, Shaka left for home to meet an adoring constituency.

The scene in Nablus was bedlam as thousands of people awaited the return of their valiant leader. When Shaka arrived, the crowd began to press in on him, and the mood bordered on mass hysteria as they carried him on their shoulders to the gate of his home. Feasting his eyes on the scene, Ibrahim Tawil of el-Bireh said to me, "Today I'm glad that Shaka was arrested. It would have taken us three years of struggle to reach this kind of mass unity and elation. Today we can say that we've won!" Shaka, recognizing me from a distance, summoned me out of the uproar and embraced me warmly. Then, right in front of the mayors of el-Bireh and Hebron, he came out with a startling discovery he had made—"You have relatives in Ramle prison!"—and burst into delighted laughter. I was not amused. First of all, Shaka's embrace of me had been immortalized by a number of news photographers, and I had to track them down later and ask them not to publish the shot. My position was precarious enough without pictures of Rafik Halabi in Bassam Shaka's arms to stir up the lunatic fringe. As for my "relatives in Ramle prison," I wasn't sure whether he meant guards or prisoners. A number of my relatives worked as wardens in various Israeli prisons, but also, as I could hardly have forgotten, some of the Halabis from the Golan Heights were among the prisoners. At any rate, to round out a day of unusual events the delirious Shaka put on a virtual banquet in celebration of his release and invited the crew from Israel Television to be his guests. I have never seen him in such good spirits, before or since.

Bassam Shaka had twice been saved from the fate of deportation: first when he marched against the settlement of Elon Moreh and then, in a sequel to that incident, because of his conversation with Dani Matt. Now that the military government had reversed itself, the mayor of Nablus was more than a local figure, more than a national one: he had become an emblem, a power to be reckoned with in the West Bank. Shaka believed there was a direct connection between the Elon Moreh affair and the outpouring of national feeling in the territories, but I cannot accept his view that the upsurge of Jewish settlement in heavily populated areas of the West Bank was the *sole* cause of the West Bank's eruption. After all, there had been countless demonstrations before the Elon Moreh affair. The public uproar it touched off merged with the direction provided by the PLO and the high morale of the people to create ideal conditions for fueling the flames of protest.

After the Elon Moreh affair, any claim that normal life could be maintained in the West Bank was more in the nature of wishful thinking than anything else. The military government might be able to manage public affairs by recourse to edicts and force, but it could hardly expect to receive the cooperation of the local inhabitants and their leaders. Haj

Mazuz el-Masri, a former mayor of Nablus, spoke to me nostalgically about the "good old days," lamenting that "under Dayan this wouldn't have happened." Perhaps he was right. Dayan would undoubtedly have made the rounds of the cities, met with local leaders, and kept a tight rein on the Israelis living in the territories. But it was hard to believe that any one man could step in now and deal with the situation in anything like the way Dayan had of charming and chaffing the traditional leadership. Men like Bassam Shaka were of a different ilk—militant, indomitable, uncompromising—and Israel must learn to contend with things as they were, not as they might have been.

I had been with Bassam Shaka at his peak, when the frenzied crowd in Nablus shrieked in ecstasy at his return. On June 18, 1980, I saw him at one of the lowest points in his life. Explosive devices had gone off in Shaka's car and that of Karim Halaf that morning, wounding both mayors. When I visited Halaf in the Ramallah hospital, he pointedly reminded me, "I told you they would try to eliminate us. They're opposed to peace and to anyone who is against the Camp David agreements." Depressed by the horror and the deepening hatred, I drove on to Nablus and asked to see Shaka, who was fighting for his life. The mayor asked his doctors to allow me in, but not my camera. "Why not?" I asked him. Shaka smiled bitterly and said, "The Israelis have mutilated me. I will not let anyone take pleasure in the sight of me with my legs amputated!" A shudder went through me, as I tried to convince him that there were hundreds of thousands of people in Israel who opposed his views but who were nevertheless appalled by the attack on his life. But I could see that his mind was made up.

The room in which Shaka lay did not inspire much confidence, for the medical equipment was sparse and largely out of date. I tried to persuade him to transfer to the Hadassah hospital in Jerusalem, assuring him that he would receive the finest medical care available. Again the mayor refused. "Not in Israel," he objected. "I won't insult the doctors of Nablus.

I am better off here among my own. Thousands of people from Nablus and the West Bank would flock to Hadassah, and it would only cause friction and unnecessary problems."

Major General Dani Matt expressed shock and sorrow on hearing of the attack on the mayors. General Ben-Eliezer called it a sad and vicious event and said he feared that the incident would destroy any chance of restoring peace and quiet to the region. And well it might, for the attack on the West Bank mayors struck a mortal blow to Israel's image in the territories. The search for the perpetrators continues, but no one has been arrested yet; and Mr. Begin's assertion that many murder cases the world over are never solved is cold comfort indeed. Worse, suggestions that the assailants might have been Arabs have infuriated the people in the territories, who remain convinced that the fugitives are to be found among the settlers in the West Bank.

I returned to the studio that day feeling a wreck. What I didn't know was that for me the nightmare was just beginning. After my report was broadcast, the studio switchboard began to receive phone calls that threatened, "Today Shaka, tomorrow Rafik Halabi!" Similar messages were addressed to my wife and older daughter at home. It wasn't the first time my life had been threatened, of course. One time during the Elon Moreh affair the Jerusalem police had waked me at two in the morning to warn me that they had reason to believe I was in danger. They had offered to station a patrol car outside my apartment house, but I turned them down—though I did promise to be cautious and to report anything suspicious. The next day the newspapers had reported that a body calling itself the "military arm of Gush Emunim" had assumed the responsibility for executing a death sentence passed on me by a "revolution court." Somehow, I couldn't take it very seriously.

But this time I wasn't so cavalier about the death threats. The television station's security staff provided me with a bodyguard and ordered me not to stay at home overnight. My car was kept in a parking lot under a special guard, and I had to travel by cab. For weeks I lost many a night's sleep, not least because I spent each night on a different friend's couch. When word of my private hell got around to the press, I was flooded with offers of help and messages of encouragement and support, so that eventually my fear was tempered by a sense of gratitude. More than ever I felt an identity with the mission on which I had set out in 1974, when I stumbled into this job. There were friends—some of them close, loving friends, people who really cared and feared for me—who advised me to quit my job and stay out of the public eye. But, after giving it long and hard thought, I knew I couldn't shrink from the battle.

I am not the stuff that heroes are made of, and it would be sheer bravado to suggest that I wasn't genuinely afraid. I still automatically check the stairwell, my front door, and my car, as if I worked for George Smiley rather than Yosef Lapid. But terror is not only frightening; it is infuriating as well. And that was what I held on to when things looked the bleakest. I was and am convinced that in serving the cause of free, objective journalism I am serving the best interests of my country and of the people in the territories. So I rode out that storm —in some ways I'm still riding it out—and have tried not to brood about it. The truth is that to yield to it would have been fatal.

7

THE CONTEST FOR HEBRON

T he Elon Moreh affair—which I will return to later in these pages—may have caused a greater change in the internal politics of the West Bank than in the map of settlements in the occupied territories, but it was far from the first or even the largest Jewish settlement to be established in a heavily populated area. From that standpoint, nothing can compare with the phenomenon of Kiryat Arba, just outside Hebron, the most populous Jewish settlement in the West Bank and the closest to being a full-fledged urban development. If anything can be called a touchstone of Jewish-Arab coexistence in the occupied territories, it is the experience of the past thirteen years in Hebron—and that is why the subject deserves closer scrutiny.

The history of modern Jewish settlement in Hebron has never been a happy one. In the wave of pogromlike riots that raked Palestine in 1929, the toll in Hebron was the grimmest of all: sixty-seven of the city's seven hundred Jews were killed and sixty were wounded as the rioters broke into homes, wantonly destroyed property, and desecrated synagogues and their contents. Seven years later, during the civil disturbances that set off the Arab Revolt of 1936–1939, officials of the British Mandate took no chances and evacuated Hebron's remaining Jews, leaving the city essentially devoid of Jews for the next thirty years. In light of that inglorious history, the Hebronites had ample reason to fear reprisals by the victorious Israeli army in 1967. While nothing of the sort happened, only a few months later, in the spring of 1968, something the Hebronites least expected was suddenly upon them: a group of Jewish families arrived and announced their intention to renew a Jewish presence in Hebron.

The call to resettle in the Hebron area can be traced back to the days immediately after the Six Day War. Although Israel believed the occupied territories would soon be returned to the Arab states, the National Religious Party demanded that the Labor-led government permit Jews to settle in Hebron and the area known as the Etzion bloc, about halfway between Hebron and Bethlehem. The Etzion bloc was a group of four kibbutzim that had fallen to the Arab Legion literally hours before the establishment of the State of Israel in May of 1948. After the 1967 war, the Labor party—the champion of collective settlement in Israel—made the restoration of those kibbutzim an important plank in its platform, especially since they had been built on Jewish-owned land and there was no large Arab community close by. But Hebron was another matter, and at first the Labor party resisted the pressure to allow Jews to settle there. The result was that a group of self-styled "pioneers" decided to take matters into their own hands and establish their presence in Hebron as a *fait accompli* (a tactic later borrowed by Gush Emunim, with a similar record of success).

Things in Hebron went steadily downhill from there, and the reasons were not hard to find. Unlike the northern West Bank cities of Nablus and Ramallah, with their thriving merchant class and sophisticated intelligentsia, Hebron was a relatively poor city, with a large population of day laborers, a tradition-oriented way of life, and a markedly religious character. Most of the settlers were observant (religious) Jews of a militant nationalist bent, who were drawn to the city because of its time-honored association with the Patriarchs. Friction need not have developed on the basis of religion alone, since Jews and Moslems have lived together peacefully for centuries throughout the Arab world. As we shall see, just as in 1929 and 1936, it was the nationalist ingredient in the equation that made for an explosive situation almost from the first day.

Except that this time, instead of the Palestinians provoking and attacking the Jews, the shoe was unquestionably on the other foot.

The sad saga begins on the eve of Passover in 1968, when seventy-three religious Jews, including women and children, arrived in Hebron to hold a Seder. They checked into the Park Hotel (owned by the Kawasmeh family) and promptly announced that by this symbolic gesture they were stating their intention to renew the bond between the Jewish people and the City of the Patriarchs—meaning that they had come to stay. Defense Minister Moshe Dayan was hospitalized at the time, and the coordinator of activities in the territories, Major General Shlomo Gazit, was observing the seven-day mourning period following the death of his father. So, in spite of the settlers' express defiance of government policy, no one made a move to stop them.

Leading the group was a young rabbi named Moshe Levinger, who was possessed of a messianic zeal to reclaim the holy city of Hebron for the Jewish nation. His opponent in the struggle over Hebron's future was the mayor, Sheikh Mohammed Ali Ja'abri, a canny man and a deft politician, who kept his wits about him and decided to deal with the situation through diplomatic means. Rather than confronting the settlers directly, he wrote to Dayan asking him to assume responsibility for their safety and well-being and expressing the hope that all the Jews of Hebron would soon be able to return to the city they had left in 1936—just as he hoped all the Arabs of Palestine would soon be able to return to the homes and villages they had left in 1948.

Ja'abri knew he had touched a sensitive nerve. Then again, so had the "returnees," and the sheikh was genuinely worried by the arrival of the settlers. A religious man himself, he feared that they might try to encroach upon the established prerogatives in the Cave of the Patriarchs, which is sacred to Moslems as well as to Jews. Nevertheless, he did not spurn outright any contact with the new residents of his city, and he even invited them to an audience. There, the mayor, while remaining characteristically courteous, reiterated his tit-for-tat philosophy on Jews and Arabs returning to their homes and broadly hinted to the settlers that it would be best if they left the city. Innocently or otherwise, the settlers took his politeness for a sign that they were welcome in Hebron and expressed this interpretation clearly. Ja'abri in his turn denied such a reading, saying that they had misunderstood him.

It was not an auspicious beginning for either side, and from then on things went from bad to worse. Rabbi Levinger had behaved from the outset like a lord in his own manor, but in May he reached a new height by bursting suddenly into Ja'abri's office and addressing the mayor in menacing tones. Levinger said that the settlers wanted to live peaceably in Hebron and were prepared to accept Ja'abri as mayor, but one thing needed to be made clear: they were going to stay, whether he liked it or not. The next day Ja'abri got another taste of what he could expect from the settlers. Noticing a Jewish couple loitering near the vineyard next to his home, he invited them to come in and partake of his hospitality, but the two refused. Ja'abri got the point and afterward kept the house guarded.

As the drama continued to unfold, the residents of Hebron joined in, sending Dayan a petition protesting the conduct of the settlers. Dayan was inclined to accommodate the Hebronites, but on that point he came up against a strong pro-settlement lobby within the government and found himself unable to resolve the problem by direct means. So the defense minister took a more subtle tack and set out to put difficulties in the way of the settlers. He ordered them transferred from the Park Hotel, at the entrance to the city, to the military government's headquarters, on the pretext that it would be easier to ensure their safety there. The settlers were cramped and uncomfortable in their new quarters, and Dayan thought the poor conditions might drive them away. But he seriously underestimated their determination, pioneering spirit—or what some might prefer to call fanaticism—and remarkable inner strength. They were certainly not about to leave Hebron voluntarily. On the contrary, the settlers wanted to consolidate their position in the city by opening shops and other enterprises; and when their requests were turned down, they went ahead anyway, opening a kiosk next to the Cave of the Patriarchs and gracing it with the sign "Settlers' Buffet." The military governor reacted swiftly to that, however, having the stand dismantled as local residents looked on in satisfaction.

The major contribution Rabbi Levinger's group made to the future of Israeli settlement in the West Bank was the lesson that sheer obstinacy wins out in the end. Under the unrelenting pressure of the settlers and their patrons in the National Religious Party, the government finally decided to build a housing project on the outskirts of Hebron. And so we got Kiryat Arba, a settlement I have visited often—though it would be stretching a point to say that I am a welcome guest there. As a matter of fact, it was from Kiryat Arba that the first call came to have me fired from my television job, and it is to the dubious credit of Kiryat Arba that I owe the honor of having been denounced as a political pervert—when, as a result of one of my stories, a member of the Broadcasting Authority's board of directors blithely commented that all Rafik Halabi dealt in was "political pornography." "Pornography," this honorable member of the board explained to an interviewer from the afternoon daily *Yediot Aharonot*, "means sex without love. Political pornography means presenting the issue of land [acquisition] in the Land of Israel without mentioning Zionist motivations." When pressed hard enough, the settlers in Kiryat Arba have conceded that their right to purchase land in the occupied territories was no more valid than the right of Arabs to purchase land in the State of Israel. How, I wonder, would the honorable board member go about cleaning up that confession for public consumption?

I mention these incidental matters merely to illustrate that the establishment of Kiryat Arba, rather than solving an issue, only seemed to perpetuate and aggravate it. The construction of housing for Israelis who wanted to reassert their ties to Hebron did not put an end to the settlers' belligerent rhetoric or arrogant behavior, which doomed from the outset any chance of a dialogue between the Jews and the Arabs of Hebron. It was therefore no surprise that violence soon threatened to predominate in the relations between the two peoples. When Sheikh Ja'abri wanted to fly the Jordanian flag in Hebron in 1975, to mark the twenty-fifth anniversary of King Hussein's ascent to the throne, a spokesman for the Kiryat Arba settlers contacted me with the warning that "if the mayor has his way, there will be bloodshed in this city." I wanted to do a broadcast on these developments in Hebron, even though the commander of the West Bank, Brigadier General David Hagoel, was pressuring me heavily to drop the idea. In the end, the director of broadcasting came to the conclusion that if the mood of the two sides was described on the air, then television might be blamed for having stirred up the bad feelings! At any rate, that's what he told me when he ordered the piece scratched, and there was little I could do about it.

A particularly alarming element in the possibility of violence in Hebron was the symmetry—or perhaps symbiosis is a better term—in the dynamics of incitement. Balancing out Rabbi Levinger and Eliakim Ha'etzni in Kiryat Arba were Sheikh Bayoudi of the city's religious council, who was a member of the Moslem Brotherhood, and Sheikh Hamouri. Sheikh Ja'abri had managed to keep his constituents under control, but as the elections of 1976 approached there was concern about how well Fahed Kawasmeh would fare on that score. The anxiety disappeared quickly enough when Kawasmeh proved to be a model mayor in the military government's eyes. He devoted himself exclusively to municipal affairs, keeping his comments on broader political issues to an absolute minimum, and tried to introduce a new tone into relations between the two peoples in his city. As noted earlier, that approach won him the respect of senior officers in the military government, who spoke of him as a brave, wise, and dedicated man, bent on forging a spirit of reconciliation between the residents of Kiryat Arba and Hebron. Defense Minister Ezer Weizman, on one visit to the city, stood before the TV cameras and paid Kawasmeh the highest compliment in describing him as "a man you can do business with."

Of course, there was a price to be paid for the romance between Kawasmeh and the Israeli authorities, and the mayor's position was precarious for his first year in office. To begin with, some circles in Hebron accused him of having plotted with the military government to remove Dr. Ahmad Hamzi Natshe from the scene so that he, Kawasmeh, could attain the coveted office of mayor. Worse, he did not boycott the Israeli press—as the PLO would have had him do—and was even known to socialize with the local military governor, Lieutenant Colonel Yehoshua Ben-Shahal.

The disappointment was therefore all the greater when Kawasmeh began to show the nationalist side of his personality. He was assailed by the "jilted" parties in the military government and accused of tagging along in Bassam Shaka's wake. But the main complaint against Kawasmeh, usually phrased in the words of a popular Arab proverb, was that he was "dancing at too many weddings and destined to fall off the tightrope in the end." The mayor's crimes seemed to be cooperating with the American consulate, maintaining secret contacts with the Jordanians, and professing fealty to Arafat—all the while doing his best to maintain good relations with the military government.

There was more than a grain of truth to the assessment, but it is hard to see why the military government was so resentful. After all, considering the tone of the election campaign, surely no one had believed that Fahed Kawasmeh was going to be a lackey of the Israeli authorities. By maintaining his links with the Jordanian monarchy, he was able to obtain substantial funds for the development of his city. By keeping up his ties with the PLO, he reinforced his standing in Hebron, enabling him to exert effective leadership in the city and influence the Palestinian movement as a whole. At the same time, he did his best to maintain a cordial relationship with the military government, which led to grants of millions of Israeli pounds for the development of Hebron and contributed to a calm and constructive atmosphere in the city. It appeared to be a brilliant strategy.

But not a foolproof one. In spite of his initial attempts to smooth out the many rough spots in intercommunity relations, Kawasmeh found himself growing increasingly antagonistic toward the extremist settlers and constantly complained that they were troublemakers who were poisoning the city's atmosphere. Curiously, the military government seems to have held a similar view, for on September 23, 1976, the commander of the West Bank signed a restriction order against Rabbi Levinger for acts of incitement and disturbing the peace. Over the preceding months, the rabbi and his followers had made a practice of entering Hebron to flaunt their presence. Carrying arms, groups from Kiryat Arba would break into song and dance outside the Cave of the Patriarchs and the building known as Hadassah House on Friday nights, stirring up suspicion and resentment. If soldiers asked the demonstrators to refrain from such activities, Levinger would respond by proclaiming that he was not intimidated by the army's power. That was provocation enough. But the breaking point came when Rabbi Levinger and his followers held a public prayer session in the ruins of the Avraham Avinu Synagogue, in brazen defiance of a standing order. Prayers had been forbidden there because the ruins were situated in the very heart of Arab Hebron, next to the vegetable market. The military governor summoned Levinger to his office and produced the order, but it did not seem to impress the rabbi. At any rate, he was not upset by the summons. He simply tore up the order in the governor's face and pronounced, "I will not accept that order because it is not legal."

145

Having delivered himself of that legal judgment, Levinger and one of his disciples, Professor Ben-Zion Tagber, "fled" from the authorities and went into hiding in an apartment right in Kiryat Arba. Mayor Kawasmeh wondered out loud who was running the city, the army or the settlers, and remarked that if *he* were on the run from the military government he would be declared a "wanted man" and the IDF would be given orders to shoot him on sight. In any event, the fugitives remained in hiding for three days, with the military government making little effort to flush them out or arrest them, though every child in Kiryat Arba knew where the rabbi was. Even *I* met with him during that time. He claimed to be willing to see me because he knew I wouldn't tell anyone about our conversation! Also present was a Knesset member, Geula Cohen, who took the opportunity to lament that "in our own country a respected rabbi cannot pray in a synagogue in the City of the Patriarchs."

Following the broadcast of my report on the meeting, on that night's newscast, some government ministers began to grumble about Levinger's brazen contempt for the law and the military government's apparent helplessness to deal with the situation. In Hebron itself, the entire affair was considered ludicrous, but nonetheless it aroused resentment. Finally the military government had to act, and troops were ordered to break into the rabbi's hideout. Hundreds of soldiers massed in Kiryat Arba, and they met with tough resistance. Even so, the troops managed to refrain from using force and swallowed all the abuse showered on them by the "defenders" of Kiryat Arba. I stood to one side and winced at the spectacle of a woman in her second-story apartment pouring a pail of water down on the commanding officer while other settlers battered and kicked his men—who still held back from using force. The entire action was immortalized on film, but it was hardly over before the military government was exerting pressure on us not to broadcast any of it, on the ground that "it might do damage to public morale"—the worst argument the army could have used with me, because it happens to be one of my pet hates. Just for the record, rather than demoralizing the public, the report aroused anger over the settlers' defiant behavior toward the IDF. Nevertheless, Rabbi Levinger was not even taken into custody. Instead, a compromise was arrived at whereby he would report to military government headquarters for questioning and be released the same day.

The Levinger affair proved to have a far-reaching effect on the mood of the two communities in Hebron. As might have been expected, the military government's lenience toward the residents of Kiryat Arba was a very sore point with the Arabs of Hebron. They observed that the settlers were allowed to do as they pleased with complete impunity, while Arabs were pounced on for the smallest infringement of regulations. The settlers, for their part, evidently came to the same conclusion, for, having established their "facts on the ground" by the very presence of Kiryat Arba, they began to think about expanding. First they tried to take over two hills adjoining the development. Then they started to press for the renewal of Jewish settlement in the heart of Hebron. They were clear about their desire for changes in the prayer schedules for the two communities at the Cave of the Patriarchs, they publicly stated their intention to reinhabit Jewish buildings in the old city of Hebron, and they demanded that the government restore the Avraham Avinu Synagogue, near the city's bustling outdoor vegetable market.

A few weeks later, in October of 1976, a definite religious factor was added to the ingredients for a confrontation when Moslems accused the worshippers from Kiryat Arba of damaging religious objects and a copy of the Koran in one of the rooms of the Cave of the Patriarchs. That accusation, on top of the frustration they felt over the Levinger episode, sent a wave of rage billowing through the city's Moslem community, and the next day a mob of students broke into the cave and desecrated some Jewish ritual objects. I am not a religious man, but when I arrived in Hebron and saw the aftermath of the rampage by religious fanatics from both camps, I was filled with horror. I suppose some of that feeling must have come through in the report I prepared, for the settlers lashed out at me for according both incidents equal weight, and even *Davar*, the daily of the Histadrut, the National Federation of Labor, called for my dismissal, in an article saying that a "conflict" had come to light between my national and religious identity and the news stories I was covering. In replying to such criticism, it is probably useless to repeat that I am not a Moslem, for facts are meant to appeal to reason, and reason is rarely in evidence once religious passions have been inflamed.

In addition to their role in dramatizing the shift in mood in Hebron, the Levinger episode and the outbursts in the Cave of the Patriarchs had the effect of pushing the new mayor further away from his moderate position and into the limelight as a Palestinian national figure. The Kiryat Arba settlers despised him for opposing their designs on Hebron, and they vilified him openly when he began collecting funds to erect a mosque near their quarter. Kawasmeh professed not to understand why Jews should be permitted to pray in Hebron and run a yeshiva in the Cave of the Patriarchs while Moslems were forbidden to pray near a Jewish community. By that time, his relations with the military government had begun to falter, and yet his fellow mayors remained suspicious of him. But I think Kawasmeh enjoyed the tightrope walking and was proud of his balancing act. When Bassam Shaka was arrested, following his notorious conversation with Dani Matt, Kawasmeh phoned me and asked whether I thought there was any point in approaching Ezer Weizman to appeal for Shaka's release. "Shaka always gets us into a jam," he complained. "Believe me, I am the only one who can say whatever I want and still remain strong." I had my doubts about Kawasmeh's strength, however, because by then the moderates in the West Bank and in the Israeli government alike seemed to be out in the cold.

For four years I watched as the mayor of Hebron edged gradually out of the center and into the radical camp. The saga of Hadassah House was what finally capped the change in him and set the seal on what today appears to be an irreparable breach between the two communities in Hebron. Hadassah House is a building that was erected in 1863 with contributions from four North African Jewish donors. At the beginning of this century it was purchased by a Jewish physician, Dr. Ben-Zion Gershon, who used it to house a clinic serving both the Jews and the Arabs of Hebron. During the 1929 riots, a mob attacked the building and murdered Dr. Gershon, his wife, and one of their daughters, Esther. A surviving daughter lives in the Galilee town of Kiryat Tivon, and in the mid-1970s, when the question of who controlled the building became a public issue, she told a reporter for *Ma'ariv* that she had wanted to return to Hebron and reopen the clinic to all the residents of the city, in the spirit of her father's work, but that the local military governor had rejected her request on security grounds.

The doctor's daughter was not the only one with an eye on the building. Members of Gush Emunim had tried several times to take it over and thereby restore a Jewish presence in the heart of Arab Hebron, but their efforts had been thwarted each time. Where the men failed, however, a group of women from Kiryat Arba, under the leadership of Rabbanit Miriam Levinger, succeeded with ease. They simply broke into the building, on April 19, 1979—and they have yet to be turned out by the authorities. Dr. Gershon's daughter bristles with indignation over the "illegal squatters who are allowed to remain there undisturbed—even their expenses are covered— while I, who would like to carry on my father's mission of serving the population of Hebron and helping to create as normal a life as possible for Arabs and Jews—I am not allowed into the building." Indignation obviously cannot compete with the efficacy of brute force.

I have been to Hadassah House often and have observed the leadership qualities of Rabbi Levinger's wife. Born in the United States, she is a highly intelligent, outspoken woman, not easily provoked or flustered. She and her group have taken over Hadassah House as the first step toward their goal of renewing Jewish life in Hebron, which she considers a Jewish city that just happens to be populated by Arabs as well. Within Gush Emunim and like-minded circles, the trespassers ensconced in Hadassah House are "heroines." Miriam Levinger was comparatively restrained when she told me that her group's presence in the building was "the bone stuck in the government's throat. Here we have proclaimed, 'Hebron will never again be *Judenrein.*'" Sarah Nahshon, one of her fellow squatters, put it more bluntly in warning, "There may be bloodshed here, but we will not leave Hadassah House!" That proved to be a chillingly accurate prophecy.

The military government was firmly opposed to the "invasion" of Hadassah House, and only two Cabinet ministers expressed support for the action. Yet no one was prepared to give the order that would send troops in to remove the women. Ariel Sharon, one of the two ministers countenancing the action, visited Hebron to demonstrate his open support for the lawbreakers. I also visited Hadassah House, but the military governor forbade my television crew from entering the building. An Arab boy helped us get around that obstacle by leading us to a side street that looked down on the place. We could see the squatters' children playing on the roof, under the supervision of Mrs. Levinger herself. I called down to her, and she called back that the women and children occupying the building were in high spirits, adding, "We won't leave until our presence in Hebron is approved." When I asked how she justified their acting in defiance of the law and contrary to the express wishes of the government, Mrs. Levinger gave me a beatific smile and told me, in motherly tones, "I honor only one law: the commandments of God Almighty. He has determined that this is the Land of Israel and it belongs to us. We are merely carrying out His divine will."

Needless to say, Fahed Kawasmeh had other ideas. After convening an emergency meeting of the municipal council, which denounced the take-over of the building, he told the press that he intended to demonstrate in front of his family's apartment, in the Talpiot Quarter of Jerusalem, by putting up a tent and squatting there until he was forcibly removed. Though everyone knew the mayor was merely posturing for dramatic effect, the military government, to be on the safe side, took measures to ensure that he could not get to the site of his projected protest. His gesture may have looked like the futile and slightly ridiculous histrionics of a powerless man, but I was haunted by the thought that whatever could bring someone as suave as Fahed Kawasmeh to such a pass did not augur well for either side in Hebron.

The people of Hebron are not as prone to take to the streets as their compatriots in Nablus or Ramallah are. Far more ominous is their tendency to keep their feelings bottled up, until one day they burst forth in a paroxysm of violence. When Israeli soldiers were sent to guard the women in Hadassah House, the fury of the Hebronites inched up another degree. Kawasmeh, fuming at this latest affront to his constituency, declared to the press that "we will agree to return Hadassah House and all the rest of the Jewish property in the city to them on condition that they return to us just half of our property in Israel. I am not responsible for the safety of the Jews in Hadassah House. Their presence there is a provocation."

Hebron simmered with sullen anger for a whole year, while its leaders worried about an escalation in the friction. Then the violence began. The first outburst came in the spring of 1980, when a local yeshiva student, Yehoshua Saloma, was murdered in Hebron's casbah. Saloma, making his way through the local market, was shot at point-blank range by an assassin who leaped out of an alleyway. The military government reacted swiftly. Tenants of nearby buildings abandoned their homes in panic, and sent their children to stay with relatives outside the casbah, as the army imposed a curfew on the entire city and instituted searches and arrests. Dozens of men were detained in the central square and subjected to nighttime interrogations. Hebronites complained about abuses, but the military government was determined to trap the assassin as quickly as possible. Its officers still believed in collective punishment as an effective means of control, refusing to see that innocent people were bound to suffer in the process. I spent a day with a family living in the casbah and tried to capture in my report what life was like under the curfew. In other cities the streets were totally deserted, but in Hebron only the Arabs were shut up in their homes, while the people of Kiryat Arba were free to walk about, with no attempts made to stop them. For days after the murder, the inhabitants of Kiryat Arba ranged through Hebron extracting their revenge by the indiscriminate destruction of Arab property. The grim scenes we filmed spoke for themselves; there was little need for any narration.

Sometime during the curfew, Kol Yisrael, the Israeli radio network, broadcast a story implying that Fahed Kawasmeh had condoned the murder of the yeshiva student in retaliation for the shooting of two Arab demonstrators in Halhul, about three miles north of Hebron. That incident had occurred a year earlier, when a command car carrying Israeli soldiers and a vehicle transporting settlers from Kiryat Arba happened on the scene of a demonstration by schoolchildren in Halhul. As the soldiers fired to disperse the demonstration, one of the settlers, Ilan Tor, also fired his weapon, and two students were hit and killed. Tor was subsequently tried and acquitted of murder, the court ruling that he had fired in self-defense. Now Kol Yisrael was ascribing to Kawasmeh a statement suggesting a direct connection between the Halhul incident and the murder of Yehoshua Saloma. Instantly, the entire State of Israel was up in arms, and a number of Knesset members called for the mayor's deportation. I rushed to Kawasmeh's home, to find him fast asleep. I told him about the radio report, and he immediately agreed to respond to it, inviting our crew into the spacious drawing room of the Park Hotel. An immense por-

trait of the mayor hanging on the wall bespoke the change in
Kawasmeh's status and self-image. Against that backdrop, the
camera started to roll and I began the interview.

"What is the connection between the Halhul incident and
the murder of Yehoshua Saloma?" I asked.

"There isn't any."

"Then why did you tell the radio reporters there was?"

"They misunderstood what I said. . . . I told them I am
opposed to violence. I denounced the killing of the demonstrators in Halhul then, and I am equally appalled by the
murder of Saloma. Violence is an unjustifiable means of action. Even if some of us are killed, we will not react in that
manner. But all these incidents should be viewed in the proper
perspective."

As we talked after the interview, Kawasmeh commented,
half in jest and half in earnest, "I think I should buy an apartment in Amman. They're surely going to deport me there."
Then his expression turned grave, and he confessed, "I'm
tired. Things are getting serious. The Jews will extract their
revenge, and the Arabs will respond in kind."

The murder of Yehoshua Saloma seemed to silence all
Israeli opposition to the women in Hadassah House, and more
and more voices were raised in favor of massive Jewish settlement in the heart of Hebron. As an indication of how far things
had gone, people were suggesting in all seriousness that Jewish settlement in Hebron was the "appropriate Zionist response" to murder. The government debate on the issue was
far from unanimous in its conclusions, but nonetheless it was
decided to restore and reinhabit two Jewish-owned buildings
in the center of Hebron. The city's Arabs interpreted the decision to mean the beginning of the "Judaization" of Hebron.
The Israelis already had other footholds in the city: an art
gallery, a synagogue in the process of restoration, the settlers'
restaurant, and Hadassah House. The addition of two more
buildings, along with the opening of a field school, was an
ominous portent to Hebron's Arabs.

Immediately after the decision was announced, I returned to Hebron to get the mayor's reaction. I found Kawasmeh in the courtyard of the high school, with all the members of the municipal council, and it happened that I was the first person to tell him about the government's decision to resettle Jews in the heart of Hebron. Not hiding his rage, the mayor stormed, "They're trying to undermine the peace. I will not stand by silently while they go about overrunning my city. I prefer to be deported, arrested, tried—anything but the Judaization of Arab Hebron!"

The next morning, March 24, 1980, hundreds of citizens and members of municipal councils in the Hebron area, along with the mayors of Bethlehem, Halhul, and Beit Sahour, gathered in the Hebron council chambers for a protest meeting. The first speaker was a member of Hebron's council, who set the tone for the other speakers by calling for a jihad—a holy war—to liberate Hebron and all of Palestine. Kawasmeh, who was acutely aware of the heavy turnout from all branches of the media, chose his words accordingly:

> Even if we are imprisoned, we are better off in jail than remaining here to witness our people being driven out of their land. If we are sentenced to prison, we can take comfort from the fact that there is nothing we can do. It is Allah's will. But to stay here and enjoy partial freedom by remaining silent in the face of the steps being taken by the Begin government—that is something we cannot do. My brothers! We have ceased to be afraid of arrests and prison. We are not frightened by the specter of deportation, for that is easier to bear than to stand by and watch the Jewish settlement of the Hebron area.

Thrilled by their leader's words, the assembled councillors broke into resounding applause. Kawasmeh seemed encouraged by the response and continued, "My brothers! It is not with words that we shall stand up to these measures. We

154

shall resist this decision with deeds, and by every means available to us. We will prove to anyone willing to understand that the people of Hebron are prepared to struggle and have been struggling ever since the Palestinian problem came into being." He went on to depict the present rulers of the Hebron area as arrogant brutes who believed in nothing but force. "But just as the British Empire collapsed and the Nazis collapsed, so will these arrogant, presumptuous men disappear." The reporter sitting next to me remarked that those were probably the most biting words Fahed Kawasmeh had ever uttered.

Once the dam had burst, extremism carried the day. The kadi of Hebron, Sheikh Rajab Bayoudi Tamimi, concluded his diatribe with this prophecy: "The day will come when our flag will fly over Jaffa, and Haifa, and Acre, and the Jews will be destroyed." Even Elias Freij of Bethlehem joined the others in denouncing the government decision. The meeting closed with a vote to send cables of protest to the United Nations, the Israeli minister of defense, and the military government.

Freij walked over to Kawasmeh afterward and said, "This time you've crossed the line." Flushed and still agitated as he left the hall, the mayor of Hebron stopped when he saw me and asked, with a mischievous smile, "Well, should I buy an apartment in Amman or not?" That time I didn't smile back, for my friend Fahed Kawasmeh had crossed a line in my eyes, too, though in a way that Elias Freij might not have appreciated. Kawasmeh's comparison of Jews to Nazis—even if only implied—was inexcusable, no matter how you looked at it.

Our close-ups of the kadi's ranting message and echoes of the other speeches to the Hebron assembly reverberated through every home in Israel, shocking many; in Hebron, the people were still in a state of exhilaration at their own bravura. In spite of a reprimand from the military governor of Hebron and warnings from the commander of the West Bank, Kawasmeh convened in his home a large gathering at which delegates from all the local councils in the Hebron mountains deliberated a proposal that they resign en masse. I was the only Israeli present, and I was surprised by the vehemence of the response to the proposal. While the discussion was in progress, a member of the National Guidance Committee, Mamon a-Sa'id, the editor of *al-Fajr,* entered with a message from the leading PLO figure in the United States forbidding the mayors to resign before the PLO leadership had an opportunity to discuss the matter. Kawasmeh accepted that ruling, but the younger people in the room demanded that he at least lead them in a mass march on Hadassah House. I smiled as I thought to myself that the *shabab*—the restive youth—of Hebron did not understand Fahed Kawasmeh. Demonstrations and clashes were not his style. I had watched him being carried on the shoulders of the crowd when Bassam Shaka was released from prison, and I cannot say that he looked comfortable there. Kawasmeh knew that any demonstration would be dispersed in minutes, and he did not want to be responsible for what might result from a brush with Israeli soldiers.

A similar gathering was held the following day in the academic union building in Hebron. There, Kawasmeh called on his audience to boycott the Jews, threatening to brand as a traitor any Arab who violated his stricture. The call to boycott Jewish enterprises had been heard before in Hebron, from no less a figure than Sheikh Ja'abri, but at the time economic realities had won out over nationalist fervor. Now, too, the battle cry fell on deaf ears.

Kawasmeh also met with disappointment in the actions taken in other West Bank cities. Assemblies in support of Hebron were held in Nablus and Ramallah, and messages of encouragement were sent to the southern city, but on the whole Hebron's fate met with a wall of indifference in the north. Even Kawasmeh's attempt to galvanize the National Guidance Committee into doing something was largely fruitless.

Left standing on his own, the mayor of Hebron poured all

his energies into protecting his city's unity and its determination to fight. Fahed Kawasmeh, the erstwhile "moderate," now found himself cast as the radical straining to revive the sputtering flame of resistance in the West Bank. At a meeting he called on April 2, 1980, he took a particularly strident approach: "There is no choice but to resist the government. It must be made to understand: an eye for an eye, a word for a word, and force against force. Our enemy is not just in Hebron but throughout the West Bank. We must come out against him and act to overcome him." In his effort to turn Hebron's problem into the cause of the entire West Bank, Kawasmeh called for a fight to the death against Jewish settlement throughout the area: "We will fight with all our might, from the depths of our soul, with our bodies and with our blood, against settlements in Hebron and anywhere else on our Arab land."

The restrained agronomist from Hebron had come a long way from the days when his only desire had been to immerse himself in Hebron's municipal affairs. His meetings with leading Israeli personalities and his talks with Yasir Arafat and King Hussein had brought him out of the shadows. The once anonymous, gray figure had become a frontline public leader, a man sought out by everyone from the Israeli Peace Now movement to representatives of the Israeli Communist party, that is, from the far left to the extreme left. He entertained representatives of the Israeli Labor party, and Israel's Foreign Ministry asked him to receive visitors from abroad. The American consulate in Jerusalem even sent him on a lecture tour of the United States. It sometimes seemed that the United Jewish Appeal was the only organization not to use him for public relations purposes!

But Kawasmeh had a natural instinct on where to draw the line. Out of loyalty to the PLO, he turned down requests to meet with American diplomats visiting in the region, though he was extremely flattered that the representatives of a superpower should be interested in seeing him.

Gradually the assemblies ran their course, and calm began to return to Hebron. But it was only the calm before the storm. The next flare-up came suddenly, if not entirely unexpectedly. On Friday night, May 2, a grim piece of news swept through Israel: terrorists had carried out a deadly attack on Hadassah House. When political observers had described the take-over of the building as a turning point in relations between Jews and Arabs in Hebron, they evidently had known what they were talking about.

The IDF has a special program that allows religious youths to spend part of their military service studying in yeshivas, and the terrorist attack occurred as a group of soldiers from that program were accompanying the women and children from Hadassah House back there after Friday evening prayers at the Cave of the Patriarchs. They were approaching Hadassah House, singing and dancing their way through the streets, when three Hebronites lying in wait near the building opened fire and hurled grenades at the group. One of the three was on the roof of a carpentry shop belonging to the Hirbawi family, fondly remembered for having saved Jews from the mob during the 1929 riots. Their deed done, the terrorists fled, leaving behind a scene of carnage. The toll was harrowing: five dead and sixteen wounded.

I was at home in Dalyat el-Carmel when I heard about the attack. Understandably, my wife was unnerved by the report and pleaded with me not to go to Hebron. But I could not repress my sense of professional responsibility, and by 4:00 A.M. I was on my way south. The area was cordoned off, and a curfew had been imposed on the city. In the offices of the military government, I learned that bulldozers were already demolishing the buildings around Hadassah House that had shielded the terrorists during their attack.

I later learned how the Israeli government's response had evolved in the course of the evening. The minister of defense first heard of the attack while at a party in Tel Aviv. He immediately phoned the commander of the West Bank, Brigadier

General Benjamin Ben-Eliezer, who recommended that action be taken immediately. "It's a traumatic thing," Ben-Eliezer remembered telling Ezer Weizman, in reconstructing the evening's events for me, "and I recommended dealing with the problem by creating a 'countertrauma'—the immediate deportation of Kawasmeh and the kadi." Weizman did not reject the suggestion, but neither did he approve it. General Ben-Eliezer then left for Hebron, and near the Etzion bloc, south of Bethlehem, he met up with a Knesset member, Charlie Biton of the New Communist List (Rakah), who was trying to reach Hebron in order to extend his protection to Kawasmeh. The police had immediately had the mayor's and the kadi's phones cut off.

Weizman was still in Tel Aviv when he received another phone call, this time informing him that the minister of agriculture, Ariel Sharon, was on his way to Hebron. That settled it. Whatever reservations the defense minister might have had about going to Hebron vanished. If Sharon was going to show up at the scene, he would have to get there first. Weizman flew to Hebron.

In the meantime, the chief of staff, Rafael Eitan, the officer in charge of the Central Command, Moshe Levi, and the coordinator of activities in the territories, Dani Matt, had also gathered in Hebron. General Levi wanted to check out the legal aspects of a deportation order before anything was decided, while Dani Matt was pressing for the immediate banishment of the entire membership of the National Guidance Committee. But Ben-Eliezer was being careful not to let the Hadassah House attack balloon into a general crisis, and he stuck by his recommendation that, if there were to be any deportations, they should be limited to Kawasmeh, the kadi, and Mohammed Milhem of Halhul, who was active in the National Guidance Committee and was known to be behind the latest wave of demonstrations in the Hebron area. After he arrived in Hebron, Weizman phoned Prime Minister Begin to inform him of the plan to deport the public figures and received his approval. The decision was also reported to the minister of justice, and when Mohammed Milhem was added to the list all parties concerned were up to date.

Three officers from Ben-Eliezer's staff brought Kawasmeh, Milhem, and the kadi to the military government headquarters in Hebron. They were told that they were being flown to Tel Aviv for a meeting with Ben-Eliezer and were taken to a helicopter, in which a force of paratroops waited. Mrs. Kawasmeh later reported that during the flight Mohammed Milhem had grumbled that the story sounded fishy. Indeed, the helicopter landed at an airfield in northern Israel, and the three men were blindfolded and taken in a military vehicle across the border into Christian-ruled southern Lebanon. From there they made their own way to Beirut.

The people of Hebron heard about the deportation the next morning. That was also when I was allowed into the city, and I made straight for Hadassah House. The place looked like a combat zone. Young people from Kiryat Arba were milling around in the streets, weapons in hand, smashing Arab vehicles at random. Nothing seemed to stop those vengeful people. All the lofty talk of coexistence between Jews and Arabs in Hebron dissipated in the clear mountain air that morning. I circled around past Kawasmeh's locked house and drove on to Jerusalem.

Now I had the task of reporting on the events of the last few hours, and I found myself in a quandary. How was I to approach the subject of Kawasmeh's deportation? Should I quote his remarks on peace and reconciliation or tell of his rash analogy between Jews and Nazis? In the narration to my filmed report, I made a reference to the settlers in Hebron—how could I not mention them?—and before I knew it there was another great outcry. People claimed that by my very mention of Kiryat Arba and the Israeli settlers in Hebron I had implied a justification of the terrorists, or at least an understanding of their motives. The vigilantes resumed their crusade against me, and the phone threats became less ambiguous. But attacks also came from otherwise peaceable citizens who seemed unable to control their emotions. A woman caller who was put through to the news department got me on the line completely by chance. She evidently didn't recognize my voice, for as soon as I said, "News room," she shrieked into the receiver, "How can you let that Arab report on our dead?" I tried not to let it rattle me. I knew all about the pain and fear behind outbursts of that kind. All the same, my belief in the possibility of reconciliation in the region was badly battered that evening.

Not content with deporting the mayors, the military government decided it had to deal firmly with all the residents of the territories and began by forbidding the remaining mayors to grant press interviews. But Hebron bore the brunt of Israel's wrath, and a particularly hard blow was an extended curfew. The restrictions had a damaging effect on commerce and left the city perilously short of food as the IDF proceeded with its relentless search for the terrorists. Hundreds of suspects were arrested and subjected to rigorous interrogations. Soldiers scoured every building in the city, and a reinforced unit was stationed in Hadassah House, turning it into a bona fide military installation. Once again the familiar scenes were played of bulldozers destroying houses and shops—this time adjacent to Hadassah House—as if by some inscrutable logic the buildings themselves were responsible for the crime. And once again I felt myself rebelling at the sheer injustice of it all. If the owners of the property were guilty of some crime, why weren't they arrested and placed on trial, like anyone else? If the military government was so meticulous about observing the letter of the law, why hadn't it removed the women squatters from Hadassah House? Because, as one of the military government officers in Hebron took pains to explain to me, the evacuation of the building would have been interpreted as a victory for the PLO, and the government of Israel could never allow that.

On the third day of the curfew, the funeral of one of the victims was held in Hebron's ancient Jewish cemetery, which had been restored after the Six Day War. There were hundreds of Jews in the streets of Hebron, but not a single Arab face to be seen. After the rites, youths again loosed their anger by vandalizing Arab property. They made for the home of Sheikh Mohammed Ali Ja'abri, shattering windows and damaging his son's car. Also, in the course of that day, there was violence of another kind in Hebron: Na'im Mor, an Israeli press photographer, was beaten up by hooligans who mistook him for "Rafik Halabi, television's Arab reporter."

In the following months Fahed Kawasmeh traveled over half the globe as an exile, but he was determined to return to Hebron. He loved his city, and had told me often that he would rather live in a hut in Hebron than in a luxurious villa in Beirut or Amman. That is why deportation is the cruelest punishment available to Israel. A deportee may win fleeting fame, but after he has made the rounds of the royal courts, and has done the lecture circuit in Europe and the United States, no one seems to care any longer about his plight. Fahed Kawasmeh had been a lord in his city, but outside Hebron he was only one of thousands in the ranks of the PLO.

On May 11, 1980, Kawasmeh attempted to re-enter the West Bank via one of the Jordan bridges. He was with the other two deportees, a number of their followers, and the veteran exile Abdul Jawad Saleh, and they were stopped by Israeli soldiers. Then a fist fight broke out between the sentries and Israeli sympathizers of the deportees who had come to give them encouragement. The episode might have been good for their morale, but the four were nevertheless turned back to Jordan.

After the failure of that attempt, Kawasmeh and Milhem decided to take a more sophisticated tack. They appealed the deportation order to the Israeli High Court of Justice, on the ground that the standard procedures had not been observed in executing it. The two mayors demanded that they be allowed to appear before the Military Board of Appeals, as stipulated in the regulations covering deportations, and, although the court rejected their petition to return, it did endorse their right to a hearing before the board. So it was that I found myself waiting at the Allenby Bridge on October 14, 1980, when Kawasmeh and Milhem returned to the West Bank. The exiled mayor of Hebron stepped off the bridge flushed with emotion and asked to be allowed to pray. Milhem retained enough composure to declare that he had returned to the West Bank with no intention of ever leaving it again. And that was all I heard either of them say, for they were promptly detained by the army and taken off to the VIP lounge at the terminal, sealed off from curiosity seekers and journalists.

At the session of the Board of Appeals, Kawasmeh and Milhem denied all the charges against them and swore that there was no truth to the statements published in their names. They maintained that they favored the establishment of a Palestinian state alongside the State of Israel, not in its place, but they reiterated their opposition to Israeli settlement in the territories, on the ground that the settlements provoked antagonism and outbursts of violence. When questioned about an article in a Lebanese paper that quoted them as calling for the destruction of Israel, Kawasmeh replied, "The reporter distorted what we said. He wanted to embellish our reputations in the Arab world. You know the Arab press . . ."

The military board rejected the mayors' appeal, and they turned back to the High Court of Justice to argue their case on technical grounds. I tried to get their reactions to the board's negative verdict, but the guards would not let anyone near them. Finally I sent Kawasmeh a note, through the lawyer Abd Asali. Reminding him that I was writing a book, I asked him to send me a few words about his present political outlook. Kawasmeh never answered the note, but, considering his ticklish position, I could well understand his silence.

I finally got to see the two mayors when their appeal proceedings opened in the High Court of Justice. Judge Moshe Landau asked if there was anyone in the courtroom fluent in both Hebrew and Arabic. I raised my hand, and the court appointed me to translate for the appellants. Milhem was a paragon of poise at all times. In fact, he seemed in exceptionally good spirits, joking and asking about the age and marital status of the attractive deputy state prosecutor. Kawasmeh's mood could not have been more of a contrast. He bit his nails incessantly and badgered me with a stream of distracted questions: "Is it possible that Begin will change his mind? What should I do? Where should I turn?" It was painful to see him in such a state, and I could do little to relieve his anxiety. Nevertheless, he was convinced of the court's unimpeachable integrity. I asked him if he was worried about the outcome of the suit, and his answer was an emphatic no. "The High Court of Justice will see the light. And anyway," he added, in a lighter tone, as if to underscore his confidence on this point, "if they deport me again, I'll murder you!"

Milhem complained about their treatment in the prison where they were being held for the duration of the proceedings. He grumbled about the shortage of cigarettes, about not having access to the prison cafeteria, and, in general, about their being treated like common criminals. But Kawasmeh's thoughts were elsewhere. At one point he offered to sign a pledge to obey the law and the regulations of the military government. Later, under the relentless gaze of the wardens, he whispered to me, "Is there any chance that the Labor party will let us back in when they return to power?"

I fell silent, but Milhem picked up the slack by asking me to send regards to his friends in Israel and to assure them that he hadn't changed his views on a Palestinian state coexisting with the State of Israel.

"How is Rabbi Levinger?" Kawasmeh broke in, as if the talk of coexistence had reminded him of something.

"Fine," I said, and in an effort to jar him out of his nervous depression I went on to ask how he felt about the West Bank's restrained response to their deportation. But it was Milhem who answered, arguing that restraint had been the proper response from a tactical standpoint. I could see that Kawasmeh did not agree, but rather than giving vent to his anger he withdrew into a deafening silence.

Finally he spoke again, asking if there was any point in agreeing to be deported for a stated period—a kind of cooling-off period—that would allow the military government to save face. This time I was the one who withdrew into an exasperated silence, while Milhem confined his response to a wry smile. I jotted down an outline of our conversation, with quotations, and asked both of them to sign the "minutes"—"so that this time you won't deny what you've said." At least they both grinned at that, and they signed.

When the court proceedings ended, a crowd of people from the Hebron area was waiting for the two men outside the courthouse and greeted them with shouts and song. The High Court of Justice recessed to consider its ruling, and throughout the period of waiting for the verdict Hebron and Halhul remained quiet, though Nablus and Ramallah were rumbling with turmoil. On one occasion, a demonstration by hundreds of pupils, Israeli troops resorted to weapons to disperse the crowd.

On December 4, 1980, the High Court of Justice convened to announce its decision on the appeal of Kawasmeh and Milhem. The two judges concurring in the majority opinion ruled that the decision to deport the mayors was faultless from a judicial standpoint, though they conceded that the obligatory procedures had not been observed at the time of the deportation. In his dissenting opinion, Justice Chaim Cohen found that the deportation was contrary to international law and should therefore be nullified. Then, in an extraordinary rider appended to their ruling, the judges stated that, in spite of the validity of the deportation order in strictly legal terms, there were grounds to reconsider it from the standpoint of political expediency.

The public and the media understood the court's comment as a recommendation to cancel the deportation order, but the government thought otherwise. At a special Cabinet session the following day, it voted to deport the mayors again without further delay, for the sake of security and public safety. A few hours after the Cabinet meeting, Kawasmeh and Milhem were again whisked off to Lebanon. They spent the night in the Christian-ruled enclave and then were driven on to Beirut. They had no legal recourse left.

The struggle for control of Hebron goes on, and it is not likely to abate. Yet the chairman of the Kiryat Arba administrative committee told me, only a few months ago, that he still believes it possible to mend relations and improve the quality of life in the city. All I can say is, blessed is he who has not lost faith.

8
MODERATES AND
RADICALS

n their attempts to explain what was happening in the territories, the news media have devised various concepts, or labels, to aid them in making an inherently complex situation more concise and intelligible to the average reader or viewer. One such shortcut to understanding was the twin concept of moderates and radicals, and its use by the media left the implication that it was possible to differentiate clearly between those two camps in the West Bank and the Gaza Strip. Until a few years ago, the concept worked fairly well. Those who expressed open support for Jordan and advocated solving the Palestinian problem in concert with the Hashemite Kingdom were the moderates. The radicals—from the Israeli standpoint, the villains of the piece—were those who, through an organization or otherwise, supported the PLO. Today it is difficult to find any public figure in the West Bank who is willing to speak out against the PLO's policies, and the hard-and-fast division into moderates and radicals no longer meets the test of reality. The true situation is probably closer to the description offered by Jamil Hamad, a journalist from Bethlehem, who agrees that there are two camps in the West Bank but defines them as PLO supporters and PLO members.

Nevertheless, it would be misleading to depict the political situation in the West Bank as strictly monolithic, for there are definite differences of emphasis and approach within an overwhelmingly pro-PLO constituency. The differences cut across traditional social lines and sometimes right through families. Occasionally public figures appear to have gone out of their way to place their people in every available camp. The late Sheikh Mohammed Ali Ja'abri, who worked hand in glove with the Israeli military authorities, had one son, Wahid, who was the director general of the Communications Ministry in Amman and an enthusiastic proponent of uniting the two banks of the Jordan, and a second son, Bourhan, who in 1978 headed the West Bank delegation in support of Egyptian President Sadat but who clandestinely joined the PLO and was a recruiter for it. To take a different kind of example, Sheikh Hashem Khuzandar, the imam of Gaza, who was murdered on his doorstep in 1979 for collaborating with the Israeli authorities and for supporting Sadat, had two sons in the PLO.

Elias Freij, the mayor of Bethlehem, is probably the most prominent and typical representative of the present-day moderate camp—perhaps more appropriately called moderate radicals. His policy of pronounced caution is indicative of the plight faced by those who try to swim against the current. (In addition to courage, a moderate leader in the West Bank must have an abundant reserve of political ingenuity just to survive.) Freij does not have any sons in the PLO, but he is on record as affirming that organization's hegemony in the territories. At the same time, his home, on the main road between Bethlehem and Hebron, has been a rendezvous for dozens of West Bank personalities interested in consolidating a moderate line—for tactical purposes or on principle. They have ranged from well-known pro-Jordan figures in Jerusalem to such leading lights of the southern West Bank as Fahed Kawasmeh, Mohammed Milhem, Hana el-Atrash of Beit Sahour, and Farah el-Araj of Beit Jalla.

One illustration of the delicate position in which the moderates find themselves, and the stratagems they must sometimes resort to, is an incident that accompanied the Bassam Shaka uproar. When Shaka was arrested, in anticipation of his deportation, the National Guidance Committee called for all the mayors in the occupied territories to resign in protest. Freij had misgivings about the move and met secretly with

Kawasmeh, who agreed that it was misguided. The two men devised a ploy to get around the committee's explicit order. Kawasmeh would leave for Amman immediately, avoiding the issue for the present. Freij, if ordered to resign, would say that Kawasmeh had gone to discuss the matter with the PLO leadership and therefore any action should be deferred until his return. Freij hoped that the storm would blow over in the meantime. The plan looked fine in theory, but it failed miserably when Kawasmeh buckled under pressure from the National Guidance Committee and resigned, leaving Freij to hold out alone. The mayor of Bethlehem had little choice but to bow to the inevitable. The episode is typical of the tight spots in which Freij has often found himself.

Freij is in a singular position in the West Bank because of Bethlehem's status as a center of pilgrimage for ministers, ambassadors, and other public figures from all over the world. They meet with the city's mayor as a diplomatic courtesy and also because they are genuinely interested in hearing his views on the problems of the region. Moreover, Freij has actively cultivated contacts with Israel-based and visiting American diplomats—much to the annoyance of both the Israeli government and the PLO.

American diplomatic activity has been a piquant ingredient in the caldron of West Bank politics. When East Jerusalem was officially annexed, in June of 1967, consuls representing ten nations whose consulates were in East Jerusalem refused to recognize Israel's control over the entire city. In consequence, they did not present their credentials to the Israeli Foreign Ministry and were not accredited by the president of Israel to function within the country. Having become "renegade consuls" in the official sense, they soon began to operate in a manner appropriate to that status. Some five months after the war, one of them, the American consul in East Jerusalem, began meeting with Arab personalities in the city and throughout the West Bank. Among other things, he wanted to feel them out on the question of establishing a Palestinian state in the occupied territories; what he heard was their desire to have the West Bank returned to Jordan. The French consul likewise met with four leaders from Nablus and presented his country's proposed solution—an Israeli withdrawal from the occupied territories, followed by international supervision for a limited transition period. The four men—Kadri Toukan, Walid Shaka, Hamdi Kenan, and Mussa Nasser—welcomed that proposal, but when the consul went on to test their opinion of an independent Palestinian state all turned thumbs down.

The consuls' activities led to a sharp rise in friction with the Israeli Foreign Ministry. When it came out that the American consul had persuaded his colleagues to boycott a reception in their honor given by Teddy Kollek in April of 1968, and had encouraged Arab women to hold a demonstration on Israel's Independence Day, the ministry began to issue blunt hints that the consuls had best stop meddling in Israel's affairs. However, the consuls continued to maintain close ties with Arab figures in Jerusalem and the territories. The American consulate in Jerusalem has been active among the West Bank's mayors—sometimes to the embarrassment of the ambassador in Tel Aviv—and has been instrumental in bringing together senior American officials and the mayors of the territories.

The mayors have been reluctant to meet with such high-ranking American visitors as Secretary of State Cyrus Vance, Donald McHenry, the ambassador to the United Nations, and Alfred Atherton, the assistant secretary of state, because of the PLO's opposition to independent contacts with the Americans and its firm rejection of the autonomy plan stipulated in the Camp David accords. But Rashad a-Shawa and Elias Freij have met with the Americans on their own initiative—and with the consent of the Hashemite court. Although these two have insisted that they came only to listen, and that if the Americans wanted to hear their views they would have to approach the official Palestinian representatives in Beirut, their protestations have done them little good with their fellow mayors, who have treated such meetings with great suspicion. Freij in particular has left himself open to charges of collaboration, and even of treason.

People who know the West Bank are only too willing to supply details about the rivalry between Elias Freij and the other mayors. Freij is not on the best of terms with Bassam Shaka or with Karim Halaf of Ramallah. They can count on his support in times of crisis, as an expression of solidarity, but that does not necessarily imply a concordance of views. On one occasion, Halaf, who is not especially noted for his self-control, went so far as to insult Freij in public. When the latter extended his hand in greeting, Halaf pointedly turned away and muttered the word "traitor." Freij wisely remained impassive, reserving his "right of reply" for a more appropriate occasion.

Such an opportunity arose in February of 1980, when a number of mayors, including Shaka, Halaf, and Freij, were invited to meet in Amman with a Jordanian government minister and a leading representative of the PLO. Sometime during the conference the PLO leader turned to Freij with a question deliberately intended to embarrass him: "Why did you meet with McHenry, Atherton, and the others during their visit to the West Bank, when all your colleagues boycotted them?" The unflappable Freij shot a glance at Halaf and replied, in a tone of undisguised disdain, "The other mayors did not meet with the Americans because they weren't invited to. They had the newspapers report it as though they had been asked and refused, but that wasn't so. As for the meetings themselves, what's the difference between meeting with McHenry in Jerusalem and meeting with Andrew Young [McHenry's predecessor] in New York? In either case, we tell them that the PLO is our sole representative." Freij's biting remarks evidently hit their mark, and in Nablus and Ramallah he would not easily be forgiven for them.

Ironically, Elias Freij's well-publicized views have not dampened the spirit of insurgency in his city. Bethlehem is susceptible to the strikes that frequently break out in the West

Bank, and Freij, who owns a souvenir and antiques shop in the town's main square, has himself taken part in them. During one protest in 1980, Israeli soldiers tried to break the strike by forcing all the shops in the city to open. They began their visits to Bethlehem's tradesmen with Freij's establishment, and when the mayor refused to open his shop the troops broke in by force. Freij emerged from the incident a loser on all counts. Not only was he castigated by the military government, but also his political opponents in Bethlehem and throughout the West Bank rejoiced over his chagrin, scoffing that even his "collaboration" with the Israeli authorities could not saved him from their wrath.

Unfortunately for Freij, that is largely true. In spite of his reputation as a moderate, he cannot claim that the military government's attitude toward him is always to his liking, and he certainly does not enjoy any special treatment from the occupying authorities. Early in 1980, for example, the military government imposed tight restrictions on the mayors, ordering them not to go beyond the boundaries of their cities. Freij, a Christian, attended mass one Sunday at the church of Mar Elias, about a mile outside Bethlehem proper. He had no sooner returned home than a sergeant, acting on behalf of the military governor, summoned the errant mayor to the local headquarters and upbraided him. After that humiliation, Freij said to me, in a voice quaking with fury, "Next thing you know they'll tie me to my gatepost. Today a sergeant reprimanded me; tomorrow it may be a sentry or the governor's cook!"

Feeling increasingly isolated, Freij of course tried to build his own network of alliances, and he began by establishing good relations with Fahed Kawasmeh. However, as Kawasmeh gained prominence in the West Bank and fell into step with the mayors of Nablus and Ramallah, their understanding suffered. Freij was honestly upset when the mayor of Hebron was deported, but he held his erstwhile ally responsible for his own downfall. "It's really a shame about Kawasmeh," he told me. "They set a trap for him and he fell right into it." That may have been so, but observers of the West Bank political scene believe that Freij has fallen into a trap of his own—though a very different kind of trap. On the one hand, the Israelis do not consider him a leader of stature who is worth cultivating; on the other, he is mocked outright by his compatriots for his unreciprocated moderation. Freij has a stable of eager rivals right in his own city. For one, his deputy, George Hazbun, a member of the Communist party, is just waiting for the moment when he can take over the mayor's chair. Moreover, the triple alliance of Bethlehem, Hebron, and Gaza has lost the Hebron factor, leaving Rashad a-Shawa as probably Freij's only remaining ally.

While Elias Freij is undoubtedly the most celebrated moderate in the territories, he is not the most trenchant in espousing his views. There are others—a vanishing breed, to be sure —who are known opponents of the PLO. They include Mustafa Dudin of Hebron, formerly a Jordanian minister, and Hussein Shiyukhi, another Hebronite, who has close ties with the military government. In spite of the ongoing dialogue between Jordan and the PLO, these opponents of the Palestinian umbrella organization have received support from Amman and from others associated with Hussein's regime. They express their opposition in statements of various kinds and by their contacts with officials of the military government—and they are rewarded by preferential treatment in such areas as the granting of import and export licenses for trade with the East Bank. But they never attack the PLO outright, for fear of their lives.

I have often heard Israelis complain that they hear no voice of moderation at all. Without doubt, a bolder and more outspoken moderate camp would profoundly affect public opinion in Israel for the better, and for that reason alone the weakness of the moderates is regrettable. Nevertheless, one cannot blame them for their reticence, since matters have reached a point where anyone in the territories who dared to express dissident opinions would do so at the risk of his life.

True, the Palestinians who encouraged the rapprochement between Egypt and Israel and backed the Camp David agreements had a positive influence on Israeli public opinion, but the events that followed their courageous statements gave ample cause for second thoughts. Open season was declared on President Sadat's supporters in the territories. Hamdi el-Kadi, a senior official with the Ministry of Education in Ramallah, was shot in the head on his front doorstep. Hashem Khuzandar of Gaza met a similar fate. A "revolutionary court" handed down death sentences against local land dealers for having truck with the Jews, and some of the sentences were carried out. Apparently one can be as moderate as he pleases, so long as he keeps his views to himself.

Following the murder of Khuzandar, Rashad a-Shawa was informed that he was next in line. A resourceful man, the mayor of Gaza made directly for Beirut, met with Yasir Arafat, and managed to get his name removed from the PLO's hit list. But the psychology that leads a "revolutionary court" to pronounce the death sentence on a man like a-Shawa is not easy to follow. When representatives of the radical camp meet with an Israeli politician, they are depicted as heroes willing to sully themselves by contact with an Israeli; but when a so-called moderate meets with an Israeli, he is denounced as a quisling.

The remarkable thing about the arcane politics of radicalism and moderation is that radicals have met with leading Israeli officials. Shortly before he resigned as foreign minister in Menachem Begin's government, Moshe Dayan met with two prominent representatives of the radical wing, Dr. Haydar Abdul Shafi of Gaza and Dr. Ahmad Hamzi Natshe of Hebron. (Fahed Kawasmeh, who had once been accused of plotting Natshe's deportation for his own ends, had intervened in 1978 with Defense Minister Ezer Weizman to have Dr. Natshe allowed back into the country. Weizman told journalists afterward that Natshe had pledged not to engage in any activity that could broadly be considered incitement; Natshe countered that he had not committed himself to anything and promptly resumed his activities in the Communist party.) When Dayan invited his guests to express their views on the Jewish settlements in the territories, Dr. Natshe's ready response was to promise the foreign minister that the Arabs would never become reconciled to the existence of the settlements. "We'll settle our refugees there once you evacuate them," he vowed unabashedly.

After his session with Natshe and Abdul Shafi, Dayan expressed an interest in meeting with other Palestinian hardliners. A disgruntled Elias Freij remarked to me, "Dayan probably wants to go to Europe and tell everyone he is carrying on a dialogue with the Palestinians. I can't avoid the conclusion that you Israelis are easily taken in by sloganeers, of all people." Mustafa Dudin, like others before him, has accused Israel of bolstering the radicals "so that you can go crying to the world that you have no one to talk to. That logic made it possible for the radical mayors to take over in 1976, and it's the way you've always acted."

Those comments are characteristic of the disappointment the moderates have expressed privately in discussing Israel's mishandling of the situation. Though many of them have developed personal ties with individual Israelis, they haven't managed to get their message across to the government. Elias Freij, for example, maintains a close relationship with the mayor of Jerusalem, Teddy Kollek, and had hoped that the government of Israel would see the benefits of such a bond and act to strengthen ties between Israel and the territories by focusing on economic cooperation, tourism, and human contacts. He got instead the new Israeli housing development of Giloh, midway between Jerusalem and Bethlehem.

Yet there is something irrepressible about Elias Freij. When Gaston Thorn, an official of the European Economic Community, visited Jerusalem to promote an EEC initiative for solving the Middle East conflict, he asked to meet with the West Bank mayors. Freij arrived early for the meeting, arranged by the British consul in East Jerusalem, and called me aside for a talk. Hammering away at his favorite theme, he said, "The PLO must be persuaded to recognize Israel's right to exist while demanding the establishment of a Palestinian state alongside Israel." Afterward, when I mentioned Freij's statement to a reporter from the local paper, *al-Fajr*, I got a warning about grasping at straws. Ingratiating statements were one thing, but reality was something else—and often quite savage. My journalist colleague, giving vent to the more prevalent view, said, "Freij has turned away from the rejectionist front and the strategy of armed struggle. He should be pulled back into line immediately."

Short of physical violence, the accepted way to pull a man back into line was a campaign of personal attacks to discredit him. The West Bank moderates are extremely sensitive about their public images, not least because the process of smearing a prominent figure is usually swift and irreversible. A person branded as a collaborator or a traitor gets no opportunity to clear himself; it does him no good to relent and begin spouting extremist slogans, because his credibility is already gone. Among such outcasts are a number of prominent and talented men whose moderation and experience can find no outlet: Professor Nafez Nazzal of Bir Zeit College, the lawyer Aziz Shihadeh of Ramallah, members of the Ja'abri family of Hebron and the el-Masri family of Nablus, the mayors of Beit Jalla and Beit Sahour, Anwar Nusseibah and Anwar el-Khatib of Jerusalem. An objective observer knows that a terrible injustice has been done them, for they are no less patriotic than the more strident leaders.

Paradoxically, the Communist party, whose official position is close to that of the moderates, is the most militant force in denouncing them. Outlawed by Jordan, the Communist party went underground until 1967, when it was granted a reprieve and soon was making an impressive comeback. The first to revive was the Palestinian National Front, the party's military arm, whose members managed to get in a few terrorist attacks before the front was declared illegal and wiped out. In

176

the face of that setback, the party's leaders initially feared for their own safety and refrained from holding any meetings. But gradually it became apparent that the military government had no clear-cut policy toward the Communist party, and before long the stalwarts were back at work building up their membership. The party's veteran leadership is composed of such well-known figures as Dr. Natshe of Hebron, George Hazbun of Bethlehem, Ibrahim Dakak of Jerusalem, Bashir Bargouthi from the Ramallah district, and Khaldun Abdul-Hak, a building contractor, from Nablus. Its strongholds are in Jerusalem and Nablus, though it has cells throughout the West Bank. In 1978 the party began to publish a weekly, *a-Tali'ah,* which helped spread its doctrine and won many converts. Also, the West Bank Communists have close ties with Israel's New Communist List (Rakah), which gives them added strength.

According to the official Communist line, the only possible solution to the Middle East dispute is the coexistence of two sovereign states: the State of Israel and an independent Palestinian entity. On the surface, that is very close to what the moderates propose. However, the leaders of the party have been known to play a double game: their declarations for local consumption have parroted the war cry of the radicals in calling for the destruction of the Jewish state, but in addressing a foreign audience they have been careful to toe the official Soviet line.*

I have met the Communist leaders in the West Bank and have always been impressed by their political acumen and level-headedness. In February of 1976, when Dr. Ahmad Hamzi Natshe was promoting his candidacy for mayor of Hebron, I visited him and his French-born wife, who is also a veteran Communist, in their home. Although the military government deported Natshe for incitement soon afterward, I

---

*The Soviet Union recognizes only the partition lines (never implemented) of the United Nations resolution of 1947, and shows these on its maps as the boundaries of Israel.

found him an extremely gracious host, whose soft-spoken manner was highly persuasive. Natshe's views are unequivocal: the division of Palestine into two states, suspension of the military government, the cessation of Jewish settlement in the territories, and the dismantling of existing settlements. None of those positions necessarily classifies him as a radical, though evidently they were potent enough to arouse the ire of the military government. At the same time, his association with the Communist party serves him as a buffer against attacks by those who might consider his views insufficiently aggressive.

The story of the journalist Mohammed Khas reflects another side of the political and personal predicament of the Palestinian Communists. Until 1948, Khas was one of the leaders of the Communist party in the region that would become the Gaza Strip. The "Reds of Gaza," as the Egyptians called them, rigidly followed Moscow's official line in supporting the partition of Palestine into two states—a position then rejected by the Arab countries. As a consequence, Khas was arrested by the Egyptians and imprisoned in a detention camp in Sinai.

The IDF captured that camp in the 1948 war, and, as a result of intervention by the leaders of the Israeli Communist party, they released Khas and brought him back to Israel. He married a young woman from the Galilee village of Shfaram and joined the Israeli Communist party. Noted for being a sharp-witted polemicist, he soon took over as editor of the party's Arab-language newspaper, *Al-Itihad.*

When the IDF captured the Gaza Strip in 1967, Khas was caught up in a bitter controversy with his local party comrades and decided to return to the region of his birth. The Israeli security apparatus, only too pleased to be rid of this scourge of the state, cheerfully granted his request, but he was forbidden from engaging in politics in Gaza. Accepting that condition, Khas broke off all ties with the Communist party and devoted himself wholly to his new job, as secretary to the mayor of Gaza, Rashad a-Shawa, a post he held until August of 1980. His son, Majid, joined el-Fatah and is now a student in Cairo. Khas himself has moved steadily closer to the moderate camp, and after President Sadat's visit to Jerusalem he came out in open support of reconciliation. In fact, he resigned his Gaza post in a split with a-Shawa over Sadat's suggestion that the autonomy plan be instituted first in the Gaza Strip. A-Shawa opposed the idea; Khas believed it should be accepted.

It was no problem for me to find a common language with Mohammed Khas. In several visits with him, at his municipal-building office and in his home, I easily related to him as "one of us"—an Israeli Arab who thought in Israeli terms. Khas believes it is time the Palestinians came to terms with reality. "Any peace process deserves our support," he says, "because there is no other way." An exceptionally brave man, he nonetheless fears for his life. Yet he knows that overt Israeli protection would disqualify him as a political factor of any consequence.

Another moderate who has been forced to yield to public pressure is the attorney Hussein Shiyukhi. I met Shiyukhi in his office in Ramallah right after he had announced his support for President Sadat's peace initiative and his intention of leading a West Bank delegation to Cairo as a gesture of esteem for the president. Two bodyguards were stationed outside Shiyukhi's office. Every car that stopped in the street below all but sent him diving for cover. He spoke with pathos about what it meant to be in his position: "It is difficult to be a moderate today, but someone must take up the baton, so I have decided to run and attract all the arrows. At least, those who come after me will know how and against whom they must fight." They were brave words, but before long Shiyukhi broke. As the pressure on him mounted, he retired to his village in the Hebron hills to wait out the storm, and all his supporters kept a low profile. Bourhan Ja'abri finally led the delegation to Egypt, though Cairo was in no rush to receive it. The Egyptians hoped that in time it would be possible to organize a more representative and more impressive group. In the end, the only result of this move in support of peace was to provide Fahed Kawasmeh with the political capital to declare that Ja'abri had failed in his bid for leadership and represented no one but his own defeated family.

By 1980, the standing of the moderate camp appeared to have reached an all-time low. Bourhan Ja'abri had joined the PLO in 1978. Hussein Shiyukhi had vanished from the scene. And Elias Freij was continuing to maneuver his way "between the raindrops" while avowing day and night that the PLO was the sole representative of the Palestinian people. Moderation, it seemed, had met its Waterloo.

To the degree that such an assessment is valid, a major share of the responsibility lies with Jordan. Not surprisingly, the forces of moderation have generally been identified with the pro-Jordan line. Most of the moderates were merchants with economic interests in Jordan or had been part of the Jordanian political establishment before the 1967 war. But, as we have seen in the case of Bourhan Ja'abri, relationships among the various camps in the West Bank have tended to be complex and fluid, and positions have been known to shift with astonishing ease. Moreover, that situation is not exclusive to the West Bank. The political dialogue instituted between Jordan and the PLO in 1978, for example, pulled the rug out from under the West Bank moderates and weakened the bond between them and the Hashemite court.

The prospect of solving the Palestinian problem through the "Jordanian option" has recently enjoyed a revival in Israel. The champions of the option—especially in Israel's Labor party—undoubtedly see it as a good way to rid Israel of the Palestinian population under its rule, which has become a considerable burden to the country, and at the same time to involve Hussein in the peace negotiations as insurance against the establishment of an independent Palestinian state. On the face of it, a return to the policy of courting Jordan ought to strengthen the hand of the West Bank moderates. But the standard-bearers of moderation have studied the Israeli political map thoroughly and seem to know by heart all its pitfalls, which have led them to take some surprising twists. Anwar el-Khatib, the embodiment of affiliation with Jordan, has complimented Prime Minister Menachem Begin, a leading proponent of retaining the West Bank, and criticized the Israeli Labor party for its murky and tortuous position on the issue. Khatib has also recalled that it was under Labor rule that the policy of *faits accomplis* was initiated in the territories: Kiryat Arba was built, the Etzion bloc was resettled, the settlements in the Jordan valley were founded, and the Gush Emunim settlers were allowed to establish a foothold in Samaria by setting up their camp at Kadum. Khatib acknowledges that Begin's Likud government has built additional settlements in the territories, especially in the more heavily populated region of Samaria. Nevertheless, it was Labor that set the precedent and formulated the ideological underpinnings of the settlement policy.

The question, of course, is whether the "Jordanian option" is still viable or is merely the vestige of a lost age in Middle Eastern politics. King Hussein's abdication, at the time of the Rabat conference, of his role as spokesman for the Palestinians would seem to have put the idea to rest as far back as 1974. But the fact that talk of the "Jordanian option" still persists after all this time makes one suspect that there must be something to it—if only by virtue of the logic that where there's smoke there's fire. Assuming for the sake of argument that the king would be willing to step back into the Palestinian imbroglio, there remains one factor that cannot be ignored—namely, the Palestinians themselves and how they feel about the option. Here I believe the experience of Aziz Shihadeh is instructive.

On August 10, 1977, Shihadeh, a lawyer from Ramallah, sent a letter to Cyrus Vance, the American secretary of state, setting forth his views on the Palestinian question. The letter was a model of balanced moderation in its assertion that "Israelis and Palestinians should recognize the mutual legitimate rights of both peoples to sovereign national statehood in the land which both claim as their homeland." It went on to warn that "Jerusalem . . . should never be divided again by a wall" and suggested as a solution "not a divided city but a shared sovereignty" of Israelis and Palestinians. Although the document repeatedly stressed that the only just solution was the establishment of an independent Palestinian state "within boundaries which will be the result of an agreement reached by [Israelis and Palestinians]," one brief paragraph paid modest respect to the place of Jordan in the greater scheme of things. It read, "We Palestinians believe that our future lies with the Arab World and particularly with Jordan. This could only be achieved by agreement with King Hussein and the Hashemite Kingdom of Jordan. We do not want to be offered a ready-made solution."

Whether because of the ambiguous "this" in the paragraph just quoted or because of his effrontery in bypassing the PLO and addressing the United States government directly, Shihadeh became the target of heavy pressure and scathing criticism. He was forced to publish an Arabic translation of the document, and in his introduction to it he reiterated the importance of a Palestinian state, while making no mention of Jordan as a party to the dispute or its resolution. In assessing the implications of the hypersensitive reaction to Shihadeh's letter, we must bear in mind that the date was August of 1977 —more than a year before the founding of the National Guidance Committee and well before Bassam Shaka's triumphant return to Nablus, the radicalization of Fahed Kawasmeh, and the resurgence of terror against both Israelis and Palestinians. Considering all that has happened since, can anyone believe that feelings on the Jordanian issue have mellowed?

Saddest of all is that the moderates have been roundly defeated in the battle for the hearts of the young, the leaders of the future, in large part because they have been unable to provide any satisfactory explanation for Israel's conduct in the territories. The glaring contrast between the punishments meted out to Palestinians and to Israelis for similar offenses was provocation enough. Such instances as the IDF's pronounced restraint in dealing with Rabbi Levinger and the "defenders of Kiryat Arba" in 1976 were infuriating enough. But, in May of 1979, matters bordered on the burlesque in the resistance of the settlers of Neot Sinai, on the north Sinai coast, to the evacuation of their settlement, as required by the terms of the Israeli-Egyptian peace treaty. The recalcitrant settlers hurled flaming torches at the Israeli troops. But when they were brought to trial for their obstructionism, countless reasons were advanced for justifying their motives and showing clemency toward them. The defendants were sentenced to only three months' imprisonment, and even that was immediately reduced to a lighter penalty. If Palestinian students run amok or throw stones at Israeli soldiers, however, they can look forward to severe sentences. Osama Sa'adeh, a nineteen-year-old student tried in December of 1978 on charges of disorderly conduct and throwing stones at military vehicles, was sentenced to one year's imprisonment, two more on probation, and a fine of 25,000 Israeli pounds—approximately $1,500.

Not that such punishments have been any deterrent to further outbursts. In the past few years Bir Zeit College became a hotbed of rebellion among the youth and intellectuals of the West Bank, and I saw the school erupt repeatedly. The atmosphere was permeated with tension; violence on both sides—demonstrators and soldiers alike—became the accepted norm. The military government brought all its power to bear in trying to limit Bir Zeit to strictly educational activities, but when all else failed the college was closed, on May 7, 1980, by order of the military governor. The reason: students and staff were engaging in incitement and attempts to undermine public order throughout the West Bank.

By now, institutions like Bir Zeit and the younger generation in general are setting the tone for the entire population of the West Bank. During one demonstration at the Amari refugee camp near Ramallah, my crew became an easy target for stone throwers, and we were lucky to get away unscathed. In the Nablus casbah, I once saw a middle-aged woman pour water from her third-floor balcony onto soldiers patrolling the streets below. I have soaked up more tear gas covering street demonstrations than I care to recall, and I can testify to just how potent a weapon it is in dispersing crowds. And still those students and their elders keep coming back for more.

What of the children born since 1967, who have never known any rule but the Israeli administration? Is there perhaps a ray of hope in them? I would not venture to speak for their political leanings, but one thing is certain: the boys and girls growing up in the West Bank today are a generation without hope. Indeed, what kind of dream can a youngster from Nablus or Hebron nurture in these times? How can one expect him to believe that science and technology will improve his lot or raise his people out of their misery? It is grotesque to speak of the "gift of science and development" in a region that boasts exactly one vocational school, mostly for show, and lacks a single advanced medical institution. Surely that is not a likely breeding ground for moderation.

In the face of such realities—not to mention the expropriation of land for Israel's settlement program or the military government's strong-arm tactics—it is next to impossible for a moderate in the territories to advocate a dialogue with Israel over the future of the area. In all fairness, it is no easier for moderates in Israel to promote the cause of understanding toward the Palestinians. For how can they possibly explain away the arbitrary use of terror as a political instrument? And how can they ask that the right of free speech and assembly be granted in the territories when every demonstration turns into a whirlpool of violence and invective focused against Israel? Can an Israeli moderate honestly support a Palestinian radical's right to self-expression if that freedom will be used to block every avenue to reason and reconciliation?

I opened this chapter with an analysis of the terms moderate and radical, and I end it with the conclusion that the distinctions between them have been reduced to a parody by the sober facts of life in the territories. Many erstwhile moderates have taken cover behind radical statements, while the few who have stuck to their views have retreated into double-talk or, more often, into total silence. No matter who calls the shots these days, the PLO comes out ahead.

9
TERROR

The PLO is a household expression today throughout much of the world, and its leader, Yasir Arafat, has become the embodiment of the Palestinian national struggle. But the organization, although it was founded in May of 1964, did not become a political factor of any consequence until well after the Six Day War, when the splintered Palestinian movement began to escape from the control of the various Arab states and come into its own as an independent political and paramilitary force. Two developments at a meeting of the Palestinian National Council in Cairo in May of 1968 led to that shift in the PLO's status and fortunes. The first was el-Fatah's bid for dominance within the PLO—which it finally achieved at the council's next meeting, in February of 1969, when Arafat's organization secured a majority of the council's one hundred seats. The other key event of the May 1968 meeting was the issuance of a document called the Palestinian National Covenant, which, by providing an ideological basis for the war against Israel and detailing the organization's aims, brought the PLO's political image into sharp focus.

The opening clause of the Palestinian National Covenant proclaimed: "Palestine is the homeland of the Palestinian Arab People and an integral part of the Great Arab Homeland, and the People of Palestine are part of the Arab Nation." In affirming the Palestinians' right to political independence and self-determination, the covenant thereby denied that same right to the Jews, who were defined as a religious sect rather than a national entity. Only by rewriting Jewish history to fit its own

186

purposes was the PLO able to conclude that there was a place for Jews in the secular-democratic state it intended to set up in Palestine, and in a burst of generosity the covenant allowed that not all Jews need to be turned out of the country. Clause 6 stated: "The Jews who were living permanently in Palestine until the beginning of the Zionist invasion will be considered Palestinians." In a later paragraph, however, the onset of the "Zionist invasion" was given as 1917. As to the means for achieving its ends, Clause 9 of the covenant said: "Armed struggle is the only way to liberate Palestine and is therefore to be considered a strategy, not merely a tactic."

The Palestinian National Covenant immediately became a categorical imperative for all who identified with the Palestinian nationalist cause. Occasionally, leading figures in the territories have spoken against the letter and the spirit of the covenant in private conversation. But anyone who challenged it publicly placed himself in great personal jeopardy—and some have paid for their criticism with their lives. True, in recent years moderate voices within the PLO have called for a retreat from the claim to all of the former Palestine Mandate and a return to the idea of partitioning the country into two states. But those voices have been drowned out by the war cries of the young lions, coming from the Lebanese refugee camps and from political rallies in the West Bank.

At the same time, the Palestinian National Covenant has been a red flag to hard-liners in Israel, who cite it in justification of their demands for a firm hand in dealing with the Palestinians. The only answer to such an extremist manifesto, they argue, is a rigid, uncompromising stand. Thus the covenant has buttressed the extremists on both sides of the dispute. On the one hand, it has provided a rationale for Yasir Arafat's aphoristic prediction that "Palestine fell in a storm of fire and steel and will be retaken in a storm of fire and steel"; on the other hand, in a different but scarcely less ominous vein, it has created a climate that has allowed Israeli settlers in the territories to suggest that "if democracy diminishes the security of the whole Land of Israel, we're best off renouncing it."

Violence as a way of solving political problems has been a standard feature of the Middle East conflict from the beginning. The rulers of the Arab states have encouraged it for decades, even exploiting the squalor and misery in the refugee camps to build cadres of irregulars willing to sacrifice themselves for their "captured land." From that standpoint, the Palestinian National Covenant merely added an ideological element to the existing reality. In contrast to the fedayeen of the 1950s, whose principal interest was vengeance and murder, Yasir Arafat has viewed terrorism as a means to gain political ends and has given stature to this form of violence by cloaking it in ideological respectability. His doctrine can be summed up in the statement "The hand that holds the gun must be the hand of a self-conscious man." In the PLO's view, terrorism was an outlet for the frustration consuming the spirit of the Palestinian refugees. Thus Arafat has legitimized murder and sabotage as the means by which the Palestinian refugee can express his resolution to overcome the apathy that breeds in the camps and to do something about changing his fate. "Falling in action against the enemy," Arafat tells his followers, "is better than dying a slow, sordid death in the tents of the desert."

Like most people in Israel, it was after the 1967 war that I became keenly aware of the resurgence of terror. But the resumption of terrorist attacks (after a long pause following the Sinai campaign) had actually come two years earlier, well before the conquest of the territories. The opening move in this cat-and-mouse war against Israel was on January 3, 1965, when an employee of the Mekorot water company discovered some sticks of gelignite set to explode in a reservoir that was part of the regional water supply. Trackers from the Border Police followed the saboteurs' trail to the Arab village of Arabeh, in the lower Galilee, and questioning of the villagers revealed that the explosives had been smuggled over the border by terrorists.

Although most of the terrorist squads crossed into Israel from Jordan, the nerve center of the Palestinian movement was in Egypt, and it was run by Abdul Rahman Abd e-Rauf al-Kadwa el-Husseini, better known as Yasir Arafat. The Husseini family is said to be descended from the prophet Mohammed, but it might be more pertinent that Arafat is a blood relation of Haj Amin el-Husseini, the former mufti of Jerusalem and the leader of the Palestinian Arab national movement until the British dismissed him for seditious activities and he fled the country in 1937. Arafat was born in Cairo in 1929, but he usually embellishes his biography with the claim that he was born in Jerusalem, near the Western Wall. His mother was in fact a Jerusalemite, from the Abu-Sa'ud family, whose home was not far from the wall. (The building was torn down in 1969 to make way for the plaza facing the Western Wall, though Jerusalem Arabs believe it was destroyed because of its association with Arafat.) The discrepancy about his birthplace aside, there is no dispute that Arafat grew up in Cairo, along with his three siblings: Gamal, one of the leaders of el-Fatah; Fathi, a doctor and the director of the Palestinian Red Crescent; and a sister, who still lives in Cairo with her family.

Arafat's name has been closely associated with el-Fatah since its establishment in 1965—though some versions have the organization dating back to 1958 and even to 1951. What is certain is that 1965 was the first year in which el-Fatah had terrorist groups operating in the field; they executed thirty-five armed incursions into Israeli territory. The organization's leaders solicited the support of all the Arab states. But in Syria, where el-Fatah was initially based, they encountered resistance to the presence of an armed force not under the government's direct control. Syria was actually interested in furthering el-Fatah's activities, but Arafat refused to accept the authority of the Ba'ath party. A showdown over the issue came in May of 1966, when a squad of terrorists crossed the Israeli border and booby-trapped a civilian vehicle without having received prior permission from the Syrian General Staff. Annoyed, the Syrians decided to put a halt to el-Fatah's activities and arrested the organization's leaders, Arafat among them. Captain Yusuf Orabi, an officer in one of the regular Palestinian units of the Syrian army, then informed all the el-Fatah cells that Arafat had been deposed and that he, Orabi, was taking over. Soon afterward, however, Orabi was murdered in the Yarmouk refugee camp—apparently by Arafat's men. At all events, the el-Fatah leaders were shortly released from detention and moved their headquarters out of Syria, which transferred its backing to the a-Sa'ika organization.

El-Fatah's determination to remain independent was especially noteworthy in an era when it was standard practice for the various Arab states to organize Palestinian contingents under their own patronage. That left the movement plagued by factional rivalries from the start. Egypt, for example, encouraged the more conservative elements in the Palestinian movement, whose leader was Ahmad Shukeiri, then the head of the PLO. Shukeiri, in turn, was sensitive to the rise of el-Fatah and to Syria's desire to dominate the Palestine guerrilla movement. Yet, along with its divisive effect, the competition among the Palestinian organizations spurred them to prove their mettle in actions against Israel—and in that they certainly made themselves felt.

On November 12, 1966, a land mine planted by terrorists on a patrol road in the Judean desert caused the death of three Israeli soldiers. The IDF traced the terrorists' base of operations to the village of Samua, in the Hebron mountains, and mounted a retaliatory action in which forty houses were blown up. But even that heavy punishment—a sign of Israel's growing exasperation with the terrorist attacks—did not halt the terror. In fact, when the Six Day War broke out, el-Fatah claimed the credit for touching it off. That, of course, was a gross exaggeration (which the Egyptian writer Lutfi el-Khuli ascribed to "el-Fatah's narcissism"). But it was certainly true that terrorism along Israel's borders in the two years before the 1967 war had contributed to rising tension in the area.

Two weeks after the cease-fire of June 10, 1967, the central committee of el-Fatah convened in Damascus to discuss the calamitous outcome of the war it had worked so hard to ignite. While the Arab states were still licking their wounds, the Palestinians began to make plans for the future. The revised map of the Middle East opened up new horizons, and the leaders of el-Fatah resolved to turn the Arab defeat into a springboard for the advancement of the Palestinian organizations. At postwar rallies Yasir Arafat tried to revive the flagging spirits of his followers with the exhortation that "a revolution that ceases to function dooms itself to extinction." On a more pragmatic level, he had concluded that the methods of combat should be revised and the base of operations against Israel transferred to the "conquered territories." In effect, Arafat had his sights set on a "popular war of liberation."

In July of 1967 Arafat himself slipped across the border into the West Bank, while the IDF was still busy mopping up and trying to restore life to normal. He set up his base in a deserted building in the casbah of Nablus and became known by various *noms de guerre*—Abu-Mohammed, "the Doctor," Dr. Fawzi Arafat, and the like. Crisscrossing the West Bank on his motorbike, he held meetings in cafés and tried to organize a command structure, all the while recruiting local young people into the ranks of el-Fatah. During that period Arafat had as his deputy "Abu-Leila," a native of Jaffa and a graduate of the military college in Baghdad, who was killed in Jenin at the end of 1967. But the men he appointed as local commanders were all natives of the West Bank. Fayiz Hamdoun, a former artillery officer in the Arab Legion, became the commander of the Jerusalem sector, which was sustained by Palestinian students who had returned from schools in Germany and Egypt. When Hamdoun was forced to flee to Syria, he was replaced by Kamal Nammri, a pharmaceutical agent from East Jerusalem, who was the child of a mixed marriage (his mother's maiden name was Yetti Kleiner). The commander of operations in Samaria was Mazen Abu-Gazala, the scion of a prominent family in Nablus (he, too, was killed in a clash with Israeli troops, in September of 1967).

Nablus was a natural base for el-Fatah's operations because of the long-time activity there of the Arab Nationalists (followers of the Syrian Ba'ath party), which made the city fertile ground for Arafat's recruitment efforts. Before long, however, cells and training bases were sprouting up all over Samaria. The price for the riotous growth, though, was sloppiness of a kind that a clandestine movement cannot afford. The dictates of secrecy were not observed, recruits did not bother to conceal their weapons, and control over the network was slipping out of Arafat's hands. Soon the military government awoke to the situation, and in September of 1967 it struck with a vengeance. Squads that had infiltrated from Jordan, as well as the local cells, tried to persuade the West Bank villagers to give them cover, but the message of the military government came through louder and clearer, and the fellahin drove the terrorists out.

Despite having become hunted men, the terrorists tried to intensify their activities. Between September and December of 1967, they carried out a total of sixty actions against Israel. The targets of the operations were strictly civilian—factories, homes, and places of public assembly, such as movie theaters. In this early stage, however, they actually achieved little, mostly because of the amateurishness of their operations. The young people operating in the field, disinclined to take great risks, planted most of their devices in out-of-the-way spots where they caused little damage. Nevertheless, they managed to create great tension throughout Israel: for months on end, the entire country was on the lookout for suspicious objects.

It was also during this early stage that internecine terror made its debut in the territories. Conceived as a means of silencing opponents and punishing those accused of collaborating with the military government, the policy had a double-edged effect: while making the population more circumspect in its behavior, the intimidation also generated antagonism toward the terrorist groups. In fact, the Israeli security apparatus benefited greatly from the fact that influential circles in West Bank society—veteran leaders, dignitaries from the villages, and urban tradesmen—opposed terrorism and the terrorist organizations. Moreover, it was clear that if the terrorists were to succeed in bringing off an armed uprising, they would need popular backing in the form of civil unrest—boycotts, strikes, and other protest actions. But their earliest attempts to stir the West Bank to revolt ended in stinging failure. Two hundred of the new recruits were killed, and a thousand others were rounded up and held in administrative detention. Arafat admitted defeat and fled to Jordan, to develop an alternative mode of operations.

Yet even the setback of Arafat's departure and the arrest of the network's other leaders did not bring the terror to a halt. On the contrary, the aim now became to mount spectacular, punishing attacks against the Israeli civilian population, as if to disprove the crippling of the terrorist organizations. On November 22, 1968, Ahmad Hassan Zomorrod of Jerusalem drove his car through the western half of the city, followed by an accomplice, Halil Husseini of Jericho, in a second vehicle. When they neared the large outdoor market in Mahaneh Yehudah, a policeman stopped their cars and barred them from driving into the area of the market proper, for security reasons (their license plates indicated that the cars were from the West Bank and East Jerusalem). Zomorrod obeyed the policeman's instructions, parked his car at the edge of the market, and left. Two hours later an explosive device planted in the vehicle went off, killing twelve people and wounding fifty-four others.

The magnitude of that "achievement" encouraged other fledgling squads. Two young women planted a bomb in what was then the main supermarket in downtown Jerusalem, causing two deaths and leaving eight others wounded. In the wake of this new outbreak of terrorism, the young people involved in it were joined by some of the cream of the local intelligentsia

—Dr. Subahi Gosha, Dr. Nabieh Muamar, and the priest Iliya Huri. As the outrage in Israel grew, the military government became increasingly determined to track down the saboteurs, and its efforts bore fruit in the uncovering of a large network in Samaria and the arrest of 172 people.

Since terror was now a political fact, the local leadership in the West Bank was forced to formulate a position on it. Curiously, reservations about terrorism and the terrorist organizations came from some unexpected quarters. The mayor of Hebron, Sheikh Ja'abri, one of the instigators of the riots against the Jews and the British back in 1929, stated his unequivocal opposition to terrorism in these words: "Enough bloodshed! Israel cannot be defeated by these actions, and we must put an end to the violence." Rashad a-Shawa of Gaza, who had served as a liaison for the Arab terrorist gangs of the 1930s, now expressed his regret over the deaths of innocent civilians. And Haj Mazuz el-Masri, a former mayor of Nablus, likewise denounced the acts of sabotage—though all of them emphasized that the deplorable actions of the terrorists did not warrant Israeli military operations against Jordan and southern Lebanon or Israel's collective punishment of the people of the territories.

The attitude toward terror and the Palestinian organizations underwent a volte-face after the 1973 war, when the number of people willing to denounce such violence declined in inverse proportion to the number who believed that Israel could be defeated by force. Not surprisingly, that was also the time when the PLO's star was on the rise in the Arab countries and the world at large. The sharp turnabout reached its climax at the Rabat conference in 1974, when the Arab world officially recognized the PLO as the sole representative of the Palestinian people. With that change in its status and the boost in its respectability, the PLO began to invest more effort in the political sphere. Though the organization was still based outside the West Bank and Gaza, its leaders understood the supreme importance of maintaining the support of the population in the territories, without which they would lose their moral right to speak in those people's behalf. The PLO therefore went all out to expand its educational and recruitment activities among young people in the territories. Its battle hymns were taught in schools, colleges, and other educational institutions, which became hothouses of recruits for the terrorist squads. The results of the stepped-up activity—which took place right under the nose of the Israeli military government —were also evident in classic political ways. We have already discussed the well-organized national blocs that ran in the local elections of 1976. Forthright in their support for the PLO, the leaders of those blocs proclaimed themselves "against self-rule and the occupation and for the establishment of an independent Palestinian state."

As we know, the pro-PLO lists scored a smashing victory in those elections. Haj Mazuz el-Masri, a supporter of King Hussein, turned his office over to Bassam Shaka, whose sentiments lay with the Ba'ath party; Mohammed Ali Ja'abri gave way to Fahed Kawasmeh; and so on, down to the smaller towns throughout the West Bank. Yet what we earlier characterized as the new generation of leaders is not homogeneous in its political affiliations within the PLO—which is made up of eight independent organizations. Some are associated with Ahmad Jabril's Popular Front for the Liberation of Palestine–General Command; others are followers of Arafat's el-Fatah. George Habash's Popular Front for the Liberation of Palestine has widespread support in the Hebron mountains and Nablus areas, and Na'if Hawatmeh, leader of the Democratic Front for the Liberation of Palestine, has a large following in the Ramallah district. Both of them are unabashed leftists, devoted to the principles of Marxism-Leninism, while Arafat—according to insiders—is an archetype right-winger, though he takes great pains to conceal his true views.

George Habash is probably the best known of the PLO's top leaders after Arafat himself. Born in Jerusalem's mixed Arab-Jewish neighborhood of Musrara, he eventually made his way to Egypt, and in the 1950s, around the time Arafat founded the Union of Palestinian Students, Habash established the Arab Nationalist Movement, which won the support of Egypt's President Nasser. Habash has many followers and personal friends in the West Bank, but probably the most outstanding of them is Dr. Hatim Abu-Gazala, a member of the Nablus municipal council and a practicing physician, who was among the founders of the pro-Ba'ath group known as the Arab Nationalists.

In his clinic near Nablus's Clock Tower Square, Dr. Abu-Gazala provides free medical services to refugees from the camps clustered around the city. "The cunning carrottop," as the members of the local military government call him, is proud of his association with Habash and tells anyone willing to listen that his friend's true intentions have been misunderstood and his image distorted. One of my uncles from Dalyat el-Carmel has been going to Dr. Abu-Gazala's clinic for years and constantly sings his praises, so on one of my frequent trips to Nablus I, too, paid the doctor a visit, to ask for his views on the recently signed Israeli-Egyptian peace treaty. My cameraman was enchanted by the doctor, and on the drive back to Jerusalem he commented, "Now, there is a charming Arab gentleman. I would be more than willing to talk business with a man like him." I couldn't help grinning wickedly as I explained to him exactly who Dr. Abu-Gazala was. An embarrassed silence filled the car, until our sound man piped up, "If that's what they're like, then there's hope. We just have to keep our fingers crossed—and our eyes peeled."

Despite the PLO's essay into politics—on both a local and an international scale—the terrorism has not abated. Quite the opposite: statistics show a steady rise in the organization's terrorist operations; since 1974 more than a hundred actions have been perpetrated each year. The attacks have been directed against Jews per se, even though, in its doctrinal proclamations for the benefit of Western audiences, the PLO has attempted to draw a distinction between Jews and Zionists.

196

"Our movement is not racist," Arafat has been quoted as saying. But attacks on a restaurant in Paris frequented by Jewish schoolchildren and on orthodox Jewish schoolchildren in Antwerp would seem to belie that claim.

Jews are not the only targets of PLO terror, however. Threats of violence as a means of intimidating fellow Arabs have, if anything, grown more common. At one rally in Bethlehem, there was ghoulish talk of "tearing the Dudins and Khuzandars to pieces," and the audience showed its wholehearted support by thunderous applause. And the strategy does not necessarily stop at threats. In 1978, three well-known moderates from Ramallah were murdered after they dared to express cautious reservations about the doctrine of the Palestinian National Covenant and to advocate a peaceful settlement between the Palestinians and the State of Israel.

One of the victims was a local merchant, Abdul Nur Janhu, who was shot to death on the main street of Ramallah on February 9, 1978. Known to have ties with the Israelis, including Mayor Teddy Kollek of Jerusalem and officers of the military government, Janhu had escaped an earlier attempt on his life by shooting and killing his assailant. A military court in Ramallah had ruled that he shot in self-defense, but the PLO would not accept the verdict and sent another youth, from the village of Silwad, to finish the job. That time the assassin succeeded. Far from deploring the murder, the pastor of Janhu's parish and the deputy mayor of Ramallah readily admitted that the PLO had been responsible for the deed—and had had good reasons for it.

While some of the West Bank mayors have expressed disapproval of the terrorism—though they are not likely to do so openly—for the most part the shift in the public mood with regard to it is unmistakable. The commander of the West Bank, visiting the village of Tul Karem on June 27, 1979, was told by the mayor, Hilmi Hanoun, that the terrorists imprisoned in Israeli jails "are not criminals. They were merely defending themselves." On June 15, 1980, a detail of terrorists attempted to seize an apartment house in the town of Nahariya and was wiped out by Israeli troops. When the identity of the terrorists was established, it turned out that one of them was from the village of Anabta, in Samaria. The next day, the local papers carried mourning notices that ran along these lines: "Do not believe that those who have died for Allah are dead, for they live"—a verse from the Koran. "Condolences on the death of a dear one." The village's official notice read:

> The mayor of Anabta, members of the municipal council, and all its residents are again honored to yield up unto the Palestinian people and the Arab and Islamic nation its pure and guiltless son, the slain Atzam Sabuba, and his two comrades who rose up to their God on the morning of June 16, 1980, after quenching with their innocent blood the holiest of soils for the worthiest of goals. Rise up, then, you and your comrades, to Paradise and Eternity, to the place where the pure and the innocent dwell. May they receive you there graciously as friends.

In another case, Ziyad Abu-Ayin planted an explosive device in the Israeli city of Tiberias, killing a number of innocent civilians, and managed to escape to the United States. When the Israeli authorities instituted extradition proceedings, the West Bank mayors came to the terrorist's defense. Ibrahim Tawil of el-Bireh maintained that "he was merely doing his duty," and Mohammed Milhem declared, "The inhabitants in the occupied homeland stand behind Ziyad and roundly denounce the decision to extradite him."

Not that there is any lack of terrorists in Israeli jails. In 1978, Israel Television's crime reporter was doing a feature on prisons, and I accompanied him to the Ashkelon prison, where we spent an hour with some convicted terrorists (dubbed "security prisoners" to distinguish them from ordinary criminals). Most of the men we met had actually committed acts of sabotage in Israel, and were not just being detained on charges of conspiracy or membership in a terrorist group. At first they were reluctant to say anything at all, suspecting that we had been sent by one of the state security agencies to wring secrets out of them. But then a few of them recognized me, and they began to open up. We discovered that the military hierarchy of the terrorist organizations is maintained even behind bars. The men take orders from a supreme commander inside the prison, who in turn receives instructions from the PLO command on the outside. Also functioning within the prisons are "revolutionary courts," which pass judgment on those who "rat" or cooperate with the authorities in other ways. One of the inmates of the Ashkelon facility had had his eyes gouged out by his erstwhile comrades-in-arms for such a crime. When asked to comment on the incident, the warden summed up his opinion of security prisoners in general in this terse but telling statement: "They don't love Israel and they're not very nice."

I admit it is difficult to talk about terrorism without sliding into the pitfall of moralizing. Nevertheless, when the leaders of the Palestinian organizations extol terror as the salvation of the Palestinian soul, they ignore its corrosive moral effects. There are countless incidents I could use to illustrate the point, but I am haunted by one in particular because of what it implies about such simple but central values as trust, loyalty, and fidelity to one's convictions. A few years ago, a West Jerusalem taxi driver was found dead in his car, his body booby-trapped. The terrorists who had murdered him—two brothers from the village of Abu Dis—had known their victim since childhood, for their mother had been his wet nurse prior to the 1948 war, when they all lived in Jerusalem. In 1967 their acquaintance had been renewed, and it was no accident that the two brothers had been riding in his taxi that day. In any event, when they returned home and boasted to friends of their "heroic deed," their mother overheard them and realized that "for the sake of the cause" her sons had murdered the man she had nursed as an infant. Agonized by that realization, she turned her sons in to the police. Needless to say, she was forced to leave her village, change her identity, and take refuge in Israel, well away from the Jerusalem area.

That incident is not a freak or isolated tragedy. It speaks for the toxic influence terrorism can have on the moral and social fabric of an entire society. Yet there seems to be great resistance to facing that fact. Even those mayors and other public figures in the West Bank who recognize the debasing effects of terror fall back on the pot-and-kettle syndrome by responding with examples of how the Jewish underground also used terror in Israel's struggle for independence. Every nation's history contains some bloodstained pages, they argue, and terror is the only way the weak can prevail in their struggle against the strong. Moreover, they keep coming back to the intimidating tactics of the Israeli settlers in the territories and to the strong-arm methods of the IDF. I would be the last to deny that the settlers have benefited from a double standard on law and order in the territories or that demonstrators in the West Bank have been beaten and even shot at. I have seen such things with my own eyes, and have been appalled by them. But there is no way I can compare those excesses with a deliberate policy of murder and destruction built on an ideological rationale.

Yet neither will I deny that Israel has surrendered to a policy of counterterrorism—though successive governments have indignantly denied such a reading of their conduct. One way the government has settled an uneasy conscience has been to slap euphemistic labels on otherwise ugly situations. The operations carried out by the Palestinian organizations are defined as terrorism, but Israel "responds," or it deals in "preventive strikes." Most citizens refuse to accept the fact that the IDF is also employing terror tactics when the air force bombs terrorist bases in Lebanon, killing and wounding women and children. Martin Buber addressed himself to just such a situation, involving the distinction between a justifiable attack and the spilling of innocent blood, when he wrote:

If a man enters the room in which his child is playing and sees a stranger at the window pointing a gun, he fulfills a duty if he shoots first—and we may hope that he will be acquitted of murder. But if a thief breaks into a house, commits a murder, and flees, and the head of the household shoots down a passerby merely because he is of the same race as the criminal, how can this deed be justified?

One can hardly expect a fair hearing for propositions like these in the emotion-charged atmosphere of the Middle East. Terror is a vicious trap, and the more prevalent it becomes, the greater the need for courageous people to rise above the slogans, the fear, the fetters of their own passions, and demand a return to reason. Reason dictates that terrorism is a bankrupt policy—if only because it hasn't worked. The Arab gangs did not scare the Jews out of Palestine in the 1930s and 1940s. The fedayeen did not frighten Israeli farmers into pulling up stakes in the 1950s. And, since 1967, the PLO's brand of terrorism has not driven Israel out of the territories, nor have the bombs falling on Lebanon caused el-Fatah to fold, or prevented further armed incursions, or deterred more and more young people from swelling the ranks of the PLO. If anything, terror only seems to make people clench their teeth and cling ever more firmly to their resolve not to budge; and to the degree that it does promote movement, the movement is in the direction of greater extremism. So when all else fails—appeals to moral sensibilities, appeals to sentiment, appeals to stark self-interest—the actual events of these fifty years should be ample food for thought on this very pressing, very painful subject.

10
THE SETTLEMENTS

The bond between the Jewish people and the land of Israel has been the heart of the Zionist movement since its inception. Nevertheless, when forced to decide between sovereignty over part of the land of Israel and continued subjection to an increasingly inimical foreign rule, the majority in the Zionist movement accepted the principle of partition —which first the British and then the United Nations proposed as an equitable solution to the Arab-Jewish conflict in Palestine. But there remained a group of diehards who never became reconciled to the division of the country and waited for decades for just the right moment to reopen the question. In 1967, most of the historical land of Israel fell under Israeli control, and the debate came alive again; in one muddled fashion or another, it has been going on ever since.

When Israel has had any policy at all on settlement in the occupied territories, it has always been deliberately obscure. Under the Labor governments, probably the major reason was a blind devotion to outdated myths as a substitute for sober analysis. One of the legacies of the successive partition plans, for example, was a vague belief that the map of Jewish settlement would determine the borders of the Jewish state. That was never strictly true. The 1937 Peel Commission, the 1938 Woodhead Commission, and the 1947 United Nations Special Commission on Palestine all drew up partition maps that left some Jewish settlements in what was slated to become the Arab state and vice versa. Nevertheless, a principle that might have been applicable during the Mandate but that had certainly lost its validity by the 1970s continued to maintain its hold on a large proportion of the Israeli public.

Another seemingly incontrovertible myth was that border settlements safeguarded Israel's security. At one time that was not a myth at all. During the 1948 war, when the IDF was still in the process of becoming a regular army and Israel was desperate for arms, Kibbutz Degania halted a Syrian armored thrust toward the Galilee, and Kibbutz Yad Mordechai single-handedly held off an Egyptian armored column for five days, giving the IDF time to strengthen its defenses closer to Tel Aviv. But in an era of bulging arsenals, including FROG and Scud missiles on the Arab side, it is hard to see how border settlements can arrest an enemy's advance or prevent it from wreaking destruction on the interior. As a matter of fact, during the 1973 war the settlements in the Golan Heights were evacuated—and it's fortunate they were, for otherwise their inhabitants would have been captured by the Syrians—and FROG missiles reached well into the heart of the Galilee.

Regardless of what bearing these myths have on current realities, they hung on and directed the thinking of the majority of Israelis for a whole decade, from 1967 to 1977. Until 1977, most of the settlements in the territories were indeed built near the borders—meaning the cease-fire lines—in the Jordan valley and the Golan Heights. The Rafiah salient, south of the Gaza Strip, was settled partly to separate Sinai and the Gaza Strip—presumably to ensure that the Strip would not revert to Egypt in any future political agreement. Outside Israel, there was constant grumbling about the settlements. But since they were located in areas without large Arab populations (with the exception, of course, of Kiryat Arba, outside Hebron), the issue never generated a sustained hue and cry. Never, that is, until the advent of Menachem Begin's Likud government, in June of 1977, when the problem was rendered more complex by the introduction of two new factors: a change in the government's policy on the location of future settlements, and a new ideology—or perhaps mystique is a better word—to replace the exhausted mythology of earlier decades. In the West, the debate has centered on the legality of the settlements and their disservice to the cause of peace. Here in Israel, in addition to those issues, the new settlements in the West Bank have raised serious questions about the health of a democratic system that permits the government to be so responsive to a relatively small segment of the public and permits that same segment to have such an inordinate influence on national policy.

The dimensions of the problem are apparent in these statistics: up to December of 1980, 110 settlements had been established throughout the occupied territories, including Sinai and the Golan Heights. They were concentrated mainly in four areas: sixty-eight settlements in the West Bank, including the Jordan valley, for a total of 17,500 people; three settlements in the Gaza Strip, for a total of 700 people; thirteen in the Rafiah salient, for a total of 6,000 people (all of them scheduled to be evacuated, under the terms of the Israeli-Egyptian peace treaty); and twenty-six in the Golan Heights, for a total of 6,500 people. Since the installation of the Begin government, the West Bank proper—meaning the more heavily populated hilly areas of Judea and Samaria—has for the first time been the focus of Jewish settlement, with forty-four new communities there and the Jewish population up fivefold in three and a half years.

Depending on how one looks at it, the growth can be considered alarming or an enviable achievement—or both. The reaction of Elias Khuri, for one, is an interesting illustration of the ambivalence. Khuri is a young Israeli Arab lawyer, whose father was killed by a terrorist bomb that exploded in Zion Square, in the heart of Jerusalem, in July of 1975. In the past few years he has specialized in representing Arabs from the territories who have appealed to the courts the expropriation of their land for the benefit of the new settlements. His own family, from the village of Malul in the Jezreel valley (it was destroyed in 1948), had hundreds of acres expropriated after the establishment of the state, so that Khuri was well able to understand the West Bank inhabitants' feeling that their land was being stolen from them. I met Khuri in Rujeib, after the verdict was announced on his appeal in the Elon Moreh case, and he made a strange confession of admiration for his adversaries. "I wish the young generation of my own people were pioneers like those settlers," he said wistfully. "They fight tooth and nail for what they want, and in the end they get it." (Ironically, I do know of one case in which a Druse named Saleh Khir, the chairman of the Peki'in local council, tried to organize a group of young Druse to establish a collective settlement in the Galilee, but unfortunately he made little headway and finally gave up in despair.)

Khuri's enviousness of the young Jews who enjoy government aid in establishing their new settlements is understandable. And it is hard to refute the claims of the radical nationalist-religious settlers that they are carrying on the glorious tradition of the Zionist pioneers. Nevertheless, the difficult issue of settlement in the West Bank must be faced squarely, because of its potent effect on the atmosphere in the territories and on prospects for achieving peace. Let us begin by taking a look at the Gush Emunim movement, the prime mover behind Jewish settlement in Judea and Samaria for the past eight years.

Gush Emunim was founded in 1973 as a faction within the National Religious Party—the NRP. In time, the members of this faction—mostly graduates of the NRP's youth movement, B'nei Akiva—managed to impose on the party an aggressive line regarding questions of peace and security. The NRP, which had always been considered dovish on foreign policy, thus became the champion of a massive settlement effort throughout the occupied territories, but particularly in the West Bank.

Hanan Porat, at one time the unofficial leader of Gush Emunim, and a man whose pronouncements have reflected the prevailing mood within the movement, set out on what he saw as his mission, to settle in the Etzion bloc. He had been born there, before the establishment of the state, and was evacuated in January of 1948 because of the bloc's vulnerability to attack by Arab irregulars. The first time I met Porat, he impressed me immediately as a determined man with a talent for leading people toward whatever goals they had set for themselves. He has organized and headed many unauthorized settlement attempts in the West Bank, and over the years he has made an effort to develop an ideological base for the movement. Something of the mystical fervor that moves a man like Hanan Porat resounded through the deliberations of Gush Emunim at a conference it held in July of 1980 at Ganei Tal, a moshav, or cooperative settlement, on the Gaza coast. Among other things, the members had gathered to discuss the question of Jewish-Arab coexistence in the land of Israel, and in the process they revealed some illuminating points about their credo. At that meeting, Porat proclaimed:

> I see the aims of the Redemption as the reform of the world in the Kingdom of God, a state in which the entire world and all who dwell therein, on these rungs and on others, will manifest the verse: "Yea, at that time I will change the speech of the peoples to a pure speech, that all of them may call on the name of the Lord and serve him with one accord" [Zephaniah 3:9]. The Jewish people has a focal role to play in this vision, and all the other nations are arranged around it in concentric circles. I see the first circle as the population here in the land of Israel. I am not talking about conversion; John Hyrcanus converted the Idumeans and brought down on us the rule of Herod and the Roman Empire. We must consider the Arab population living in our midst as a decisive test of the Jewish people in terms of how it relates to them and as an indication, to some degree, of the Redemption of the entire world. In conclusion, I wish to make it clear that I have not found in any Halakic source any precept which or-

dains that Gentiles must be expelled from the country.

That ostensibly benevolent statement speaks volumes about the attitude of Gush Emunim toward the people of the territories—not to mention the Arabs of Israel proper. In their basic assumption that the territories are Israel's incontestable dominion, Porat and his comrades do not seem disconcerted by the fact that there are only about 17,500 Jews in the West Bank, among a population of a million Palestinian Arabs. They also choose not to acknowledge that the Palestinians, rather than being passive agents of the Redemption, have national aspirations and demands of their own. And not everyone in Gush Emunim or living in one of the settlements is as politic or rhetorically polished as Porat in talking about a solution for the Arabs of the West Bank. The lawyer Eliakim Ha'etzni, one of the earliest settlers in Kiryat Arba (who is not religious), is downright blunt; he told the Ganei Tal meeting that he addresses his Arab neighbors in these terms:

> Look, there never was a Zionist program that called for Jaffa to be a Jewish city. But when the Arabs of Jaffa began to strut around the streets of Tel Aviv bragging, "This house will be mine, this woman will be mine," they saw to it that Jaffa would be Jewish. Today, too, we have no plan to make Hebron a Jewish city at your expense. But if you think that Kiryat Arba will not prevail, you'd better remember Jaffa.

Ha'etzni does not try to disguise the undertones of threat in his message. As he explains it, he is merely searching for a "Zionist" solution to the problem of the Arabs of Israel. If such a solution does not please the rest of the world, well, that's too bad—especially since he believes the people of Israel are incapable of arriving at anything but a moral solution.

More unsettling, however, is the attempt to anchor this revanchist attitude in the Jewish religion. When I was a student at the Hebrew University I took some courses in Judaism. While I would hardly claim to be a scholar on the subject, I did study the Bible, the Talmud, the Mishnah, Jewish philosophy, and the cabala, and I firmly believe that the Jewish religious outlook is essentially humanistic. Moreover, the outspoken support I have received from Israeli writers and other intellectuals when I was attacked by fanatics and radical nationalists has reinforced my belief that the people of Israel have an extraordinary moral sensibility. At a time when anti-Semitism is again rampant in the world and neo-Nazism is rearing its ugly head, it was particularly disconcerting to hear these words of Aharon Halmish, from the settlement of Ofra, near Ramallah:

> I believe that in the final analysis the land of Israel will be predominantly Jewish, and it is in accordance with this belief that I relate to the Arab minority therein. There is, of course, disagreement over exactly what is a *ger ve-toshav* [the biblical "stranger and sojourner"], who must be accorded equality by law. If I could, I would annex all the territory in our hands to the State of Israel today and let the Arabs choose whichever Arab citizenship they prefer. It's not necessary to throw grenades in the casbah of Shechem [Nablus] or drive the Arabs out. But there's nothing wrong with making life difficult for them in the hope that they will emigrate. What was permissible for Hussein— under whose reign 300,000 Arabs emigrated from Judea and Samaria—is permissible for us. In the end, perhaps those who remain will truly and honestly desire to be loyal citizens of the State of Israel, and then—let them convert. Why not? Whoever is unable to believe in this vision might as well admit that he does not believe we are already on the way to Redemption.

Though couched in different terms, that kind of thinking is reminiscent of the xenophobia that fed the Spanish Inquisi-

tion. Still another approach suggested at the Ganei Tal conference was to learn the language and life style of the Arabs, thus
forcing them to maintain neighborly relations, whether they
wanted to or not. What's more, the same people who spoke of
the "dawn of the Redemption" and the rights of the Jewish
people as deriving from religious sources have been the first
to denounce any expression of opposition based on Moslem
religious sources as "Khomeinism." It has never occurred to
them that Islam does not have a monopoly on that kind of
attitude.

Perhaps trying to make their claims more comprehensible
to an international audience, Gush Emunim and its supporters
have attempted to turn the settlement question into a human-
rights issue by portraying the Arab opposition to Jewish settlement in the territories as a denial of the Jews' right to live
wherever they wish. They even go so far as to depict such
opposition as racist. But a closer examination reveals that the
dispute is not over residence restrictions at all. What is really
at stake in the territories is national sovereignty. As Eliezer
Livne, a former leader of Gush Emunim, wrote, in a book
published by the movement, "This country is the land of Israel, and no one is a partner to sovereignty over it—except for
our brothers in the Diaspora, who need its expanses to save
themselves and to save us." (Incidentally, Livne supplemented
his declaration of faith with some very down-to-earth recom-
mendations, namely, that eight cities be built in the Sinai, five
in the vicinity of Jerusalem, two in the Hebron mountains, two
in the Golan Heights, two in the Jordan valley, and two in
Samaria.) Gush Emunim believes that large-scale Jewish settlement in the territories will put the question of sovereignty to
rest once and for all, in Israel's favor. All that is perfectly clear
to the Arabs in the territories, and it is precisely why they
oppose the Israeli settlements so fiercely.

The philosophy and methods favored by Gush Emunim
perhaps can best be illustrated by the long history of the Elon
Moreh affair. Benyamin Katzover and Menachem Felix, two

leaders of Gush Emunim, have been credited with the idea behind Elon Moreh, which dates back to 1973. In essence, the two envisioned building in Samaria a settlement equal in size and influence to Kiryat Arba in the Hebron area. Twenty families signed up for the projected settlement, and on June 5, 1974—the seventh anniversary of the Six Day War—they occupied a preselected site near an army camp in the Samarian mountains. Accompanying the families to their place of settlement were their spiritual leader, the elderly Rabbi Zvi Hacohen Kook, and three Knesset members, Yehudah Ben-Meir, Zevulun Hammer, and Geula Cohen, as well as Ariel Sharon, then a major general in the army reserve. Since the government had not authorized the move, Defense Minister Shimon Peres issued orders that the settlers were to be removed from the site.

Act two of the drama opened on July 26, when the settlers tried again. This time they called for aid from their thousands of supporters, who duly assembled at an abandoned railway station near the ancient site of Sebastia. Afraid of what might happen if it tried to remove the demonstrators by force, the government hesitated, leaving the settlers in place for three days before it reached a decision to clear the site. The resulting clash between settlers and troops was a painful sight to Israelis. But the members of Gush Emunim were less sensitive to their bruises than they were to the signs of government indecision, and they decided to just keep on, again and again, until they got their way. Meanwhile, the government was left with the problem of how to exercise its authority without engendering civil strife or divisive struggles between its own citizens.

In December of 1976 the Gush Emunim settlers returned to the site at Sebastia, and that time they forced the government to negotiate with them. Under heavy pressure, the Cabinet yielded and allowed them to remain "temporarily" within the confines of a nearby army camp outside the quaint village of Kadoum (which, in one of those exquisite twists of Middle

Eastern irony, is the birthplace of Farouk Kadoumi, head of the political department of the PLO). I visited Kadoum immediately afterward to get the villagers' reactions. The village is a collection of ancient courtyards, stone houses, and dirt paths, with a well at the center. A few yards away from the accommodations for the Jewish settlers was an elderly fellah plowing his land. I had a hard time getting him to talk, but eventually, fury shining in his eyes, he offered this pronouncement: "Today they take land; tomorrow they'll drive us out!" An old man could hardly be expected to understand what was required of him at the "dawn of the Redemption."

The settlers at Kadoum greeted the Likud's election victory with unbridled elation. Immediately after the election, the prime minister–designate, Menachem Begin, visited the camp and, carrying a Torah in his arms, joyously proclaimed, "There will be many Elonei Moreh." Still, the settlers were impatient for the new government to make good on its promises, and when it looked to them as if the Likud were dragging its feet they decided to take what they believed was their due. On January 7, 1979, in a maneuver reminiscent of the ones used against the Rabin government, a convoy of cars set out for the site that the settlers had chosen for Elon Moreh. The convoy was stopped at an IDF roadblock near the village of Rujeib, but Gush Emunim had made its point to Begin and his ministers. After five more weeks of delay and consultations, the settlement group received firm assurances that within three months it would be allowed to move to a permanent site.

The military government investigated all the land in the public domain ("state lands") in the area of Rujeib in the intervening months, but it could not seem to find any suitable for a settlement. On June 5, 1979, the commander of the West Bank therefore signed an order expropriating 175 acres of land—some of it under cultivation—from villagers in Rujeib. Just two days later, the settlers of Elon Moreh, aided by the IDF, were at work on those acres. To add insult to the villagers' injury, the owners of the land did not officially receive the expropriation order until June 7, the day on which work on the settlement began. But the lightning speed of the operation failed to intimidate the villagers. A week later, seventeen of them appealed the expropriation order to the High Court of Justice. In their decision, the justices had this comment on the timing of the take-over: "One has the impression that the physical establishment of the settlement was organized like a military operation, replete with exploiting the element of surprise to forestall the 'hazard' that this court would intervene, in response to an appeal by the landowners, before work had begun on the site."

I happened to be at home on leave from my reserve duty when the Elon Moreh story broke, and the editor of Israel Television's "Weekly News Magazine" called and asked me to go to Rujeib to get the reactions of the villagers. Right after her call, the director of the news division, that guardian of the sacred precept of balance, was on the line to remind me that it would be best if I also quoted some settlers. The report I prepared was just three minutes long, and in it I noted that until then the Likud government had tried to avoid taking over private property for settlement purposes, but that this time the expropriated land not only was privately owned, but some of it was under cultivation. By the next morning that remark had stirred up a full-blown storm, with the minister of agriculture, Ariel Sharon, charging that the report had not been faithful to the facts. I offered to accompany him to the site and show him the land I had referred to. But, as the following week's Knesset session showed, the minister was less concerned with the facts than with pursuing the attack. Taking the rostrum, he railed that no "fifth column was going to halt the march of Zionism." When challenged to identify that alleged fifth column, he referred to me by name, revealing that he had already complained to the director of the Broadcasting Authority about the piece on Elon Moreh by "that trustworthy reporter, Rafik Halabi" (heavy sarcasm on the "trustworthy"). The barb elicited outraged shouts from the floor, with Knesset member

Zaydan Atshe, a fellow Druse, calling out, "That is racism!" Atshe demanded that Sharon retract his remark, but the minister only added fuel to the flames by gibing, "Neither you nor the likes of you will ever get me to retract the truth." Afterward, in reply to a question about me from a *Ma'ariv* reporter, Sharon snapped, "His being a Druse does not give him special privileges."

The consensus in the press seemed to be that the scene in the Knesset had been a discredit to that institution and the entire State of Israel. At the time, though, I was too stunned to take any comfort in editorials. My colleagues stood staunchly behind me. The director of the news division issued a statement saying that the affair had exceeded the bounds of a personal disagreement and was now a matter of public concern. However, I had come to the conclusion that the only course open for me was to resign. After all, a senior government minister and high-ranking reserve officer had not only deemed it proper to make a reference to my origins in the context of a very sensitive issue; he had also in effect accused me of treason for reporting something that was inconvenient from the government's position and his own. I was in no position to fight back, and I felt stultified as a journalist, belittled as a man. I went to one of the executives of Israel Television to tender my resignation, but he sat me down for a long talk and, with a mixture of gentle coaxing and occasional appeals to my professional pride, got me to relent. I did insist on taking a leave, though—not as a gesture to make anyone's life -easier, but because I needed time to put my own thoughts and feelings in order.

For a while the affair followed me home to Dalyat el-Carmel. I wanted to keep the details from my elderly, ailing parents, but the messages of support and encouragement that kept pouring in gave me away. Besides, feeling was running high in the village, and many of my friends and neighbors were champing at the bit to take action of some kind. There was talk of a demonstration; some of the local radicals wanted to close the village to outsiders and hold a general strike and mass rally. But I was afraid that what I regarded as a struggle to safeguard the principles of democracy in Israel would turn into a general confrontation along ethnic or national lines—and nothing could have been further from my desires. So I urged my friends and relatives not to do anything to aggravate the situation.

Tempers cooled, I put my time to good use, and in a few weeks I was back at work again. Meanwhile, the center of attention had shifted to the place where it belonged—the High Court of Justice, which was deliberating the appeal by the Rujeib villagers. The court battle over Elon Moreh is of particular interest because of the way in which the settlers managed to undermine the government's case. State Attorney Gabriel Bach argued the government's right to expropriate the Rujeib villagers' land solely on the basis of security needs. In an earlier and similar case, the High Court had ruled that the seizure of private land to establish two settlements had not contravened Israeli or international law because the settlements were founded for military purposes. In light of that precedent, Bach logically decided to pursue the same line again, and Chief of Staff Rafael Eitan gave a deposition, on behalf of the government, defending the location of Elon Moreh on strictly military grounds. Anticipating the state's approach, the lawyers for the appellants had solicited and received contrary professional opinions from the former chief of staff, Chaim Bar-Lev, and from Matityahu Peled, a major general in the reserve, who explained why they believed a civilian settlement at Elon Moreh would not contribute to the security of the state.

It should have been a cut-and-dried affair, and if left to its own devices the government might have won—especially since the court was not inclined to decide between the arguments of military professionals. However, the grounds for a ruling on the case changed radically when two settlers from Elon Moreh, Menachem Felix and Avraham Shevut, both members of the settlement's administrative staff, requested and were granted the right to reply to the suit. Felix claimed in his testimony that the members of the settlement group had established Elon Moreh "in fulfillment of the Divine Commandment to take possession of the land given to our forefathers." He went on to say that "the act of the people of Israel settling in the land of Israel is the most concrete, effective, and genuine insurance of security. Yet it derives not from military considerations or physical needs but from a sense of mission and the imperative of the Jewish people's return to its land." Therefore, as the settlers told the court, "with all due respect to the security consideration . . . in our eyes it has little bearing on [the real issue]."

The court's verdict, published on October 22, 1979, seemed to agree with that assessment. While not discounting the chief of staff's arguments regarding the location of Elon Moreh, the court ruled that his professional judgment had not in and of itself engendered the decision to establish the settlement. The real moving force behind the decision, the ruling continued, was pressure on the government from Gush Emunim, which was determined to settle in the heart of Samaria. In such a context, the court found it pertinent that the initiative to establish a settlement in the vicinity of Nablus had come not from the IDF but from the government; the army had merely been asked for its professional opinion on which of five possible sites would best serve the military interests of the state. Finally, in the most compelling argument in the decision, the court noted that the settlers themselves had refuted the state's contention that "the civilian settlement can exist on that site only as long as the IDF occupies the area," and yet the state had not contradicted the settlers' reading. Hence, the court concluded the government had in fact decided to establish a settlement "designed to remain in place permanently— or at least beyond the life-span of the military government." If the settlement was slated to outlive the military government and its interests, the judges reasoned—and so ruled—then "the crucial factor motivating the political echelon to decide on the establishment of said settlement was not the military consideration." Consequently, the precedent on expropriating private land for military purposes did not apply, and the government was given thirty days to remove the settlers from the site.

I returned to Rujeib soon after the High Court announced its decision. Curiously, Elias Khuri, who had pleaded the villagers' case before the court, had never met any of his principals, and I asked if I could accompany him on a visit to the village after the court's verdict in their favor. Rujeib is a very primitive village. There was something about it that haunted me—perhaps its power to stir up childhood memories of my father working the rocky soil of the Carmel to eke out a subsistence for his family. The inhabitants of Rujeib live in run-down houses and still use the ancient farming methods. Suddenly they were in the eye of a public storm, and many of them couldn't understand why they should have been singled out for that dubious honor. Naturally, the meeting between Khuri and his clients was an emotional one, and I admit that I shared in their joy, because I had believed that the justice of their cause would win in the end. The members of Gush Emunim who had staked their claim outside Rujeib had argued that they were manifesting their historic right to settle anywhere in the land of Israel. That part of their message had been abundantly clear. What was less clear—to me, at least—was why it had been necessary to do so at the expense of these simple fellahin.

In a brief, rather pathetic coda to the Elon Moreh affair, the settlers threatened that, court or no court, they were not going to leave their settlement—even though the government was pouring fantastic sums into the preparation of another site for them. They did remain in place for well over the thirty days granted by the court, and their threats to resist evacuation by force, if necessary, were taken seriously. That the whole minidrama may have been nothing more than bluster, for psychological effect, is not beside the point; it *is* the point. The emotional climate is an important political factor in this part of the world. Once, when I tried to explain to Fahed Kawasmeh that the people of Gush Emunim were only a loud but tiny minority in Israel, and that most Israelis wanted a workable solution to the Palestinian problem, he retorted that Gush Emunim's lack of numerical strength, which he was well aware of, had little to do with the movement's impact on the mood in the territories.

He had a valid point, for the settlements and their inhabitants appear to exert an influence out of all proportion to their actual size and strength. In spite of Gush Emunim's cascades of words and soaring vision, its accomplishments in the territories have not done much to change the demographic character of the region. To date, forty-five settlements have materialized in the mountainous areas of the West Bank, most of them small communities supporting fewer than a hundred people. But the Arabs of the territories are not reassured by those figures, and it is easy to see why. The West Bank (including East Jerusalem) covers 2,270 square miles, and of that only about 175,000 acres—or about one-eighth—are defined as state lands. Yet there has been talk of settling between a million and a million and a half Jews in the region, and somehow land must be found for them. Since the state lands will not suffice, the obvious conclusion is that any such program will have to entail the mass expropriation of privately owned land. From that perspective, the Arab inhabitants of the West Bank are right to fear that the small settlements of today are the nuclei of future urban concentrations, which will dispossess them and destroy their dream of an independent Palestinian entity.

That is why the settlements wield a much greater influence than the cold statistics would suggest is possible. Driven by their feeling that time is short and much remains to be done, the settlers have succumbed to a bad case of land mania and cannot seem to satisfy their craving. The residents of Kiryat Arba, in the Hebron mountains, are trying to expand their settlement at the expense of landowners in the neighboring villages of Tarkumiyeh and Shayukh. In Samaria, a recent expropriation controversy has centered on the village of Anabta (where Bassam Shaka again demonstrated his pluck by joining in a protest rally). To their credit, the fellahin are not taking the encroachments lying down, and in most cases they have turned to the High Court of Justice, which is glutted with suits. All attempts to settle the claims through military boards of appeal have failed, for those committees are staffed by IDF officers subordinate to the local or area commander, and the Arab appellants do not put much stock in their impartiality.

The settlers, meanwhile, are pulling in exactly the opposite direction with their arguments that the Israeli government cannot afford to be hamstrung by the finer points of the law; if land cannot be purchased from the Arabs, it must be expropriated and settled quickly. The truth is that land is hard to come by in the territories these days. In 1979, for example, less than seventy-five acres were purchased from Arab sources—little wonder, when the Jordanian government and the Palestinian organizations have threatened to dispatch anyone who sells land to Jews. The dearth of available land is what has prompted the settlers' contention that Israel has no choice, if it intends to extend Jewish settlement in Judea and Samaria, but to seize Arab property at will, discarding the argument based on security considerations—the one that failed to win the government's case in the Elon Moreh suit.

Beyond what such an approach augurs for the future of Arab-Jewish relations, it betrays a new and appalling attitude toward the rule of law in the State of Israel. Indeed, Gush Emunim's sights are so firmly trained on its ends that the nature of its means has been reduced to mere expediency. If the government is responsive and approves its plans, fine; if not, Gush Emunim is quite prepared to resort to force and chicanery. A few years ago, for example, a group of alleged archaeologists arrived at the site of Shiloh, with the declared purpose of setting up a dig. The result: a settlement stands there today, its members gloating about how they managed to get their way over the government.

Whether or not the settlers are to blame for tarnishing the image of the Begin government by drawing it into these power games, one sure casualty of Israel's settlement program is the autonomy clause of the Camp David agreements, which most Palestinians reject precisely because it does not rule out future Jewish settlement in the territories. The Israeli government's insistence that autonomy applies to the inhabitants of the West Bank and Gaza, and not to the territories per se, shows that Israel does not really intend to lower its profile in those regions and that the autonomy arrangements will not be binding on the Jewish settlers. In that case, the prognosis in Arab eyes is that the Israelis will be free to keep on doing as they please, with the Arab agencies of self-rule powerless to react in any way. In September of 1978, after the signing of the Camp David accords, Anwar el-Khatib expressed the bitterness shared by many Palestinians when he wrote, "We were deceived into believing that the Israelis are interested in coexistence and do not harbor expansionist ambitions. Today they say there's no room for the Palestinians on their land, and they have gone back to talking about their own historic rights. The Israeli policy has managed to drive the moderates to extremism."

The true state of affairs is considerably more complex, for the autonomy plan has driven both camps to extremism: the Palestinians reject the plan because it prevents them from realizing their dream of independence and sovereignty, and the settlers regard it as the first stage in the establishment of an independent Palestinian state. Likewise, the National Guidance Committee has called on the Palestinians to oppose the Camp David agreements with every means available, and the settlers are preparing for the possibility that the government might actually implement the accords, which stipulate "a withdrawal of Israeli armed forces" from the territories and "a redeployment of the remaining Israeli forces into specified security locations." At two conferences, held at Alon Shevut, in the Etzion bloc, and at Kiryat Arba, they resolved to form a settlers' police, so that they could defend themselves in the event that the government limited the IDF's presence. Eliakim Ha'etzni of Kiryat Arba spelled it out clearly when he said, at an assembly in Jerusalem in January of 1979, "On the day that Jews in uniform leave the cities, Jews out of uniform will enter those cities. In order to effect that plan, we will register a reserve corps of Jews willing to answer any call. If tomorrow, Heaven forbid, a bus carrying Jews is stoned at Halhul and the IDF is closed up in 'security locations,' it will be necessary to respond to Halhul, and we won't be able to do that alone. If we don't help ourselves, no one else will. The government of Israel certainly won't help us."

In the atmosphere created by moves and proclamations like those, it should surprise no one that relations between the Jewish settlers and the Arab villagers are far from cordial and accommodating. When some Arabs stoned a Jewish vehicle, settlers from Shiloh cut off the electric supply to all nearby villages. When children from the village of Beit Or threw stones at the settlers of Beit Horon, the settlers, taking the law into their own hands, broke into the village, barred the door to the schoolhouse, and cut off the electricity. The settlers of Ofra routinely terrorize neighboring Arab villages, going so far as to detain anyone who appears to them to be "a threat to public safety." By far the most brazen of all these displays of the settlers' contempt for their neighbors and the military government came at the beginning of 1980, when a group of settlers from Beit El (ironically, one of the settlements for which the High Court had approved private-land expropriation, on the ground that it served "military purposes") were caught in the streets of Ramallah carrying hammers and clubs. Before they were stopped and arrested, these vigilantes had managed to smash the windshields of forty Arab vehicles, as their response to the stoning of one Israeli car. The detainees gave their interrogators no cooperation, but they were released anyway, prompting the mayor of Ramallah to call the settlers the "real regime" in the territories.

I have given ample coverage to the settlers' "rule" in the territories in my television reports, and that may be why I am considered *persona non grata* in most of the new settlements. On a visit to Hebron, for example, a resident of Kiryat Arba accused me of destroying the dream of a land of Israel. I shot back that I probably loved the State of Israel as much as he did, but he was more likely to smother it with a bear hug.

That exchange took place outside Hadassah House, which senior officers in the military government regard as the crucible of Arab-Jewish relations in the territories. With their "live-in" at Hadassah House, the members of Gush Emunim had adopted a new method of warfare, placing women and children on the front line in their battle for hegemony in the West Bank. For nearly two years, more than thirty women and children have lived in Hadassah House under atrocious conditions: the building contains one kitchen, two bathrooms, and a single shower. Instead of dispersing this "settlement" by force, the military governor of Hebron placed his faith in the ravages of nature and waited to see if a brutal winter wouldn't send the women packing. But winter came and went, and the women's hold on the building only grew firmer. Then came the terrorist attack in May of 1980, strengthening their determination even more. Hadassah House has been surrounded by sandbags and a permanent military guard. Many of the adjacent buildings have been demolished or appropriated by order of the military governor in order to reinforce control over the site. The roof was walled off after the terrorist attack, but before then children in the neighboring houses used to sit on their roofs in the summer singing children's ditties in Arabic, to which the squatters' children would respond, in Hebrew and in march rhythm:

> We shall live in Hadassah forever,
> And we shall never return Hebron.

We shall bring on the Redemption,
And then salvation will come.

Eviction of the women and their offspring was unthinkable—the Israeli government reasoning that such a move
would only set the PLO propaganda mill into high gear by
allowing it to claim a victory. Then, following the terrorist
attack, three men joined their wives in Hadassah House, making the live-in a family affair. One of them was Rabbi Levinger,
who had at one time been banned from Hebron because the
military governor considered him a menace to the peace.
Every move Levinger makes is motivated by ideological conviction, and he gave a *Ma'ariv* reporter this explanation for his
presence in Hadassah House:

> I am fighting against the conventions of Israeli society: the
> pursuit of material wealth, sagging morale, the use of
> drugs, murder for monetary gain, a rise in the incidence
> of rape and crime. We must return to our mission, to
> being a Chosen People. I am against elitism and murder.
> But I understand those who murder for an ideal. . . . For
> whoever kills a Jew will be murdered in turn, and I under-
> stand and admire those who undertake this mission.

Rabbi Levinger of course has the right to understand and
admire whomever he chooses. But I cannot shake the notion
that it was for advocating precisely what Levinger advocated
in this quotation—"according moral legitimacy to murder"—
that Fahed Kawasmeh and Mohammed Milhem were deported
from their country.

Early in 1981 the Hadassah House "settlement group"
yielded the building to a group of families from Kiryat Arba.
The top floor now houses the yeshiva of Shavei Hebron, and
the guard duties have been turned over to the settlers. A
number of unpleasant incidents have occurred between the
settlers and their neighbors since the original take-over of the

building. But none of them matches the bizarre episode in March of 1981, during the holiday of Purim, when the roof caved in on the entire Hadassah House affair because, literally, the ceiling fell on Ibrahim Dandisi, the proprietor of a dry goods shop on the ground floor of the building.

The Dandisis, father and son, had rented the shop for thirty years—first from the Jordanian Custodian of Enemy Property and then from his Israeli successor in the military government. They closed the shop on Fridays, to observe the Moslem Sabbath, but were of course open for business on Saturdays, like all the rest of the shops in Hebron. Upon opening the shop on Saturday, March 21, 1981, however, they discovered a strange alteration in the status quo with regard to their upstairs neighbors: a hole approximately three feet square gaped at them from the ceiling of the shop, which was also the floor of the quarters occupied by the Kiryat Arba settlers. Ibrahim Dandisi, the son, reported their discovery to the police and the military government, and was told—on the basis of the settlers' explanations—that the damage had resulted from some exuberant dancing during the Purim celebration. But Dandisi took that story with a grain of salt, since the floor was constructed of reinforced concrete. Inviting a representative of the military government into the shop, he pointed to telltale evidence that an unknown party or parties had been at work with a pickax, which tended to belie the settlers' assertion that the floor had given way under the sheer thrust of their ecstasy.

Naturally, the Dandisis wanted to repair the hole as quickly as possible, but when they set to work on it they were assailed by blows from none other than Rabbi Levinger, who was incensed that they should be working on the Sabbath. (No matter that the Dandisis worked on Rabbi Levinger's Sabbath every week, and had been doing so for thirty years.) At the end of the day, having accomplished little in the way of repairs, the Dandisis locked their shop and returned to the police station to file a complaint against their neighbors for obstructing their efforts to restore the ceiling. Their greatest worry was that the hole left the shop wide open to intrusions from the settlers' floor above. But the duty officer assured them that not so much as a pin would be missing and that they could resume their repair work the next day without interference from their neighbors.

Unfortunately, it was not that simple. As the younger Dandisi subsequently claimed in a damage suit filed with the High Court of Justice, when he and his father returned to their shop the following day, they met armed settlers at the door—which was locked from the inside. The steel beams they had purchased to support the patch in the ceiling had been thrown into the street. But the worst shock was still ahead: when the Dandisis finally got into their shop, they found the ceiling gone altogether and in its stead a staircase the settlers had built leading up to their living quarters on the next floor. Mattresses were scattered around the floor of the shop—which was completely bare of merchandise—and the telephone was broken. Before the Dandisis could recover from the shock, the settlers informed them that there was no use in their returning to Hadassah House. The settlers did offer to buy the shop, out of fairness to their former neighbors, but the Dandisis were in no mood to sell. They refused to leave, and things turned nasty. According to his son's complaint before the High Court, when the elder Dandisi sat down on the new staircase he was beaten, trampled on, and forcibly ejected from the shop by the armed settlers, including Rabbi Levinger. As for the dry goods that had been removed, they were found in another room of the building, strewn around the floor and badly soiled. As Ibrahim Dandisi's lawyer noted in her court brief, the settlers' objectives could be deduced from an article published in *Ha'aretz* on March 24, in which they claimed that the shop was part of their domain because it was located in the original Hadassah House foyer.

The Purim caper may have been the last straw, because, after two years of forbearance, eleven parties living or working near Hadassah House decided to file suit calling on the minister of defense and the commander of the West Bank to show cause why the settlers from Kiryat Arba, who were violating the law by trespassing on the premises of Hadassah House, should not be removed from the building forthwith. Sections of the suit read like a catalogue of harassments, with complaints ranging from the settlers' refusal to repair faulty sewage pipes leading from Hadassah House, thus causing damage and anguish to a neighbor, to their willful obstruction of trade in the commercial establishments around Hadassah House by blocking access to the shops and even by stoning customers from their windows.

As we have seen, the outrageous behavior of the Kiryat Arba squatters toward the Dindisi family was certainly not the first instance of the settlers' use of harassment and intimidation against their Arab neighbors, and it will probably not be the last. In fact, Rabbi Levinger and company have been facing stiff competition on that score from another rabbi with a growing following in the West Bank settlements: Meir Kahane, the leader of the Kach Movement. Kahane was the founder and head of the Jewish Defense League in the United States before immigrating to Israel in September of 1971. His supporters will not hear of any compromise over the borders of the land of Israel, and they are quite frank about their ambition to drive all Arabs out of Israel and the occupied territories. Falling short of his goal, the outright expulsion of the entire Arab community, Kahane has tried instead to persuade individual Arabs to emigrate, even promising to pay their plane fare and help them find work abroad. His followers, not so affable, have been known to send threatening letters to Arab public figures in the territories. Toward the end of 1979, a few of them broke into some Jewish-owned but Arab-occupied houses in Hebron, beat up the occupants, and "recommended" that they evacuate the houses. A few months later the security services in Israel got word that Kahane was planning a sensational action somewhere in the West Bank. With tension already running high, the government decided to take no chances and held Rabbi Kahane in administrative detention for about six months. On his release, he was quick to declare that "we have much work ahead of us" and set about booking appearances at the universities of Tel Aviv and Haifa.

Meir Kahane enjoys little public support in Israel, but nevertheless his activities are a nuisance to the government and troubling to many citizens. The Arabs believe that, like Rabbi Levinger and many of the settlers in the territories, he enjoys favored treatment from the authorities, which encourages him to pursue his aims. Early in 1980, a large weapons cache was uncovered over a synagogue in the Jewish Quarter of Jerusalem's Old City, not far from the Western Wall. The Arab residents of Jerusalem were afraid the weapons belonged to Rabbi Kahane's people and were meant to be used in an attack on one of the Old City's mosques during Friday prayers. No direct link has ever been established between Kahane and the arms, but the fact that Israeli citizens were collecting and stashing weapons was in itself disquieting.

In December of 1978 I received a letter from one Yosef Dayan, the secretary of Rabbi Kahane's Kach Movement. I have kept it as a curiosity because, more than what it said, I was impressed by the style of the missive, which I think of as "classic punk":

> The Kach Movement—the Jewish Defense League in the land of Israel—has decided to make it clear to Rafik Halabi, the Arab reporter of Israel Television, that there is no such thing as Palestine; there is only the land of Israel. The secretariat of the Kach Movement has decided to do so following the report broadcast by Halabi on Wednesday, in which the citizens of Israel were informed that Kiryat Arba is illegal and has been built on Palestinian soil. . . . If the Arab reporter Rafik Halabi does not understand that there is no such thing as Palestine, only the land of Israel, so be it. We will prove it to him. . . . What is

beyond understanding is how such hate-filled reporting gets past all Israel Broadcasting Authority (or is it the Palestine Broadcasting Authority?) channels of control. The telecast of this report was another phase in the battle that the Fascist Left is waging against the Jewish community in the land of Israel through its agent planted in the Israel Broadcasting Authority. We will carry out an action against Rafik Halabi to show him exactly who the exclusive proprietors of the land of Israel are!

A few months later, the members of the Kach Movement evidently decided to carry out their threat. Two girls—one of them a minor, the other armed with a Kalachnikov rifle—turned up at the information desk of Israel Television's studios in Jerusalem and asked to see me. One of our security officers was immediately alerted and called the police, who took the girls into custody but released them on bail after questioning. The girl with the gun was Mazal Cohen, who had already won a reputation of sorts by spitting in Defense Minister Ezer Weizman's face during the evacuation of Neot Sinai and by doctoring his coffee with salt when he paid a visit to Elon Moreh, of which she was a member. After her release from custody, she told a reporter from *Yediot Aharonot* that the whole thing had been a joke that had gotten out of hand. (No one at the television studios seemed amused by it; in fact, that was when the administration first offered me a bodyguard.) Then she added, in utter seriousness, "Rafik Halabi should be thrown out of this country. He's a man who turns everything into a lie. He isn't a Jew. He's a *goy* and doesn't deserve to be here. But of course I wouldn't use a weapon against him. I'd have to be crazy to waste twenty years in prison because of an *Arab.*"

Meanwhile, I continued to receive threatening letters, and the police continued to suspect members of Kach. One of the more articulate of these "love notes," mailed from the town of Afula in the Jezreel valley, read as follows: "To the filthy Arab reporter: We will kill you. Death is the end!"

Since the inauguration of the Begin government, most of the attention surrounding new settlements has been focused on the West Bank. But an issue that is just as emotional in Israel is the fate of the settlements in the Rafiah salient—including the city of Yamit—which are destined to be abandoned and dismantled as one of the provisions of the Israeli-Egyptian peace treaty. The settlers have been promised that twelve replacement communities will be built in the Shalom bloc, within Israel's pre-1967 borders, but they seem unappeased by that. The chances are excellent that within a short time the new bloc, like the Rafiah salient before it, will be flourishing, with hothouses, chicken coops, small industry, and choice agricultural produce all financed by generous government and Jewish Agency loans and grants and worked by cheap Arab labor. Even so, the settlers of the salient are in no hurry to move and are holding up the government for heavy reparations.

The transformation of the Rafiah salient into a green and prosperous corner of Israel was bound up with the long and painful process of "clearing the land." In the past that meant removing stones from the rocky soil in order to plow and plant; this time it meant removing the thousands of Bedouins who pitched their tents on the sand dunes. There is no getting around the fact that the Bedouins were summarily driven out, sometimes by the use of force and threats, so that agricultural settlements could take their place. Anyone visiting the area today is filled with wonder at the sight of the settlers' achievements. The desert wastes have been turned into verdant, blooming expanses. Only the Bedouins camped at the entrances to the settlements (membership in these collectives is, of course, not open to them) serve as a reminder of the upheavals that took place there.

The situation in the Golan Heights differs from that in the other occupied territories for a number of reasons. First of all, settlement in the Golan, as in the Rafiah area, was motivated not by a religious or nationalist ideology centering on the whole land of Israel but by the belief that a cordon of kibbutzim and moshavim would truly enhance Israel's security. Naturally, the idea of annexing the Golan Heights to Israel focuses on those settlements. Close to 6,500 people, including some 2,300 children, make their homes in the twenty-six kibbutzim and moshavim (three more are under construction) and in the development town of Katzrin, and the government has provided them with 18,000 acres for cultivation and 700 acres for their herds. Still, the Israelis in the Golan do not feel that their future there is secure—especially since the signing of the Camp David agreements—and they have tried to enlist support for their cause by organizing a mass petition against an Israeli withdrawal from the area.

That was a formidable project, but when the petition campaign was over, Shimon Sheves, one of the most active members of the Committee of Golan Settlements, was able to display a document signed by almost 750,000 Israeli citizens who believed that it would be a national catastrophe to relinquish the Golan Heights. Among the signatories were seventy members of the Knesset, including ministers in the Begin government and the leaders of the Labor opposition—Shimon Peres, Yitzhak Rabin, Chaim Bar-Lev, and the late Yigal Allon. A number of Knesset members even organized a "Golan lobby" to guard against any future peace treaty with Syria being contingent on the return of the Heights. As far as the lobbyists were concerned, the security value of an Israeli presence in the Golan far outweighed the benefits of a peace treaty.

There is another reason why the political mood in the Golan is quite different from that in the West Bank or the Gaza Strip. Unlike the Jordanians and the Egyptians in their respective areas, the Syrians never succeeded in establishing firm hegemony over the Golan. The Moslem population of the area fled across the cease-fire line in 1967, leaving only a community of Druse—who have always lived apart in their mountain villages and are proud of their tradition as farmers. As a persecuted minority in the Middle East, the Druse have learned to be prudent in calculating their moves. Many of the Golan Druse, like their new Israeli neighbors, want the region annexed to the State of Israel, but there is also a large group that considers itself Syrian. Relations between the Druse and the Jewish settlers range from civil to friendly. Aided by the absence of friction, the energetic Sheves has tried to persuade local leaders to press for annexation. "If the Druse demand Israeli sovereignty over the area," he told me candidly, "it will make things easier for us in the Knesset." However, few Druse in the Golan are inclined to subordinate their own interests to those of the Israeli settlers; and their unofficial leader, Sheikh Suleiman Kanj, constantly reminds his flock of their interlocking ties with Syria and its people. The future of the Golan therefore remains firmly in abeyance.

I have lectured at scores of kibbutzim and moshavim in Israel proper over the last few years, and time and again the members of those communities have lectured back to me to the effect that I had failed to grasp the profound significance that settlement on the land has in the Zionist world view. I beg to disagree, for I fully appreciate the historical, sociological, and psychological impact of settlement as a factor that has helped to shape a revolution in Jewish life here. But I continue to believe that a fundamental distinction must be drawn between Jewish settlement within the State of Israel and settlement in the occupied territories. I see no contradiction in fighting with supreme conviction for the Jewish people's right to maintain their state within the land of Israel and at the same time opposing the extension of Jewish settlement to the occupied areas heavily populated by Arabs. As for what that might imply about the "difference" of my "Israeliness," I can only say that not long ago 100,000 other Israelis—Jewish Israelis—marched through the streets of Tel Aviv roaring, "Better peace than the whole of the land of Israel," and no one raised any questions about their identity or loyalty or anything else.

That was in the autumn of 1979. Meanwhile, the debate

over the future of the territories and Jewish settlement goes on, and the government continues to establish stark "facts on the ground" in the form of more and more settlements each year. We have already seen their influence on the political climate in the territories. Just as important is the effect they have had on political thinking in Israel and on the tough decisions that must be faced in the near future. In May of 1979, when the time came to evacuate the settlement of Neot Sinai, the settlers barricaded themselves in one of the buildings and bombarded the IDF with whatever came to hand, including flaming torches and poisonous insecticides. An Israeli politician who must contemplate the prospect of evacuating any or all of the settlers in the West Bank is not likely to forget the lesson of Neot Sinai.

All the same, it is clear that at some point a democratic decision will have to be made—assuming, of course, that extremism will not have impaired the democratic process—for neither the most daunting expectations nor the most florid rhetoric can erase the experience of the past fourteen years. There is little hope of establishing peaceful or even correct relations between the Israeli settlers and the Arab inhabitants of the territories. Since the hostility between the two peoples borders on covert war, there would appear to be only two choices left: a struggle to the end or a solution pointing toward pragmatic compromise—and that would mean deliberately disregarding the question of whose historic right is more valid. The greatest danger we face now is that the very scope of settlement in the territories may mislead Israelis into thinking that we are past the point where territorial compromise is still possible. Prophecy has never been my stock in trade, but I'll venture that the adage "discretion is the better part of valor" will never have been sounder advice than in the days ahead when we must deal with the fate of the occupied territories.

11
THE NAZARETH-NABLUS
AXIS

Detractors of the State of Israel consistently claim that the Zionist movement from its inception has systematically ignored the existence of the Arabs of Palestine. The point of the charge is to deny that the Jews have ever made any effort to reach a modus vivendi with the indigenous inhabitants of the country. Anyone who delves into the history of the Zionist movement knows that the accusation is a gross oversimplification, deriving from a refusal to admit the complexity of a problem that has been so long in the making. Quite early in the story of renewed Jewish settlement in Palestine, the leaders of the Zionist movement were disabused of the notion that the country was mostly an empty wasteland. To European eyes, it may have looked like a wasteland, but it certainly wasn't an empty one; and the Jewish pioneers and their backers in the Zionist political establishment were keenly aware of both the existence of Palestinian Arabs and the need to establish peaceful relations with them. By 1925 David Ben-Gurion was addressing that issue when he wrote, in these unequivocal terms:

> There was a time when the Zionist movement tended to ignore the question of the Arab community in Palestine and calculated its moves as if the country were totally unpopulated. But the age of that kind of naive Zionism has passed forever. . . . The Arab community in this country is an organic, integral part of the land of Israel. It is rooted in this country, labors in it, and will remain in it.

Zionism has not come here to take its place or be built on its ruins.

The year Ben-Gurion made that statement, there were about 600,000 Arabs and 120,000 Jews in Palestine. The Jewish immigrants who arrived during that period encountered a politically weak, tradition-oriented Arab community. Most of the Arabs of Palestine were fellahin who worked the land as tenant farmers for the effendis—feudal landlords of large estates, who lived in the cities or abroad. The harsh realities of life in this backward, poverty-stricken country forced the newly arrived Jews to confront the problem of what their relationship should be with their Arab neighbors, and in grappling with it the ideologues and policy makers of the Zionist movement had to ask themselves whether the Jews were coming to Palestine as a ruling class, with the intent of subjugating the country's other inhabitants. The answer comes out clearly in the attitude of Berl Katznelson, one of the pillars of the Labor-Zionist movement, who affirmed with absolute certainty that Zionism "has no desire to create in Palestine a new Poland with one minor difference, the Arabs taking the place of the Jews and the Jews assuming the role of the Poles, perhaps with a slightly stronger sense of noblesse oblige toward the minority race."

By the time Ben-Gurion and Katznelson spoke, however, the dream of peaceful coexistence between the two peoples had already been punctured by a wave of bloodshed, which set the pattern of relations for decades to come. Clashes between Arabs and Jews became more frequent and more vehement as the British Mandate wore on, and by the mid-1930s the country was inundated in violence and was witnessing the outbreak of what Palestinian historiography calls "the Great Arab Revolt." The Arabs of Palestine fought on many fronts, defying the British authorities with a six-month general strike, trying to arrest the growth of the Jewish community, and, in the process, lighting the first sparks of a struggle within Arab society itself. For it was during this period that the Arab tenant farmers began to rebel against the feudal conditions imposed on them by the effendis. On that plane, at least, the Jews and the Arabs of Palestine might have been able to find common ground, since one of the aims of Zionism was to effect a revolution in the age-old patterns of Jewish economic life. But even here the divisive national struggle far outweighed the supposed solidarity of the working classes; in spite of repeated efforts, the Labor-Zionist movement never managed to forge an alliance with the fellahin or with the Arab blue-collar population.

The latent struggle between the two national camps in Palestine continued into the 1940s, and then it broke out again in all its virulence when the United Nations voted to partition the country. On the day the State of Israel was proclaimed, May 14, 1948, there were about 1,200,000 Arabs in the territory of the Palestine Mandate (as against some 650,000 Jews). During and after the 1948 war, about 650,000 of them fled or were driven out of the areas that came under Israeli rule, leaving 150,000 crushed and terrified Arabs within the borders of the newly founded Jewish state. The remaining 400,-000 lived in the West Bank and Gaza, which had originally been designated to become part of a Palestinian Arab state. In 1950, however, the West Bank was unilaterally annexed by Transjordan, making the establishment of that state an impossibility.

The Arabs in Israel faced an uphill road to recovery, for the war and the mass exodus had left their social and political structures in a state of collapse and their leadership broken and scattered. Many villages had been damaged or totally destroyed in the fighting, their ill-fated inhabitants doomed to become refugees in Jordan, Egypt, or Lebanon, or even in their own country. Reliable figures are lacking on the number of villages demolished or abandoned in the 1948 war, but it was no secret that in most cases Jewish settlements soon sprouted up on the land previously owned or worked by the departed villagers. When the fighting ended, the Arab citizens of Israel found themselves sealed off from the Arabs in the West Bank and Gaza—and, for that matter, from the entire Arab world. Worse yet, the new state imposed a military government on them and restricted their freedom of movement. Those restrictions were gradually rescinded, over a nineteen-year period, and the military government was abolished altogether in December of 1966. To put it bluntly, it was getting in the way of economic growth. The Jewish economy needed workers, and there was an abundance of them in the Arab villages, which suffered chronic economic deprivation. The removal of the barriers symbolized by the military government opened the way for Israel's Arabs to emerge from their economic, if not their social, isolation.

The fate of two villages, Ikrit and Biram, is probably the most troubling example of the mistakes Israel has made in dealing with the admittedly thorny problem of its Arab citizenry. In "Operation Hiram," an IDF campaign to secure the Galilee in 1948, a company manned mostly by soldiers from local kibbutzim and moshavim moved on the Christian Arab village of Ikrit, in the center of the northern Galilee. As they approached the village, three persons carrying white flags came out to meet them. Bible in hand, the village priest, Jeries Khuri, blessed the "children of Israel" standing before him. He was followed by the *mukhtar* of the village, Mibada Hana Dahoud, who distributed bread and salt—a gesture of respect —among the men of the Israeli unit. Then the villagers invited the soldiers into their homes as a sign of their goodwill. After receiving explicit assurances that they would be allowed to return when the fighting ended, they complied with the order to evacuate the village for the duration of the war.

The fighting drew to a close, peace returned to the area, and the border with Lebanon was stabilized, but the residents of Ikrit were not allowed to return to their village. In July of 1951 they appealed to the High Court of Justice, demanding that the guarantees made to them be honored. The court recognized the validity of their claim and ruled that they should be permitted to return to their homes, but again they were not allowed to. The people of Biram suffered a similar fate, and the names of those two villages became linked as a byword for the bitter experience of Arabs who believed they were serving the interests of their country but were treated like enemies. Some of the land belonging to these derelict villages has been cultivated by nearby kibbutzim and moshavim. The villagers themselves were relegated to the singular status of "present absentees"—present in the country but absent from their property. When Menachem Begin assumed office in June of 1977, he expressed the opinion that justice should be done to the villagers of Biram (for some reason, he neglected to mention Ikrit). One would naturally assume that the government is responsible for carrying out a ruling of the court; but nothing has happened to this day.

Israel's proclamation of independence declared the state's intention to grant equal rights to all citizens, but somewhere along the way that noble plan went awry. Paradoxically, the difficult war and the terrible tragedy that struck the Arab population of Israel had created extremely favorable conditions for reconciliation and the integration of the Arab minority into the new Jewish state. Today, thirty-four years later, one cannot avoid the sad conclusion that Israel let this sterling, and perhaps singular, opportunity slip by unnoticed. Some Israelis now question whether the idea of fully integrating Israel's Arabs into the life of the state was ever anything more than an impossible dream. But Zvi Al-Peleg, formerly the military governor of the heavily Arab-populated area known as the Triangle (around the old armistice line in the northern half of the West Bank), remains convinced that by 1967 the Arabs of Israel were well on their way toward becoming an integral part of Israeli society. He has a collection of photographs of various Independence Day celebrations in Israeli Arab villages, and he recalls that "schools used to compete furiously for the honor of carrying the national flag on Independence Day." Unfortunately, however, the many gains in the direction of genuine rapprochement were more than offset by the rule of the military government, which left deep scars on the Arab sector of Israeli society.

Among its other duties, the military government unfailingly quashed any hint of radical political activity and stymied all attempts of the Arab public to organize behind an independent political banner. El-Ard, a movement that advocated the repatriation of the Palestinian refugees and the institution of a binational state, was outlawed for seditious activities. The Arab members of the Communist party were subject to restrictions—even though their Jewish colleagues were free and often respected members of the Israeli political establishment —and Communist activists often found their freedom of movement severely curtailed during election campaigns; some would even be arrested for the duration of a campaign. One result of the not so subtle manipulation of the political scene in the Arab villages was that the ruling Mapai party received 67.9 percent of the Arab vote in 1951 and 64 percent in 1955 —startling figures, in light of the current political mood among Israel's Arabs.

Even with the many restrictions and obstacles, the Arab minority displayed a great willingness to come to terms with its fate. But the road to acceptance was soon blocked by a practice that became all too common, and that stuck in the throat like no other: the large-scale expropriation of Arab land. That was, and is, by far the sorest point of dispute between the Arab minority and the Israeli national authorities. In 1951, the government expropriated 1,875 acres from their Arab owners to establish the town of Upper Nazareth. Today over 40,000 people live in Arab Nazareth, in an area of 2.8 square miles, while less than 20,000 Jews live in Upper Nazareth, in an area of 3.5 square miles. Land was also expropriated from the villages of Ba'ana, Dir el-Assad, and Nahaf, in the western Galilee, to establish the development town of Carmiel. The government explained the expropriations on the basis of a need to develop the Galilee, but the Arabs in the area saw them as a calculated move to dispossess and uproot Arabs so that their land could be turned over to Jews. The more radical Arabs in the Galilee even devised a theory about a sinister government plot to destroy Arab rural life, as a step toward the final goal of getting the entire Arab minority to emigrate from the state.

The sorry truth is that contradictions, confusion, and evasion have characterized Israel's official policy toward its Arab citizens for decades. Until 1967, the Arabs of Israel lived in a social and cultural ghetto; Israel had been established as a Jewish state and by its very nature placed obstacles in the path of any non-Jew who wanted to share in its way of life. That paradox has put the Israeli Arab in a frustrating position, on both the psychological and the sociopolitical levels. The government has said it wants proud Arab citizens who are loyal to the state, without sensing that that might be a contradiction in terms. Meanwhile, forced into the status of a marginal group set apart from the rest of society, the Israeli Arabs have continued to nurse their collective resentment. The few who have tried to break out of the constricting framework and make their way in Jewish society have been stigmatized for their "assimilation and national betrayal," and sooner or later they have returned home shamefaced and crestfallen.

On March 8, 1973, nearly twenty-five years after the establishment of the State of Israel, Shmuel Toledano, the prime minister's adviser for Arab affairs, sent Golda Meir a classified memorandum in which he explicated the position of the Arab minority. It said:

> As long as a state of war exists between Israel and the Arab countries, there does not seem to be any radical solution for the difficult problems that face the Arab national minority in Israel. On the other hand, it is undoubtedly possible to alleviate the problem and perhaps decelerate the rate of decline if we are intelligent enough to give the Arabs of Israel a sense of belonging to the

state. That can be achieved by involving them on the planning, decision-making, and operative levels—whether in government ministries, public institutions, or other branches of the political system—at least regarding issues that touch directly on their lives.

That seems like a very modest formula, and yet it did not emerge even as a proposal until 1973. Actually, before 1967 there had been much loftier visions of the role that Israel's Arabs might play in advancing the welfare of their state. One of those visions conceived of them as a bridge leading the State of Israel to an understanding with the entire Arab world, but that metaphor was never translated into policy. Worse, the Arabs' efforts to become an essential, productive part of Israeli society were met by a wall of indifference. They stood by the state in 1967, in its hour of peril; despite the grim forebodings that were rife throughout Israel, there was not a single act of insurgency or attempt to exploit the country's vulnerability during that crisis. The government advisers and "experts" who had consistently portrayed the Arab minority as a fifth column had to admit they were wrong and had simply slandered a peaceful and loyal segment of Israel's population. Yet no one stopped to consider that the time might have come to reciprocate for that loyalty by adopting a new policy toward the state's Arab minority. Years later, government officials would beat their breasts in contrition and wonder why, say, not one Israeli Arab had been appointed to a civilian post in the occupied territories. No one seemed to have an answer.

That vague policy of not-so-benign neglect is why the Israeli Arab has learned to treat government proclamations with a healthy dose of skepticism. Israel is a free and open society, and government spokesmen speak of equal rights and one law for all citizens. But the Arab minority has discovered that what is perfectly acceptable for Jewish society does not necessarily hold true for them. Every announcement about land expropriation, for example, seems to be accompanied by a declaration of noble intentions. For years the government has talked about boosting the prosperity of the Arab community, developing new sources of employment, and solving housing problems. That was also the line when the government expropriated Arab land to establish Upper Nazareth and Carmiel. But if an Arab should try to move into one of the new towns, he would be received with pronounced hostility. The unwritten law has been that any Arab who wanted to get ahead in life must do so within the confines of his village—which, as everyone knew, was decades behind the rest of the country. And so, once the official fanfare died down, the brutal facts remained: many villages were deprived of their lands.

While military rule was still in effect within Israel, the security services played an active role in village affairs and had a hand in every important decision: who would be hired as a teacher and who run the school; who would have his army service deferred (in the case of the Druse) and who not; who would get a steady job in the Prison Service or the Border Police and who be left to fend for himself. The military government not only sealed off the Arab villages; it also blocked information about them from getting out to Israeli society at large. In high school and at the university, I was astounded by how little Israel's Jews knew—or cared—about the country's Arab minority, from any angle, political, cultural, or social. My classmates were almost completely ignorant about the industrial and agricultural revolution that, for example, had turned villages like Taybeh and Tira into major exporters of strawberries. They knew nothing about the gradual decline of the patriarchy as the ruling social order and were quite oblivious to the discrimination and deprivations the Arab community endured. Um el-Fahem, the largest Arab village in Israel, had a population of about 20,000, whose living conditions were unspeakable—no electricity, no sewage facilities, and precious little fresh air in the houses crowding its narrow alleyways—but the Jews of Israel were blissfully unaware of all that.

Though most Jewish Israelis lump all the minority groups in this country together as "the Arabs," in point of fact Arab society is far from homogeneous. Even the various subgroups are showing signs of strain and tears in their social fabric. A good many of the Bedouins have adopted a stable life, in permanent housing, and some of those who have kept to their tents have equipped them with generators and have brought television sets to the desert wastes—though they still maintain their traditional mores and have aspirations different from those of the Arabs of the Triangle or the Galilee. Druse society has its fair share of internal strife, with competing camps pulling in opposite directions (within my own family, my brothers consider themselves part of the Arab minority in Israel, in spite of all my father's efforts to imbue them with the consciousness of belonging to the separate and distinctive Druse community), and Christian Arab society is severely factionalized.

Unlike the man in the street, the Israeli authorities were quite aware of the sore lack of unity and uniformity among their Arab citizens and tried to exploit it as a means of exercising control over Arab society—the ancient tactic of divide and rule. The official attitude toward the Druse, for example, has differed markedly from that toward Moslems and Christians. When the Druse complained loudly and bitterly that they were treated like Arabs when it came to rights and like Jews in terms of obligations, the government got the message and took measures to improve the community's lot. Today, the order of preference for financial allocations is almost a reflex: at the top are the Jewish local councils, which receive relatively large budgets from the Ministry of Interior; next come the Druse; at the bottom of the ladder are the Moslem and Christian Arabs. Naturally, those who are considered to be "good Arabs" receive more.

The first modification in the political and social status quo of Israel's Arabs came when they encountered the Arabs of the West Bank in 1967. After nineteen years of division and isola-

tion, branches of families from both sides of the border met again—and some eye-opening experiences were in store for them. The Fahom family of Nazareth found that some of their relatives were high-ranking leaders in the PLO. Israeli Arabs took advantage of the medical services in Jenin and Nablus, and West Bank newspapers flooded into the Arab villages of Israel, a sign of the thirst for an intrinsically Arab press. At the same time, Israeli Arabs were shocked by the subhuman living conditions of relatives who had spent nearly twenty years in the refugee camps of the West Bank or Gaza. The total effect of the encounter was overwhelming, and perhaps that was why moderation and caution prevailed at first. Familial ties were renewed, but the Arabs of the Galilee and the Triangle continued to see themselves as a separate entity, whose destiny was bound up with that of the State of Israel.

The first signs of rebellion in the territories—demonstrations, burning tires, mass arrests—roused some of the dormant firebrands among Israel's Arabs as well, but it was not until 1973 that the real turnaround came. When the Egyptian army crossed the Suez Canal and struck at the Bar-Lev line, it undermined the image of the IDF's invincibility for the Arabs of Israel as well as for those in the territories. Yasir Arafat's appearance at the United Nations and the international recognition he won for the PLO accelerated the process of Palestinization among Israel's Arabs. For the first time, Israeli Arab students stood up before television cameras and openly declared themselves Palestinian-Israeli Arabs. The steady accumulation of cracks soon caused the dam to burst, and the subsequent outpouring of feeling flooded the entire Arab community. Today it is hard to find an Arab in Israel who does not define himself as a Palestinian in one way or another; when the PLO is mentioned at mass rallies, the crowds moan with delight. Neither did it take long for the symptomatic shifts to be reflected on an organizational level. In 1974, the National Council of Chairmen of Arab Local Authorities was founded to lead the struggle for equal rights. It was followed shortly by

the National Council of Secondary School Students, and in 1975 by the National Union of Arab Student Councils. At the end of 1975, however, came the organization of the most influential body of them all: the National Council for the Protection of Arab Lands. Forthright about their nationalist aims, the public figures and groups that united to form this council claimed that it was neither a party nor an independent political organization—though few observers doubted that the moving force behind it was the New Communist List (Rakah), Israel's Communist party.

The clarion call to join in the struggle for equal rights signaled a far-reaching change in the Israeli Arab's political posture. In almost a single stroke, passive resistance gave way to a political activism that did not shrink from confrontation with the government. I had grave misgivings about where it all might lead, for a showdown with the authorities could easily crescendo into violence and jeopardize the many gains scored by Israel's Arabs—besides creating a deep breach within Israeli Arab society. I soon saw that I was not alone in my concern over the new trend. Jamal Abu-Tuama, formerly the head of the Bika el-Arabiya local council, was one who tried to maintain a sense of proportion. He told me, in a private conversation, "I support the Communist party's struggle against expropriation of our lands, but from there on our paths part. I am an Israeli Arab."

Such sentiments notwithstanding, there was no stopping the process set in train in 1967 and given increased momentum since 1973. Within the last few years, tensions between various factions in Israeli Arab society and between Arabs and Jews in Israel have become almost palpable. In the summer of 1980, I gave a lecture on recent developments in the West Bank before a mixed audience of Arabs and Jews at Kibbutz Givat Haviva. The Arabs included members of the (Zionist) Israel Labor party, members of the (non-Zionist) Communist party, Rakah, and adherents of a loose political association known as the Villagers, which parrots the PLO line in advocat-

243

ing the establishment of a secular democratic state in Palestine. As soon as I began to speak, I noticed that the audience
was seated according to political affiliation. In the middle of
my remarks, a young man from the Villagers movement suddenly jumped up and—referring to the Israeli authorities—
stormed, "They act like Nazis toward us!" The kibbutzniks, cut
to the quick, were immediately on their feet demanding an
apology. The young Arab backed down, the audience settled
into a sullen silence, and I tried to keep going as if nothing had
happened. But the incident was a sobering lesson in the feelings and orientation of the upcoming generation of Arabs in
this country.

The predicament of the Israeli Arab seems to be manifesting itself much more frequently, and in a greater variety of
settings, and the radicalization overtaking the community is
alarming. Seif a-Din Zu'abi, a former Knesset member and an
outspoken proponent of mutually constructive relations between Arabs and Jews, went to the heart of the problem when
he said, "My country, Israel, is at war with my people, the
Arabs. That is the dilemma we face." The Villagers have gotten around the dilemma by regarding Israel as an occupying
power at war with their people and by refusing even to listen
to any other reading of the situation. In 1978, at a lecture I
gave before Haifa University's Student Club, two Arab students from the town of Shfaram stood within earshot, but
announced that they would not enter the hall. Out of curiosity,
I asked what the trouble was, and one of them looked me
straight in the eye and spat out, "You're a liar who calls PLO
freedom fighters terrorists!" The tragedy of that sort of sanc-
timonious drivel is that in glorifying terrorism these young
people are undermining the position of those Israeli Jews who
support their demand for Palestinian self-determination. The
two students were right not to attend my lecture: there was no
basis for a dialogue between us.

The radicalization and Palestinization of the Israeli Arab
community may have been touched off by contacts with the

Arabs of the territories, but there is no denying that the shift has been abetted by the policies of successive Israeli governments—with the issue of land expropriation still the sharpest thorn. Early in 1976, for example, about fifty acres of land north and east of the village of Kafr Kassem were cordoned off by order of the Israeli Lands Authority. I should explain that the village had been the scene of a horrifying episode that had poisoned the air between Jews and Arabs for years, and it had come to symbolize an extremely ugly phenomenon and a sore wound. The incident occurred during the Sinai campaign of 1956, when Kafr Kassem—which is located near the 1948 frontier with Jordan—was placed under a curfew and the Border Police were ordered to shoot on sight anyone found breaking the ban on movement. As evening fell and the curfew went into effect, some overzealous policemen opened fire on a group of fellahin returning from the fields, taking the lives of forty-eight (including women and children) and wounding scores of others. It was an incredibly shocking affair, especially in a country where the refrain "I was only following orders" still rankles the entire nation. The soldiers and officers responsible were brought to trial and found guilty, but they were let off with relatively light sentences, which were further reduced on appeal.

Considering that Kafr Kassem was a catchword for the more gruesome side of the Israeli-Arab conflict, it should have been obvious that this new attempt to restrict the village's development would set off a storm of protest among the country's Arab population. Furthermore, by 1976 there was an organizational tool for transforming their anger into concrete political action. The steering committee of the National Council for the Protection of Arab Lands visited Kafr Kassem and committed itself to a head-on clash with the authorities if they failed to retract their action. The seventy people who owned land in the fenced-off area vowed that they would fight to the end, and eventually the prime minister and the minister of justice ordered the operation halted.

That closed the matter—but it did not close the process of land expropriation that has played such a focal role in raising the consciousness of Israel's Arabs. Shortly afterward, the Ministry of Defense decided to resume combat maneuvers in the region known as Area 9, bordering on the vineyards of Sahnein, Dir Hana, and Arabeh, in the Galilee. The zone was already the object of a heated dispute between the villagers and the government, and the resumption of maneuvers meant that restrictions would again be imposed on farming in the region. On February 14, 1976, residents of the three villages gathered in Sahnein and decided to hold a protest demonstration and strike against the restrictions. Then the Ministry of Defense reversed itself and granted the villagers special permission to work their land. Even so, the government's muddled, flip-flop policy appeased no one, serving its own interests least of all. As the late Hana Muwas, then the chairman of the Rama local council, noted, at a later meeting in Sahnein, "The government's retreat—modest though it may be—was achieved by unity in the ranks and the dedication of the Arab community to protecting its lands. . . . Your stubborn fight in defense of your lands and the graves of your loved ones has forced the government and the Israeli Lands Authority to back down on the expropriation actions at Kafr Kassem . . . and Area 9."

If Muwas meant to imply that a precedent had been set, he spoke too soon. On February 29, 1976, the government struck again, announcing a decision to expropriate land in four areas of the Galilee: 1,175 acres in Nazareth, 77 percent of them Arab-owned; 1,875 acres in the area of Carmiel, 26 percent Arab-owned; 525 acres near the village of Makar, 35 percent Arab-owned; and 1,450 acres in the area of Safed, all of them state lands or Jewish-owned property. Even before learning of that plan, however, the steering committee of the National Council for the Protection of Arab Lands had called for a general strike to be held on March 30, 1976. In its appeal, the committee characterized the strike as

. . . an expression of the burning anger throbbing in the hearts of our people against a policy that attempts to uproot us from every plot of our land. . . . We call upon the Arab residents of Israel to declare a general strike and turn [March 30] into "Land Day," when the Arab masses will raise their voices in a call to rescind the official policy that poses a threat to our future in this country. . . . The time has come for us to say to the rulers of Israel: Enough! The remnant that is left to us must not be lost!

The strike call had a powerful impact, though not all the Arab leadership joined in the procession toward extremism. Chairmen of local councils and other moderate public figures feared the consequences of violence and strikes, but they could neither deny nor control the militant mood of the Arab community. Some of those leaders tried instead to persuade the government to act with caution and reason—though their tones of admonition were unmistakable. Zaki Diyab, a former member of the Knesset and the chairman of the Tamra local council, uttered this warning during a meeting at Sahnein on February 14, 1976: "The responsible parties must understand that if we, the moderates, feel deprived, we will nurse our resentment until the time comes to act. And when we act, we shall do so in a way that will transform Israel's Arabs into a force more dangerous than the hundred million Arabs living beyond Israel's borders."

Diyab and Abdul-Rahim Haj Yehiya, the chairman of the Taybeh local council, worked tirelessly to restore a sense of calm, and they did manage to persuade most of the local council chairmen that a strike was both unnecessary and hazardous. But the Arab students' union responded by branding them "agents who do not represent the will" of the people and denounced the "performance of the defeatists" as "nothing but a fraud and diversionary tactic. Their intention is to delude the public into believing that the Arab community has placed the conduct of its affairs in the hands of these outdated peo-

247

ple." On March 25, when forty-five chairmen of Arab local councils who opposed the strike met in Shfaram, a large crowd of young people gathered outside the hall and showered abuse on the meeting. As the delegates filed out, one of the youths elbowed his way up to Zaki Diyab and spat in his face. The division among Israeli Arabs appeared to be turning into a full-fledged confrontation across the generation gap.

Despite the attempts to put a damper on the passions, the extremists proved to have the upper hand this time, for the strike did take place and was highly effective. The news clips and photographs of violent demonstrations, burning tires, stonings of vehicles and troops, and counteractions by club-wielding Israeli soldiers in combat dress were reminiscent of similar events in the West Bank, and the story got banner headlines. The demonstrations also took a terrible toll: six Arab citizens were killed—three in Sahnein, one in Arabeh, one in Kafr Kana, and one in Taybeh—and scores of others wounded, along with many soldiers.

The violence began on March 29, the eve of the strike, when a truck filled with soldiers traveling along the Dir Hana–Sahnein–Arabeh road came upon an improvised roadblock of stones. A few of the soldiers climbed down from the vehicle to clear the way and were met by a hail of rocks and burning torches. The besieged troops opened fire. Mohammed Nimmer Hussein, the chairman of the Dir Hana council, later charged that the soldiers then "arrested young men in their homes, beat them, subjected them to abuse, and humiliated them in front of their parents. They even beat the women who tried to protect their sons. The soldiers also opened fire and wounded many people." Jamal Tarabei, the chairman of the Sahnein council—and once an enthusiastic supporter of the Mapai party—testified that "between eight and nine in the morning, three people were killed in cold blood for no reason at all. They just walked out of their homes and were shot down. A girl who came out of her house and was ordered to go back inside was shot in the back while carrying out the order."

248

A curfew was imposed on the three restless villages, but now the rest of Israel's Arabs joined in the strike, with redoubled conviction and ardor. Life in the Arab sectors came to a complete halt on March 30. No schools opened, employees did not show up for work, factories were totally paralyzed—and the standing of those who had opposed the strike hit an all-time low. Stung by the government's intemperate action, Tarek Abdul-Hai, the chairman of the Tira local council, grumbled to me, "They have shamed us. We have nothing left. We are hollow men now. But we won't make the same mistake twice, for we are being portrayed as the agents of a policy that has harmed the Arabs of Israel for thirty years."

But it was already too late for men like Abdul-Hai. After the radicalizing events of "Land Day," Israel's Arabs turned their backs on the community's moderate leaders and voted them out of office. In August of 1976, Abdul-Rahim Haj Yehiya was unseated in Taybeh and replaced by a Rakah man. Zaki Diyab, who had been beaten up by Israeli troops on "Land Day," was deposed by his fellow members of the Tamra council—though the minister of interior ruled the action void, disbanded the elected council, and appointed a new body in its place. Even Jamal Tarabei of Sahnein, once the leader of the moderates who denounced the radical upstarts, has since changed his tune. Sometime in 1978 he asked me for Fahed Kawasmeh's phone number, and shortly afterward the two men met to discuss the united destiny of the Palestinians and the need to establish an independent state that would embrace them all. Tarabei was a man who had repeatedly declared that he would never abandon the Jewish State of Israel; now he was choosing to float with the current rather than flail against it. Some other leaders of the moderate camp drew different conclusions and officially joined the Democratic Front for Peace and Equality, an amalgamation of Rakah and like-minded groups.

All credit is due to Tawfik Ziyad for the success of "Land Day." The temperamental poet, a Knesset member and the mayor of Nazareth, was a prime mover behind the diffusion of the new militant spirit among the Arabs of Israel. As a leader of the Democratic Front for Peace and Equality, he appeared at all the rallies preceding "Land Day" and, in his hoarse, dramatic voice, called on his people to enlist in the cause. He never lost his sense of proportion, however, and was careful to warn against an excess of zeal. In a leaflet circulated in Nazareth on the eve of "Land Day," Ziyad told his constituents, "We must prove we are a people that is not afraid and does not kowtow," but he also stressed the need for restraint. His polished rhetoric is suffused with nationalist slogans like *"ard el-watan"* ("the soil of the homeland"), and he has a penchant for such epigrammatic constructs as "Without land there can be no homeland, no home . . . only endless wanderings in search of work. We don't want to become the nomads of the twentieth century."

I spent "Land Day" in Nablus trying to record the reactions there to the events then unfolding in Israel. Not once since 1967 had the Arabs of Israel expressed open support for the protest activities in the territories, but now that they had decided to air their own grievances they were getting the wholehearted support of the West Bank. The PLO shrewdly encouraged the show of solidarity, with the result that the merchants of Nablus and Ramallah also shuttered their shops and walked out on strike. Thus "Land Day" was remembered as another milestone in setting the seal on a tacit alliance between the Arabs of Israel and the Arabs of the territories.

Evidence of the new nexus could be seen in the statements published by the National Council for the Protection of Arab Lands. In a manifesto issued on May 29, 1976, the council declared:

> The Arab inhabitants of Israel, who are an indivisible part of the Palestinian Arab people, continue to demand that the Israeli authorities honor their national and human rights and rescind the policy of national discrimination

against them—expressed first and foremost by the expropriation of Arab land. It is impossible to differentiate between the aggression against the Arabs of Israel evidenced on "Land Day" and the aggression against the Arabs of the occupied territories that has been going on since 1967. This is but another aspect of the policy designed to deny the rights of the Palestinian Arab people and seize their lands by force!

Considering the tone and content of such declarations, it was only logical for the executive committee of the PLO to begin channeling funds into what it called "the Arab uprising in Israel," and the PLO's official organ, *Falastin a-Thawra*, made reference to "our people in the Galilee" as "a weapon of the movement to liberate the Palestinian people." It should be remembered that "Land Day" fell just a few weeks before the elections that were to bring Bassam Shaka, Karim Halaf, and Fahed Kawasmeh into office in the West Bank, and the area was awash with pro-PLO election propaganda. While the pre-election frenzy might not have had any direct bearing on the mood of the Arab community in Israel, it is certain that the advent of the PLO-backed mayors served to strengthen the links between the Arabs of Israel and the territories, for Shaka and Kawasmeh made a point of fostering the Nablus-Nazareth axis. When the Lebanese Druse socialist leader Kamal Jumbalat was assassinated, in March of 1977, Nazareth held an official public assembly to honor his memory. Shaka turned up for it and was received like a national hero. He spoke of the need for unity in the ranks of the struggle against "imperialists and usurpers," bringing the crowd to its feet in an outburst of cheers. After the rally, the mayor of Nablus remarked to me that he felt at home in Nazareth—with a reception like that, I wasn't surprised.

Rakah has also worked steadily to reinforce ties spanning the "Green Line"—the 1949 armistice line, which constituted Israel's border until the Six Day War. In fact, Rakah's activity became so conspicuous that the military government, worried about the possible consequences of the alliance, began to prohibit Israeli party members from entering the territories. Nevertheless, such leading Rakah figures as activist lawyer Felicia Langer and Knesset members Tawfik Toubi and Tawfik Ziyad have visited the cities of the West Bank often, and cooperation between the respective branches of the party has been particularly evident in the Communist press, with Israeli Arabs contributing articles to organs published in the territories and vice versa.

Rakah considers the PLO the sole representative of the Palestinian people, and a meeting in Sofia, in September of 1980, between its Knesset members and Yasir Arafat was merely the climax of a process that had been going on for years. At the same time, since the party's moves are guided by both the Soviet Union's official line and the sharp challenge Rakah faces from young, radical circles in the villages, confusion is inevitable. For example, the Arabs of Israel may be an integral part of the Palestinian people, but by no means is the PLO their sole representative.

In June of 1976, a few of Rakah's leaders issued a puzzling statement demanding that Israel be reconstituted as a binational state. I say puzzling because such a notion was a blatant contradiction of the Communist party's official line; indeed, a few days later the same leaders published an explanatory letter in *Ha'aretz* backtracking on their position. The letter clearly stated that "Israel was founded as a Jewish state, and recognized as such, and it should remain as such. We are fighting for the rights of the Arab minority in Israel, which we view as part and parcel of the Palestinian nation, just as we are fighting for the right of [the Palestinian] nation to a state of its own alongside the State of Israel." I sometimes still wonder whether the original text was just an embarrassing gaffe, prompted by an excess of zeal, or was meant to signal a change of heart within the ranks of the party.

Either way, the symptoms of radicalization did not go

unnoticed by politically attuned Jews in Israel. Startled, per-haps, by the force of the rhetoric emanating from the Triangle and the Galilee, some circles resorted to hyperbole of their own. According great significance to the new spirit of militancy among Israel's Arabs, they spoke of the "disappearance of the 'Green Line.' " Now it was clear, they charged, that there was no real difference between Nablus and Nazareth. But such a gross distortion of the situation ignored one cardinal fact: the Arabs of Israel remained loyal to the State of Israel even when they spoke of themselves as being part of the Palestinian peo-ple. Jews who referred to "the Arabs of Palestine" as a single, indivisible entity, without applying the criterion of national citizenship to distinguish between various sectors of the Pales-tinian population, were only contributing to the vitality of a dynamic that they would have preferred to arrest.

As we have seen in other aspects of the Palestinian-Israeli conflict, the forces at both extremes of the political spectrum have tended to nourish one another. In the same manner as this antithetical symbiosis has affected the PLO and Gush Emunim, so has any inclination toward separatism among Israel's Arabs met with a backlash from hard-line Jewish na-tionalists. There have even been calls to reinstitute military government over the Israeli Arab population, in order to nip in the bud any attempt at secession. While Meir Kahane's Kach Movement demands action to encourage Arabs to emigrate from Israel, Tawfik Ziyad has threatened that if the state does not grant its Arab citizens equal rights "they will publish ads in the papers . . . proclaiming that the Arabs of Israel are looking for a country that will be good enough to accept them —and their land!" Even Ziyad, virtuoso that he is, might have been taken aback by the vehemence of the Israeli reaction, however, for in September of 1980 he issued a statement reaffirming Rakah's determination not to deviate from the pol-icy that recognized Israel's right to exist. "The Arabs of Israel view themselves as part and parcel of the state," he avowed, "and not a single serious voice calls for secession from it. The

253

Arabs of Israel are the only Arabs who officially recognize the State of Israel, and they wish to remain therein because it is their home and their homeland."

The relatively cautious line adopted by Rakah was never more evident than on the first anniversary of "Land Day," when the Villagers movement tried and failed to effect a replay of the previous year's events. The Villagers had hoped to whip up the Arab masses, but Rakah worked hard to funnel the sentiment of protest into "constructive" channels—quiet demonstrations and tightly structured rallies that would leave little room for spontaneity. All the same, it appears that the Communist party in Israel is fighting a losing battle; the turbulent events in the area and the upsurge in the West Bank of nationalist feeling, awash with romanticism, have drawn the young people in the villages away from Rakah. Indicative of the shift was a manifesto published in March of 1980, in the village of Um el-Fahem, by a body calling itself the National Progressive Movement. Throwing temperance to the winds, the manifesto spoke of "the struggle against the racist Zionist authorities who are waging a war of physical, political, and cultural annihilation against the Palestinian Arab people. . . . 'Land Day' is a day of struggle, not of ceremonies. Down with the occupation, the settlements, and the Jews! Long live the Arab-Jewish struggle against the occupation and expropriations!"

That kind of literature is hardly likely to foster an atmosphere of calm and reason. Then again, to dwell on the dangers posed by such excesses would be a typical instance of treating the symptoms rather than the cause. The young extremists cannot be held responsible for a policy that has exacerbated the problem tenfold. It is the government of Israel and its related agencies that are chiefly responsible, by their appalling lack of sensitivity and consideration, for the isolation of the moderate element among the Arabs of Israel. A case in point is the government's campaign to "Judaize" the Galilee. Although the Jewish settlement agencies have tried to explain that such "Judaization" would not be at the expense of the district's Arabs, it is obvious that the purpose is to undercut any Arab national claim to the Galilee and vindicate the Jewish claim of exclusivity there.

I recently came across a Jewish Agency document that attempted to explain the need for Jewish mini-settlements—called "lookouts"—in the Galilee. The memorandum was titled "The Establishment of Lookouts in the Mountainous Galilee: The Struggle to Protect the Nation's Land and Ensure the Character of the Area for the Future." It went on to unravel the meaning of that rather elliptic language with the explanation that 70 percent of the residents of the Galilee were not Jewish and that, due to the objective demographic situation and the distribution of the Jewish population in the area, an undesirable situation existed. In fact, the situation "poses a major threat to the character of the area as part of the Jewish state, to Jewish control thereof, and even to Israeli sovereignty over it. There is a chance that in the autonomy talks [with Egypt], the Arabs may demand that this region be included in [the area to be granted autonomy]." The authors of the document seemed totally unaware that their own analysis implied that there might be grounds for reconsidering the rightness of Israel's sovereignty over the Galilee. More than that, even someone like me, who firmly believes in Israel's right to exist as a Jewish state and is prepared to fight for that right, has difficulty accepting the style adopted by the Jewish Agency. If that august body has come to see the Arabs of Israel as a collective enemy, which must be opposed on a national basis, why should anyone be surprised that more and more young Arabs are going over to the Palestinian camp?

Even a brief, superficial tour of the Arab villages in Israel suffices for a keen-eyed observer to sense the profound bewilderment of their people. Fourteen years have passed since the roads were opened and the Arabs of Israel were reunited with their relatives in the West Bank, but the Israeli Arab still feels like a stranger in Nablus or Hebron. Further, this inability to feel at home in the West Bank has sharpened his sense of alienation and superfluousness with regard to Israeli society as well. Prior to 1967, the knowledge that there was no other choice forced the Arabs of Israel to try to integrate into the life of the state. Now they supposedly have another option, but it has only left them more skeptical and distraught than ever. The result often is an unfocused anger and a tendency to grasp at political straws.

On March 6, 1980, a mass meeting was held at the municipal building in Shfaram. The participants included public figures from across the political spectrum, representatives of the Bedouins in the Negev, twenty mayors and local council chairmen from the Galilee, leftist poets and writers, and three Arab members of the Knesset. Rakah activists stood at the entrance to the hall distributing handbills that protested the occupation of the territories and promoted the establishment of a Palestinian state alongside the State of Israel. No one objected, or even asked what the leaflets had to do with the subject at hand: the grievances of the Israeli Arab community against the government. Indeed, when Rakah's ideologue, Dr. Emil Tuma, took to the podium to denounce the discrimination against Israel's Arabs and to call for a PLO-ruled Palestinian state alongside the State of Israel, the audience broke into wild applause. I slumped down in my seat, completely at a loss. Could it really be that the Arabs of Israel wanted to pick up stakes and remove themselves to an independent Palestinian state? When I turned to the man next to me—another Israeli Arab journalist—and asked the question aloud, he smiled confidently and assured me, "That's just lip service— or, if you prefer, a moral obligation. If a Palestinian state is established in the territories, not a single person in this room will move over to the other side."

At the end of the meeting, I discovered that I was not the only one in the hall who had felt out of place—or perhaps out of step was a better way to put it. One of the Knesset members approached me and murmured in my ear, "I had a strong

speech prepared, but they—the nationalists—would have exploited it for their own ends. I felt very uncomfortable
throughout the meeting." Tarek Abdul-Hai, the chairman of
the Tira local council, confessed to similar feelings during a
private conversation we had, grumbling, "Not everyone who
speaks of Palestine understands exactly where its borders are!
I want to remain an Israeli Arab." On the other hand, Abdul-
Hai has his own ax to grind with the State of Israel. In that
same conversation, he complained that "successive Israeli
governments have humiliated me and spun a web of lies
around me, and I won't stand for it." Abdul-Hai, a graduate
of the prestigious Kadoorie Agricultural School—once the
labor movement's finest training ground—was known for
years as the Israeli government's "man in the Triangle." He
had always enjoyed easy access to the ministries—though he
seemed to have been less successful in reaching the hearts and
minds of his constituents—and had been an outspoken advocate of peaceful coexistence. But in recent years his disillusion-
ment with Israeli policies has driven him into the arms of the
Democratic Front for Peace and Equality, whose warm embrace has evidently soothed his political and social chagrin.

In a follow-up to the Shfaram meeting, the delegates decided to reconvene in Nazareth, for a national conference, in
November of 1980. Before the convention could be fully organized, the Israeli government, on the recommendation of the
security services, intervened to prevent it from taking place.
The first reaction among Israel's Arabs was stormy, but they
soon calmed down. Jewish public opinion in Israel sided with
the government, because of the widespread belief that things
might get out of hand at the convention—meaning that the
secessionist and pro-PLO radicals might set the tone and
sweep up the less sophisticated, more susceptible masses in
their wake. Moreover, a pronounced silence from official Arab
quarters only reinforced the feeling that the government's
decision had been the right one. But it was painfully obvious
that the breach between the Arabs of Israel and the Israeli

government was growing wider every day, and the decision to prohibit the Nazareth conference—which would surely have called for the creation of an independent Palestinian state in the territories—has only sharpened the estrangement between the two peoples who inhabit the State of Israel.

Considering that the Arab population of Israel has lived in a social and cultural ghetto for years, perhaps it is poetic justice that those who have the most sustained contacts with the Jewish population—the university students—are among the most radical elements in the nationalist camp. There are currently about 2,000 Arab students attending Israel's universities, or about 4 percent of the total student population, whereas Israel's Arabs make up some 15 percent of the country's overall population. Until 1967, the Arab university students met with a frigid reception on campus, not to mention the trouble they had finding decent living quarters in Jerusalem and the menial jobs they were reduced to accepting. Since then conditions have changed considerably: there has been a resurgence of national pride among the students, and over the past few years a virtual industry of radical literature has flourished on the campuses. Today's Arab student is perfectly aboveboard about his support for the PLO and may even emblazon it on his T-shirt.

One consequence of that assertiveness has been repeated episodes of violence on the country's campuses. Self-appointed guardians of law and order among the Jewish students have seemed only too eager to settle ideological differences with their fists, causing far too many confrontations across national lines to end in brawls. In fact, it would be no exaggeration to say that the institutions of higher learning—envisioned as vehicles for achieving mutual understanding between the two peoples—have become hot-beds of animosity. If the atmosphere prevailing in the universities should spread to the broader framework of relations between Jews and Arabs throughout the State of Israel, I regret to say that we can look for many difficult years ahead.

The Arabs of Israel, who have grown in number from 150,000 to about half a million since 1948, have been struggling to preserve their identity and way of life for almost thirty-five years. The 1948 war brought them tragedy, as the military government attempted to quash any manifestations of national spirit, but they nevertheless managed to preserve their distinct consciousness. At the same time, technological advances were greatly improving their economic and social status. But that has not been enough. For the Arabs of Israel find themselves in a trying national dilemma, and all citizens of this country have an obligation to understand that dilemma and help bring about its resolution.

Over the years, Israel's Arabs have come to appreciate the benefits of democracy and the meaning of a life of freedom. Immediately upon meeting their brethren from the West Bank and Gaza in 1967, they perceived the tremendous gap that separated them. The traditional, patriarchal social structure still applied in Jordan and Gaza. The two groups no longer saw eye to eye on political questions or shared the same aspirations. When they look at the bottom line, it is not surprising that few Israeli Arabs are prepared to give up their land and their lives in Israel and cross the "Green Line," in spite of the beguiling visions of a Palestinian renaissance awaiting them there.

At the same time, much patient mending remains to be done if Israeli society is to be spared the ravages of fragmentation, and the purely technical solutions that have been proposed do not show much promise. I, for one, would place little faith in a proposal for extending the draft to all the Arabs of Israel, as a way of providing Arab youth with a greater feeling of "belonging." The IDF has proved to be the great melting pot for the pluralistic Jewish community of Israel, but the same remedies do not necessarily work for Arabs and Jews. After all, the Arabs of Israel are hardly convinced that the state is prepared to accord them equal rights. Why, then, should they agree to assume equal responsibilities?

Until a solution to their many problems is hammered out, the Arabs of Israel have no choice but to continue wrestling with the ambiguities and paradoxes that have become the hallmarks of their national identity. They are not in an enviable position. Then again, who in today's Middle East is?

12
A REVOLUTION
IN ARAB SOCIETY

F or close to a century now, the labor market has been an arena of confrontation between the Arab and Jewish communities in this country. The Zionist movement, bent on revolutionizing the economic patterns of Jewish life, aspired to create a well-rounded, stable Jewish economy in Palestine; and the Jewish pioneers, in their attempt to strike roots in the soil and establish dominion over the country, had to compete against the products of Arab labor and try to keep the Arabs out of the labor market. Matters reached a point where the refusal to employ Arab labor became the test of a farmer's or builder's loyalty to the principles of Zionism. On the other side, with the declaration of a general strike in 1936 —which lasted for six months—the Arab nationalist movement tried to use economic sanctions as a weapon to cripple the vulnerable Jewish community. The plan backfired, however; the strike only served as a fillip to the development of an independent Jewish economy—and that, of course, furthered the cause of establishing an independent Jewish state.

Now, long after the establishment of that state and the consolidation of its economy, Arab labor has again become an issue, the import of which extends far beyond the strictly economic sphere. Those concerned about the moral vitality of their country fervently and justly argue that a society that has allowed itself to become dependent on the work force of another nation—as Israel has, by its mass infusion of unskilled labor from the territories—not only vitiates its moral posture but also jeopardizes its national security. That is all the more

261

true when those two people are locked in an enervating struggle for national supremacy.

The Jews and Arabs of Israel meet today in workshops, fields, factories, construction sites, and other places of work. The interdependence of the two economies within Israel proper has grown rapidly, the result of an economic revolution that has transformed the fellahin—unable to squeeze a meager living out of their small plots of land—into day laborers working outside their villages.

By 1980, 90 percent of all the Israeli Arabs aged fifteen to forty-five were employed as salaried workers. As a child, I had witnessed the transformation taking place. Dalyat el-Carmel came to life at 5:00 A.M., when scores of men in dozens of vehicles—taxis, trucks, and vans—set out for their places of work along the bay in the Haifa area and in the industrial zone near Tirat Hacarmel, or to gardening and landscaping jobs in Haifa and the kibbutzim of the area. In time, young women also began to go out to work, mainly in the textile factories being built in and around the villages. The fellahin became laborers and contractors, garage mechanics, restaurant workers, and hotel waiters. At first the new labor force was directed into jobs that Jewish workers spurned; now Arab professionals and highly skilled workers virtually dominate entire segments of the Israeli economy.

The daily outflow of Israel's Arabs from their villages into economic and social contact with Jewish society engendered thoroughgoing changes in village life, for in addition to their salaries the Arab workers brought home new ideas about getting along in the modern world. Especially radical was the sea change in the self-image and status of the Arab woman, who was no longer content with the role of an inferior creature relegated to the depths of the kitchen. Many of the women who took jobs to supplement family income came to view their economic contribution as grounds for social and political equality as well. At the same time, the changes also brought certain benefits to Jewish society—or to those Israeli industrialists and farmers who became proficient at exploiting the labor of their Arab employees for their own gain. It took the intervention of the Histadrut—once the champion of the Jewish work force in its struggle against cheaper and more experienced Arab labor—to halt or mitigate the crude exploitation by organizing the Arab workers and ensuring that they received equal social benefits. So fundamental was the labor revolution that Israeli Arabs eventually became the mainstay of certain services and branches of industry, leading their Jewish compatriots to wonder how the economy had ever functioned without them.

Those fellahin who remained on the land soon began to part with their primitive methods, in favor of mechanized agriculture. The Triangle was transformed into a center of agricultural exports, with the farmers of Taybeh, for one example, taking in millions of Israeli pounds in profits. Even my father was caught up in the surge toward modernization. Trying to find his place in the new order, he uprooted the few gnarled olive trees on his land and attempted to increase his yield by adopting the new methods of cultivation. Unfortunately, the results of the experiment did not live up to his expectations, and eventually my brothers abandoned agriculture altogether for the world of commerce.

In time, even the ugliest of the ingrained attitudes began to change, and the put-down expression "Arab labor" seemed to disappear from the language. Then, after the Six Day War, Israel was inundated with thousands of laborers from the territories—Bedouins from Sinai and Palestinians from the West Bank and Gaza—and the exploitation of Arab labor resumed on a greater scale than ever.

I had been vaguely aware of that distasteful aspect of the occupation, but it wasn't until 1978, when I visited the Gaza Strip to film a report on the local labor market, that I fully realized how far and how deep the blight had spread. My crew and I reached the crossover point on the border between the Gaza Strip and Israel proper at 3:00 A.M. one morning, in time

THE WEST BANK STORY

to see an astonishing scene unfold before us. Hundreds of unskilled day laborers were huddled around campfires waiting for the arrival of the labor contractors *(ra'isin)*, hoping to get a day's labor for a meager wage. In the beam of the one electric light, I could see dozens of boys peering forward expectantly as they marched north toward the crossover, lunch bags in hand. Some of these children had come more than six miles on foot from the Jebalya refugee camp to the "slave market" at the Ashkelon junction. Soon the *ra'isin* arrived and began to dole out agricultural jobs. The going price for a day's labor was appalling—30 to 100 Israeli pounds ($1.60 to $5.50)—but the children jumped at the offer. They made no special demands and were willing to work from early morning until late afternoon, when they would be transported back to their homes. Similar scenes were taking place at the labor markets in the Musrara Quarter of Jerusalem and in downtown Gaza, where scores of trucks and pickups stood waiting to carry thousands of unskilled laborers to places of work in Israel.

I walked over to one of the crowded vans and found fifteen children inside. "Where to?" I asked, and one of the children piped up proudly that they were going to work. Picking tomatoes! Then I turned to the *ra'is* and asked him why the children weren't in school. "Those kids are idiots," he sneered. "They wouldn't learn anything in school anyway."

"How much are they being paid for their work?" I pressed.

"Plenty. Four to five pounds"—between twenty and twenty-five cents.

"And what can you get with that?" I blurted out, flabbergasted by his hard-boiled cynicism.

"It's enough to buy some food. Anyway," the *ra'is* added, "if they're working they can't run wild in the streets. It's good for Israel, because that way they won't bother you."

The children's faces were wreathed in eager smiles for having secured a day's work. The *ra'is,* convinced he had done everyone a favor, had a clear conscience. But I returned to my hotel room in Ashkelon livid. There were labor laws in Israel expressly forbidding the employment of children under the age of sixteen, but evidently word of those laws had not reached Israel's "Wild South." I assumed that the children had been hired by the newly established moshavim of the Rafiah salient. But as we drove south, in pursuit of our story and to check out working conditions on the spot, we passed Kibbutz Yad Mordechai, a well-established community inside the "Green Line," and saw another group of Arab children, who told us they were working in the kibbutz's flowers-for-export operation.

The associations that go with the name Yad Mordechai made that discovery particularly disillusioning. Founded in 1943 by a group of young pioneers from Poland, the kibbutz was named in memory of Mordechai Anielewicz, the commander of the Warsaw ghetto uprising. Five years later, the settlers found themselves up against the same kind of hopeless odds that the Warsaw fighters had faced—except that this time the enemy was the Egyptian army advancing northward from the Sinai. With the same brand of heroism, a sprinkling of kibbutzniks held their ground for six days before the settlement fell, in May of 1948. Yad Mordechai was retaken by the IDF five months later, and the kibbutz was rebuilt. Ever since, it has been a double symbol of Jewish valor in the face of overwhelming, if not impossible, odds. Now, not only had the plague of vulgar exploitation spread to the kibbutzim—which for years had refused to employ hired labor of any kind, because of their principles of self-sufficiency and for fear of taking advantage of such workers, wittingly or otherwise—but even a respected community like Yad Mordechai had succumbed to the vice of employing Arab children! Hard as it was to believe, the evidence was right there before our eyes. And it was cold comfort to recall that the kibbutzim that did employ outside labor usually paid their hired workers well above the going rate and were scrupulous about including the standard social benefits.

We drove on to the Rafiah salient, and at each stop my camera recorded the grim testimony it would soon present to the Israeli people. When the report was screened, on the "Weekly News Magazine," it caused a wave of consternation throughout Israel. One Knesset member introduced an urgent motion to debate the employment of Arab children in the newly established "plantations of Israel's southland." In asking that his motion be given special priority, Yossi Sarid of the Labor party said, "If the realization of the Zionist ideal rests on the backs of six- and seven-year-old Arab children, it's better to leave the hay to scorch in the fields and the tomatoes to wither on their stems." The Knesset decided that the subject was indeed worthy of attention, but was not urgent and would be taken up in due course.

Public pressure did, however, set off alarms in the Ministry of Labor, and supervisors were sent out to check the situation in the field. The farmers of the Rafiah salient soon found themselves in an uncomfortable position, to say the least. Bedouins had once lived on the land on which their prosperous new moshavim now stood, and the "landed gentry" of Rafiah were employing the very Bedouins they had dispossessed. But what defied any standard of decency was that they were padding their bank accounts from the labor of Bedouin children. When I asked one of the settlers of Moshav Dikla if his conscience ever bothered him for employing children, he replied, "This is embarrassing. You've caught me in a very compromising position." Another settler, from the moshav of Netiv Ha'asarah, was not at all contrite, answering my question with a snort of indignation: "I pay a child very well—100 pounds for a day's work." Since the law did not distinguish between well-paid and poorly-paid child labor, his alleged generosity did not lessen the crime. Still, the arrogance of the answer made me skeptical about his claim, so I turned to one of the Arab youngsters and asked how much he earned. The child, who had not understood my conversation with his employer, replied without hesitation, "Forty pounds." I could only conclude that a man who had no qualms about exploiting children was even less squeamish about lying.

When my crew and I arrived at Netiv Ha'asarah, we had a hard time finding any settlers, though scores of laborers were milling around. The driver of our taxi, who prided himself on knowing the local scene, explained that as soon as we left the squires of Rafiah would appear and lead their field hands off to work. The laborers proved to be incorrigibly camera shy, because they knew that scores of others were waiting in line to take their places if they were fired.

The employers of these Bedouins had been sent to the Rafiah salient to erect a cordon of settlements that presumably were vital to Israel's security. But, speaking as one who has delved into the way of life that has evolved in these settlements, I am haunted by the thought that Israeli farmers who employ Arab laborers and children to work their land could well end up leasing out the land and conducting their enterprises as if they were kulaks or effendis. It has happened before. Meanwhile, the hired labor lived on the periphery of the agricultural settlements. In another throwback to America's antebellum South, large families were crowded into improvised tin shacks and tottering wooden huts, which looked out on the villas of Israeli landlords waxing rich off the sweat of Arab brows. "Compromising" was not quite the word I would have chosen for such a position.

The Knesset debate requested by Yossi Sarid eventually was held, and fiery speeches rang through the hall—yet little changed in the field. Forty farmers were brought to trial for violating the labor laws, but they were let off with ridiculously light sentences; a settler who employed dozens of children all year round had little to lose if a fine of a few hundred pounds was slapped on him for not hiring his workers through the state Labor Exchange. Of course, every one of those settlements is now slated for evacuation, and there are Israelis who consider that a national tragedy; but there are many others who are relieved, in a way, that the sordid side of the Rafiah story is also coming to an end. If justice has been done in the Rafiah salient, the divine kind seems to have prevailed where mere mortals faltered.

In all, the Israeli economy employs some 64,000 Arab workers from the occupied territories, about 80 percent of them processed through the Labor Exchange. It is a highly diversified work force and has recently begun to include well-educated young people who cannot find work commensurate with their talents and skills. Most of the 64,000 return home at the end of the day's work, but a good number prefer to remain in Israel's large cities—even though they break the law by doing so, and risk being sent back across the "Green Line" and punished.

Two weeks after my report on child labor in the Israeli settlements near the Gaza Strip, I went to Jaffa in search of a story on the living conditions of Arabs who worked in Tel Aviv but lived in the shadowy corners of that sprawling coastal metropolis. I began by approaching gas station attendants and restaurant owners for clues as to where their workers lodged at night, but they all dodged my questions. Finally I came across a young man who directed me to a workers' hostel in one of the dank alleys of Jaffa. The door was padlocked, and when I found the landlady—a strident old woman—she informed me that the workers were kept locked in the dormitory for their own protection. "Their living conditions are good," she assured me. "You'll see for yourself in a minute. I lock them in because of the police and thieves."

The padlocks were removed, and we entered a large room resounding with a cacophony of snores. The room contained about twenty beds lined up side by side, squeaking and sagging under the weight of their occupants; the bedding would not have passed inspection under the weakest of hygienic standards. A number of the men woke up when we switched on the overhead lights and added our own camera lighting. I knew our presence was a rude intrusion, but I dispensed with good manners and set about trying to persuade the men to talk.

That was no easy feat. The first person I approached, a youth of about eighteen, from Gaza, asked not to be disturbed because he had to get up at three o'clock to start his shift as a porter in Tel Aviv's open-air market. Most of the others in this particular hostel were construction workers, but here, too, we found a smattering of frightened children from the refugee camps of Gaza.

On balmy summer nights many of these laborers saved the cost of lodgings by bedding down in public parks or at the seashore, where at least the air was fresh and the accommodations of nature were often cleaner than what man offered them. They had become accustomed to humiliating searches and aggressive treatment by the police patrols along the shore and in the alleys of the open market. As I continued my tour, I came to one garage whose proprietor told me, without blinking an eye, that he locked his workers on the premises overnight. Aside from the gross disregard for human dignity, the practice was particularly abhorrent because it could so easily end in tragedy—as in one case where workers were trapped on the premises of a plant when a fire broke out. I needn't elaborate on the horrific outcome.

Every hostel I visited while preparing that report had the same execrable features: filth, stench—in short, subhuman conditions. At each place I had a hard time convincing the lodgers that I was not working for the police. Once I did convince them, though, they would let loose with a barrage of grievances about degrading treatment by their employers, low pay, and harassment by the police. After every hostile action in the city, the Arab laborers would be rounded up for interrogation. Never, it seemed, did their employers come to their defense, and rarely did one hear of a boss who looked out for his employees' welfare or housed them decently.

I have set out from the premise that exposing the seamier side of the occupation—especially in the economic and social spheres—would make people stop and examine what was happening to their own self-respect. There was a time when the

IDF camps in the Sinai employed local Arabs in their kitchens and for any other work that the soldiers considered "beneath their dignity." When that practice was brought to the public's attention, it met with a storm of protest—and today Bedouin boys no longer wait on Israeli officers. There are still people in Israel who cling to the belief that an "enlightened occupation" is possible, and many others who are profoundly troubled by the moral rot that inevitably attends an occupying regime. Periodic howls from the watchdogs of such fragile properties as social justice and moral integrity have helped keep the more flagrant transgressions to a minimum. Even so, callous and demeaning behavior toward the workers from the territories—whose ability to stand up for their rights is inhibited by their tenuous political position—is still far too common for us to relax our guard.

Although my own work naturally led me to focus on the abuses, it would be wrong to suggest that the Palestinian experience in the Israeli economy has been a totally negative one. After fourteen years, it is possible to see some definitively positive trends in the integration of workers from the territories into the economy. The unskilled laborers in the service industries and agriculture occupy the lowest rung on the economic ladder, but there is a growing body of blue-collar workers who have found places in large industrial concerns and have acquired technical skills—the key to upgrading their status as well as their wages. On the socioeconomic level, the fruits of working in Israel can be seen throughout the cities and refugee camps of the West Bank. In the camps, for example, TV antennas bristle on the roofs, many people have electrical appliances, and there is a wave of housing expansion and refurbishment. Economic growth has brought a steady rise in the standard of living, with real per capita consumption climbing by an average of more than 7 percent each year since 1967. There have been corresponding demographic shifts. The exodus from the villages to the cities has mounted year by year, and thousands who learned occupational skills through courses offered in Israel are now contributing their talents to enterprises in Jordan and the Persian Gulf.

Such advances in the economic sphere have left their stamp on living conditions and health standards. The infant mortality rate has declined sharply; it now stands at 42 for every 1,000 infants in the West Bank and 47 per 1,000 in Gaza, whereas the corresponding figure in Lebanon is 59 per 1,000, in Jordan 86 per 1,000, in Syria 93, in Egypt 116, and in Saudi Arabia 152. The statistics on housing construction are even more startling. In 1968, building starts covered a total of 580,-000 square feet; in 1979, they accounted for 10,300,000 square feet—a rise of close to 1,700 percent in an eleven-year period.

Widespread economic growth is plain to see throughout the territories, and its effects have not been overlooked by the residents. Yet there are Palestinians who believe it would detract from the honor of their national cause if they were to concede that the military occupation might have played any role in fostering the growth. I recently accepted an invitation to review the record of Israeli agronomists working in the West Bank. The yields they had achieved were most impressive, and they had been responsible for introducing both new crops and the latest methods of cultivation. Nevertheless, a Palestinian employed in Nablus by the Agriculture Ministry categorically denied to me that there was any connection between the contributions of the Israeli experts and the vast improvements in West Bank agriculture. To judge by the present mood in the territories, I would say that such a refusal to give credit where it is due may well become the predominant attitude among the Palestinians.

In a much less deliberate fashion, the occupation and the work of the military government have prompted or accelerated a number of social trends in Palestinian society—some them nothing short of revolutionary. The most noticeable of the shifts relates to the status of women in the occupied territories. When Zuleikha Shihabi, the president of the Women's Union in the West Bank, helped to initiate the public struggle against the occupation back in 1967, the social precedent she set as a woman was just as seismic as the political upheaval. Traditional Arab society has forced its women into a passive role, requiring them to stay within the province of the home. Since 1967 that model has been severely battered as women have assumed the role of political activist and attained the status of national heroine. The poetess Fadwa Toukan of Nablus once met with none other than Defense Minister Moshe Dayan in an effort to open new channels of dialogue on the Middle East dispute. But the masterstroke was the enlistment of women in the civil rebellion, for they galvanized the protest movement in the territories.

Led by the wives of political figures and the mothers of "security prisoners," women have taken the initiative in everything from sitdown strikes in the local offices of the Red Cross to mass funeral processions for youths killed during disturbances. When the National Guidance Committee was founded, Samiha Halil was elected a full member, and she was the star speaker at the rally following Bassam Shaka's arrest. Flouting the dictates of tradition, "Um-Halil" ("Mother Halil") strode up to the platform and delivered a rousing speech—after which the impassioned women of Nablus poured into the streets to prod the young into demonstrating against the military government. When the wives of the deported mayors of Hebron and Halhul went on a hunger strike, a fellow journalist who had joined me in covering the event commented appreciatively, "These women will be our nemesis, not the students or the politicians."

But the Palestinian woman has not limited her sights to formal political protest. The most celebrated heroines have been the young women who have joined the Palestinian terrorist organizations and "seen action" against Israel. Posters of the skyjacker Leila Khaled adorn the rooms of many a Palestinian young woman. High school students boast of their intention to follow in her footsteps or in those of Fatmeh

Barnawi and Maryam Shahshir, who executed several deadly terrorist actions in Israel. Young women have been a moving force behind student demonstrations throughout the West Bank. Taking up the Palestinian flag, they have swept out to confront Israeli soldiers, hurling stones as they marched and working themselves up to a peak of nationalist fervor. Not long ago it would have been an unspeakable scandal for a Palestinian girl to clash with armed troops or be taken into custody. Today even the most traditional and conservative of parents take pride in a daughter's arrest by the military government. And the line isn't drawn even there, for dozens of young women seated in the docks of the military courts have gamely faced stiff prison sentences. It all adds up to an irrevocable break with the past: today's Palestinian girl will not follow in her mother's path as girls did in countless generations gone by.

Three women—the wives of three West Bank mayors—have come into prominence recently for their impressive displays of dignity, grace under pressure, and the ability to handle crises on their own. What the women did was to file appeals with the High Court of Justice on their husbands' behalf. Inaya Shaka, an attractive, extremely gracious woman, made the first approach to the High Court, following her husband's arrest, and set a precedent that was later followed by Yusra Kawasmeh and Jihan Milhem. Mrs. Kawasmeh, an educator by profession, is a woman of traditional tastes and conducts herself according to the rigid norms of Hebron, which is noted for its religious atmosphere. It took the crisis of her husband's deportation to draw her in a single stroke out of her traditional feminine modesty into the glare of public renown. I was a regular visitor in Fahed Kawasmeh's home for four years, and not once in all that time did Mrs. Kawasmeh join her husband in my presence. In fact, amazingly enough, I had never even met her until he was deported. But when I finally did make her acquaintance, I was immediately impressed by her quiet determination and great inner strength.

Samiha Halil was also involved in the suit of Yusra Kawas-meh and Jihan Milhem to have their husbands' deportations reversed, working behind the scenes and attending to the administrative details. "Um-Halil" is a singularly remarkable woman, whose reputation as a dedicated Palestinian nationalist rests not only on her unabashed political activism but also on an extraordinary social welfare enterprise that she founded and runs. Her experiences over the last sixteen years reflect the Palestinian woman's emerging role in public affairs. In 1965, with a loan from the local government of el-Bireh, she established her Family Aid Society. Today, it has grown into a large institute whose annual budget is more than $100,000. In 1965, eight girls took the courses "Um-Halil" organized; today, 225 young women attend her institute, which graduates about 150 each year. The Family Aid Society started out in two rented rooms and now holds its classes in a spacious, well-designed building with proper classrooms and lecture halls. The students are taught sewing, embroidery, weaving, home economics, and cosmetology. Mrs. Halil also supervises an enterprise dedicated to the development of Palestinian folk arts. It employs about 15,000 women in a cottage-industry program to produce the traditional peasant embroidery, which is marketed through outlets run by the Family Aid Society.

In the summer "Um-Halil" opens her institute to hundreds of girls who want to supplement their regular studies with brief courses in English, Hebrew, and "national guidance." Most of the summer students are the offspring of Palestinian emigrants who have returned to the West Bank for their annual vacations. Mrs. Halil gladly explains that her aim is to forge the personalities of young Palestinian women "so that they can take care of themselves and protect their homeland." Each year Samiha Halil expands the scope of her activities, and increasing numbers of people benefit from them. She lends support to Palestinian students throughout the world and provides welfare allowances for orphans and for about 130 needy families that have lost their breadwinners. But she categorically rejects any thought of accepting aid from the Israeli Ministry of Welfare or from the United Nations welfare agencies. She once told me, with unshakable finality, "I won't ever open my palm to those who work against the aims of the Palestinian nation, even though we need every cent we can get."

The new breed of Palestinian woman has broken the barrier of fear—an achievement that has been well exploited by the Palestinian national movement. But a closer examination of the social dynamics that prevail in the territories reveals that, in spite of the breakthrough on the psychopolitical plane, the status of the Arab woman remains essentially unchanged. The same women who lead strikes and go into the streets to demonstrate against the oppression of their people find that their own basic rights to proper and equal political representation are still not recognized. Raymonda Tawil's experience in that regard is symptomatic. Probably one of the best-known Palestinian writers, Mrs. Tawil was an early leader of the women's protest movement in Nablus. When she tried to negotiate an entry into politics, however, she found her way blocked by the traditional prescriptions of male dominance. It therefore appears that the militant image of the Palestinian woman is no more than an eye-catching symbol, lacking real content. The notion of "women's liberation" certainly has not seeped into the refugee camps, where mothers still train their daughters to carry water jugs on their heads and are content with keeping house and caring for their children. Although female students extol the memory of such fallen sisters as Lina Nabulsi and Muntaha Hourani and sing paeans to their valor, the struggle for recognition of their own right to social and political equality remains to be waged within Palestinian society. Meanwhile, there is not even a whisper of a claim to those rights. Many young women have entered institutions of higher learning in the West Bank in recent years, but they have yet to identify with the spirit or symbols of the feminist movement that are so common in the universities of Europe and the United States. More and more Palestinian women, pressed by their husbands to help relieve the strain on the family budget, have begun to take full-time jobs; but they have yet to demand even the social recognition that should accompany this new role.

I cannot believe that the impulse toward equality will remain dormant much longer, however, and Israel is bound to play a role in furthering the process. For one thing, the opportunity to work in the Israeli economy is transforming the Palestinian woman into a financial force to be reckoned with. Her departure from the confines of the home has already altered many firmly rooted conventions, and her contacts with Israeli society have left her questioning other rubrics of her social environment. The transition stage, like many such passages in our personal lives, is likely to prove bewildering and painful at times, and outstanding or pioneering figures can expect to feel isolated or misunderstood.

Raymonda Tawil, known for her outspokenness, has been brutally frank in all her dealings with officials of the military government. Yet, in spite of her anger, she has been equally frank in admitting what a tremendous impact her encounters with Israeli society have had. The daughter of a wealthy family from Acre, Mrs. Tawil had some acquaintance with Jewish society in Palestine even before the establishment of Israel. After the Six Day War, she took the bold step of enrolling in the Hebrew University, and there she came into close contact with Israel's open society. Her brief and abortive foray into the all-male province of Palestinian politics has left her estranged from the mainstream political movements in the West Bank. Equally unfortunate were her statements in support of "progressive leftist circles in Israel" and her attempts to establish a dialogue with the Israeli left, which have damaged her standing among her own people.

The novelist Sakhar Khalifa, of Bir Zeit College, has kept her finger on the pulse of social revolution in the territories. Her first book, *The Cactus,* was translated into Hebrew—rare for a Palestinian work of fiction—and her new book, *The Sun-*

flower, traces trends that have taken hold in the West Bank, with special attention to the problems faced by the Palestinian woman. Perhaps that was why she was in such a diffident mood when, after reading the manuscript, I went to see her in her Ramallah home. "The publication of the book will probably do me harm," she brooded. "I have a feeling that it won't be properly understood."

The currents affecting the role and status of the Palestinian woman run parallel to those of another process that is having the same kind of stressful effect on society in the territories—the growing antagonism of Palestinian youth toward the rigid codes of the patriarchal social system. Thousands of young people who work in Israel return in a defiant mood from their daily stints in its Western-oriented cities. The gloom of the casbah depresses them, and the thought of resubmerging themselves in a society that denies its young a right to their own views drives them to rebellion. The trend has been accompanied by some particularly sad gestures that testify to the extent of their confusion. Young Arabs working in the cities have adopted Hebrew names and tried to pass for Israelis—understandable enough as attempts to blunt or evade the patent hostility directed at them by Israelis. Nevertheless, nationalist circles in the West Bank are deeply concerned at their choosing camouflage over the psychological shield of demonstrative national pride.

In Jerusalem, the largest city in the West Bank, all the changes are felt with redoubled force. Young women walk about the streets in the latest fashions, and skin-tight jeans are gradually replacing the modest, conservative dress that was once the sign of a proper upbringing. Young men and women who work in West Jerusalem often return there at night to frequent the city's entertainment spots. They do not get a very cordial reception from the Israelis, but that does not deter them from trying to melt into the crowds on the streets of the Jewish city. But time is not working in favor of this tendency to assimilate with and placate the Israelis; it has proved to be

not a very rewarding tack, and the frustration and disappoint
ment of these young Arabs grows from day to day.

Future chroniclers of social history will undoubtedly have
much to say about the ways in which the Israeli occupation
changed the face of Palestinian life in the West Bank and Gaza.
Paradoxically, the crux of the whole upheaval in Palestinian
society is that, alongside the social ferment and economic
growth Israel has precipitated, it has also precipitated, without
planning or even being conscious of it, the development of a
Palestinian national consciousness and, inevitably, a Palestinian national entity. There is a startling similarity between
the mood that took hold in Jewish society during the period
of the British Mandate and the current mood in the West Bank.

People in the territories have even begun to speak of the
Palestinian "state-in-the-making," just as the Jews of Palestine
did in the 1930s and 1940s.

Evidence of the trend can be found in all spheres of life.
The Palestinian theater, which sometimes operates underground, has staged productions on aspects of the Arab experience in the Israeli labor market, on the expropriation of land,
and, of course, on the "Palestinian hero." Suleiman Mansour,
an artist from Ramallah (who used to work as a film editor for
Israel Television, but left because of threats on his life from
the PLO), has done many works depicting the hardships of the
common man in the West Bank. In 1978, he painted a master-
work showing a suffering Arab stooped under the weight of a
gigantic teardrop with Arab Jerusalem inside it. Mansour
opened a gallery to show his work, but the military government immediately closed it on the ground that he was engaging in political activity. "The very air we breathe is political,"
he responded angrily. "We eat and drink nationalism, so how
can I avoid doing 'political' paintings?"

Mansour's point has not been lost on Israel, and sometimes it almost seems as if the dedication of the West Bank's
leaders and people to the cause of national independence
might have brought about a change of heart in this country.

High-ranking IDF officers, political figures, and academics have softened their implacable stand against the creation of a Palestinian entity, and some have gone so far as to admit that there is no getting around the eventual establishment of an independent Palestinian state. Whether such a state comes into being in the foreseeable future depends on a broad constellation of factors, including superpower rivalries, clashes of interests within the Arab world, and other factors that go far beyond the will and desires of either the Palestinians or the Israelis. But internal developments in that direction are quite unmistakable. The first time I saw the Palestinian flag unfurled during a demonstration was early in the 1970s. Today no public gathering is held without that flag in evidence. Even schoolchildren have grown adept at producing homemade versions of it out of sheets painted with watercolors. The West Bank is awash with nationalist literature featuring the Palestinian colors, on book jackets and elsewhere; the PLO anthem resounds through the halls of Bir Zeit and other schools. Israel has offered the inhabitants of the occupied territories an autonomy plan as sketched out in the Camp David agreements. But anyone at all in touch with reality knows that the inhabitants of the West Bank believe they already exercise a greater degree of self-rule than the Camp David plan envisions.

A few statistics will give a feeling of where things stand in the West Bank today. The educational system has undergone a total revolution. In 1967 there were 6,167 classes being held in the West Bank; today the number has risen to 11,187. Since the occupation began, the number of pupils has increased from 250,000 to more than 400,000. The number of Israelis holding civilian jobs with the military government—507—has hardly grown at all, while the number of Arab employees has risen fourfold: 16,378 officials, administrators, and professionals are currently overseeing various spheres of activity in the West Bank. Moreover, West Bank political leaders maintain that this body of officials is capable of running a complex government bureaucracy.

Distracted by the frenzy of the disturbances and the strident sloganeering, people in Israel have tended to overlook the growing self-confidence of the Palestinians and the advances they have made in the economic, educational, and cultural spheres. The military government has taken credit for these developments, but it is loath to admit that the same processes it characterizes as "positive" have other implications that counteract any aspirations the Israeli government has to maintain a hold on the West Bank and Gaza. Like shamans placing their faith in the power of symbols to control events, the military governors demand that their thousands of Palestinian employees refer to the West Bank as "Judea and Samaria" in all official dealings and documents. While the Palestinians accede to such bizarre rules, the effect of them is to intensify the longing for independence.

Lately, however, I have sensed a shift in mood from the festering resentment that grows out of dismay to the kind of upbeat tone that comes when a dream starts to take shape. "It doesn't matter what they call the area—Judea and Samaria or even the 'liberated territories,'" an official of the Agriculture Ministry in Nablus recently told me. "Beneath their name, whatever it is, Palestine is coming into being." After returning from a meeting with Yasir Arafat, Fahed Kawasmeh, who can hardly be considered a callow dreamer, said to me, with the utmost confidence, "In another year, you'll need a passport to visit us." But I was struck most of all by the musings of Nazieh Hijazi, a journalist from Hebron, who used to work for Israel Television and has suffered at the hands of Arabs and Israelis alike. "We are undergoing a process of renaissance," he said, "just like the Jews did before the state. And like the Jews, we will bring in our exiles; we will bring Palestinian experts to the territories—professors from the universities in the United States and the Persian Gulf—and we will establish a magnificent state."

13
A RETURN TO SANITY

When my friends heard that I was writing a book about my encounters with the Arabs of the West Bank and Gaza, many of them cautioned me against taking a clear-cut stand either for or against any of the possible solutions to the problem of the territories—the autonomy plan, the so-called "Jordanian option," an independent Palestinian state. They needn't have worried, for I wouldn't presume to tell the inhabitants of the West Bank and Gaza what is best for them or how to map out their future. That is something they will have to decide for themselves. However, I do stand on my right as an Israeli to warn my own countrymen, in no uncertain terms, that a broad segment of the population is misreading the state of affairs in the territories and leading us deeper into a morass that can only be to our continuing detriment.

A Border Police patrol car parked in front of the Red Cross headquarters in East Jerusalem may seem to be keeping the peace there, but its presence actually exacerbates the mood of hostility and whets the appetite for national independence. The arrest of hundreds of schoolchildren, the smashing open of locks on shops closed by strikes, the acceleration of Jewish settlement in the territories—all these actions may appear to restore calm and strengthen Israel's position in the territories. But peel off the thin veneer of order and control and you find a welter of turmoil that seems to be spreading wider every day. In recent months I have seen nine- and ten-year-olds marching with protesters and waving the Palestinian flag, their high-pitched voices piping out "My Country, My Country" in the most devastating rendition of that anthem I am ever likely to hear.

But it is not just unrest that is spreading. There is also a perceptible growth of certitude among the Palestinians that the more repressive the Israeli rule becomes, the closer they are to seeing it ended. In November of 1980, an officer of the military government visiting Bir Zeit College ordered the administration to dismantle an exhibition of drawings by Palestinian prisoners on the ground that "they're prisoners, not artists." Whatever logic the IDF saw in that order, the organizers of the exhibition saw it as another sign of Israel's weakness —that the military government could be intimidated by an art exhibit! About a month later, I saw an Arab girl who had been wounded in the leg by Israeli fire during the breakup of a demonstration. She was hopping along on her other leg, calming her friends with shouts of "It's OK, it's OK!" I couldn't take my eyes off her: the calmness, the presence of mind, the look of triumph on her face despite the pain, all seemed to sum up where things stand in the territories. The Palestinian people are coming together in the shadow of Israel and in response to Israel's efforts to snuff out their spirit. The same was true of the people of Israel when they faced down the British in the 1940s—so we really should know better. The harder the blows, the more they signal desperation, and the Palestinians are confident that time is on their side.

They may well be right, for the reaction in Israel to the evidences of a bankrupt policy is, above all, confusion. Some of my countrymen still fall back on the shabby cliché that "the only language that kind understands is the language of force." Others feel helpless to cope with the absurdity of a young, proud, vibrant country like Israel—the product of a determined nationalist movement—expending so much of its energy trying to suppress a kindred nationalist movement. Let me be clear: I do not suspect any of my countrymen—least of all those I have served with in the Israel Defense Forces—of

malice in their attitude toward the Arabs of the occupied ter
ritories. In fact, I suspect that most Israelis, looking at what is
happening in the West Bank and Gaza, secretly wish the whole
Palestinian problem would just go away. However, we may be
surrounded by myths and symbols, but we are not living a fairy
tale, and no magic wand or lord of the rings is going to banish
that gremlin from our national life and leave us free to live
happily ever after. We will have to forge our own fate. The
people of Israel have been doing that for decades, taking the
bit in their teeth and creating something quite extraordinary
here. To suffer a failure of will at this juncture would be more
of a tragedy than I am prepared to contemplate.

Yet not only must we act; we must act soon. The relentless
friction between Israel and its neighbors, in the territories and
beyond, is causing positions to harden and polarizing the
camps ever more drastically. No longer is the enmity between
the two peoples perceived as just the side effect of a political
dispute that can be solved by negotiation. Many Arabs now
impute to Zionism and the State of Israel secret racist designs,
while Jews have begun to speak of an unbridgeable chasm of
hatred of the Arabs. Fahed Kawasmeh sincerely accepts the
spurious *Protocols of the Elders of Zion* as genuine and believes
in the existence of a plot by the Jews—"that presumptuous,
arrogant people"—to take over the world. His neighbors in
Kiryat Arba—and farther off in Tel Aviv—call him definitely a
Nazi. Rather than talking to each other, both sides retire behind their barriers of self-righteousness and hurl racist epi-
thets. Incredibly, no one stands up and shouts, "Stop! We
won't tolerate this anymore." Whatever are we waiting for?

For the past seven years, my work has been based on the
premise that if the Israeli public is consistently and faithfully
informed about what is happening in the territories—complex
or unpleasant as the truth may be—it will be able to face the
problem and deal with it sensibly. Today my own primary
conclusion—drawn from an intimate knowledge of what has
been going on in the West Bank and Gaza since 1967—is that

there are no simple answers, only simple-minded formulas. I respect the security concerns voiced by officers in the military government, but I am nonetheless convinced that it is a mistake to base policy in the territories solely on security considerations. In fact, I have more than once been astounded and enraged by the operations directives that have followed from discussions taking only security needs into account.

The military governors protest that it is not their job to make policy; they merely must see to it that law and order are maintained. Yet, in the name of law and order, human rights are trampled on, respect for the law is undermined, and order is systematically subverted. In the name of law and order, soldiers broke into a school in Beit Jalla and fired tear gas at the pupils (who got little comfort from the fact that the officers responsible were subsequently punished). In the name of law and order, hundreds of students have been arrested, curfews have been imposed, body searches have been carried out—and today there is less respect for the law and less faith in the virtue of order than ever before. And still the military government continues to intone those words, as if they were an incantation that would make the moral, social, and political ramifications of its stubborn, brutish policy disappear.

Exasperated by the present impasse, but frightened, I think, by the vigor of the Palestinian national movement, some people in Israel delude themselves that it is possible to turn back the clock and place the West Bank under Jordanian sovereignty again. I find it hard to believe that this solution, or any other, could be imposed on the Palestinians, any more than a solution could be imposed on Israel. But the same error is committed by nationalists in the Arab camp when they speak of turning the clock back to 1948 and denying the Jewish people a sovereign political existence. The irony is that the extremists in both camps are united in their outlandish belief that the *other* side can be forcibly denied a creative and independent life. Intellectuals and humanists the world over have offered solutions to our problem, but too often the formulas proposed from afar, which may look good on paper, have failed to take into account the particular sensitivities of those who must live with the results. Anyone who presumes to advise us on the subject must show an equal measure of understanding for the wounds and aspirations of the Jewish Holocaust survivors and those of the Arab refugees scattered throughout the Middle East. That is why I am convinced that the peoples of this region and this country will somehow have to hammer out a solution by themselves, for themselves, and together.

Exactly how that will come about is much less easy to predict. But as one whose interests run more to how the problem is approached than to the details of a solution, I think it wouldn't hurt us to examine some of our ingrained patterns of behavior and our assumptions about ourselves. In writing this book, I have focused on how my status as an Arab Israeli has put me in a unique position to examine the various sides of the Middle East dispute. Torn by loyalty to their country and an identification with their people, the Arabs of Israel are particularly conscious of the need to find a sane solution to the problem. For decades, the assumption has been that if the sides would only sit down and talk to each other, reason would prevail. President Sadat's breakthrough trip to Jerusalem and the peace agreement later reached by Israel and Egypt give further credence to that assumption. But as a professional observer of the dynamic that applies between Israel and the territories, I have been impressed by the power of a force that operates on another, deeper level and that exercises a great hold over our lives: the might of symbols. The stock images for Israelis are the sensitive soldier and the young pioneers who built this country, hoe in one hand and rifle in the other (for a time, our currency even depicted two such figures, as the embodiment of the State of Israel). No matter how hardened our soldiers may have become today, or how differently our contemporary settlers behave, just let someone invoke the symbol of settling the land and immediately those two noble, starry-eyed young people who used to gaze out at us from the fifty-pound note come to mind. The Palestinians have adopted as their symbol the daring guerrilla, kaffiyeh wrapped around his face, rifle in hand, body taut in a pose of defiance, and more recently they have supplemented it with a martyrology of young people who have died in the civil strife in the West Bank.

I do not mean to mock such symbols. On the contrary, I have enormous respect for them, because I know how powerfully they hold sway over our minds, lead us into instinctive reactions, seduce us to think in terms of one-dimensional, either-or, uncomplicated stereotypes, when life is not like that at all. The symbols I would choose to epitomize the present experience of our peoples are far more complex, as befits the complexity of the situation, and far more authentic, I think. Of course, mine is a very personal choice; both these symbols that I think apt touch on me directly and reflect aspects of my own identity. One of my symbols is an Israeli soldier, the other a Palestinian journalist. Neither, I am sure, will go down in history as heroes. Both are casualties of the Israeli-Palestinian conflict—as we all are, in some way. Perhaps that is why I think their fortunes are symbolic for us all.

In June of 1980, Suleiman Khirwabi, an IDF demolition expert from the Druse village of Julis in the Galilee, was sent to defuse an explosive device planted in the home of Ibrahim Tawil, the mayor of el-Bireh. (Bassam Shaka and Karim Halaf were wounded the same day by similar bombs.) Before he could dismantle the device, however, it went off and badly wounded him, leaving him blind. Tawil and the councilmen of neighboring Ramallah wanted to visit Khirwabi in the hospital as a gesture of gratitude and respect. But they hesitated—and rightly, for Khirwabi's parents were so distraught with grief over their son's tragedy that they were as likely to lash out at the mayor as to thank him for his kindness. When Odeh Rentisi, the deputy mayor of Ramallah, called to ask my advice, I hinted that it would be best to stay away, for fear the gesture would backfire on the well-meaning visitors.

Nazieh Hijazi, the journalist from Hebron whose winsome, glowing words about the Palestinian renaissance I quoted earlier, has been buffeted by other winds of fortune. Immediately after the 1967 war he was drawn to the cause of the el-Fatah groups operating in the Hebron area, but when he saw the ruinous effects of the violence he broke off all ties with el-Fatah and went to work for Israel Television. He remained with the Arabic programming division for eight years, and that was where I met him—quiet, unassuming, reliable, and fastidious in his speech. In time Nazieh left to work in Abu Dhabi, to build himself a nest egg for the future. But he remained in touch with his friends. In fact, he used to write to me in Hebrew, and that may be one reason he fell afoul of the el-Fatah intelligence operation. At any rate, he was taken off to Beirut for interrogation. Alarmed, his father organized a delegation of notables from Hebron to go to Lebanon and sue for his release. Fortunately, their mission succeeded, and Nazieh returned home and rejoined the television staff.

When he was rehired, he of course told the Broadcasting Authority's security officer about his recent past, and that, presumably, was the end of it. Then, a few days later, Nazieh was arrested—this time by the Israeli authorities—and some of the newspapers published stories about the "entrapment of a television reporter suspected of terrorist activities and espionage." His working colleagues were incensed that one of their own had turned traitor, but I was not so easily convinced of Nazieh's guilt. I went to see him in the Hebron prison, and, sure enough, the prison commander (a Druse officer from Usifiyeh) told me that there was no evidence, and not even any grounds for suspicion, of Nazieh's alleged terrorist activities. A few days later my friend was released. And the press that had made such a big splash about his arrest was satisfied with a scant few lines buried on inside pages to note that he had been freed for lack of evidence.

Nazieh went back to work as a journalist, but an item he wrote about Fahed Kawasmeh's personal bank account in

Amman incurred the anger of his fellow Hebronites (it could have been inferred from the story that the mayor had embezzled public funds), and his life was threatened. He finally knuckled under to the pressure and quit his job. Now Nazieh plans to emigrate to Europe, as a last chance of escaping his hapless fate. Some 20,000 Palestinians a year emigrate from the territories to the Arab countries, Europe, and the United States, and few ever return to their homeland.

Perhaps that is the last symbol we should examine: "the land"—that mixture of homeland, country, soil, with all its attendant allusions and connotations. It is surely the most powerful of all symbols for both of the peoples that inhabit this country, and I believe that much of what we do to each other is a function of being under its spell. Spring has come to Israel and the West Bank with a vengeance this year. The countryside is a dark, lush green (by late May that color will be bleached away by the Mediterranean sun), and on the coast between Mount Carmel and the Judean hills the heavy perfume of orange blossoms drenches the air. Soon honeysuckle will be in bloom, and then jasmine, filling this country with new colors and scents. It is easiest in the spring to understand the passion that its warring inhabitants feel for this land. But the sheer power of this particular spring has made me think that perhaps the land is mocking us for accepting the fallacy that we can possess it.

The Zionist pioneers came to this country to build and be built by it. They drained the malarial swamps of the northern valleys and turned the rich soil into patchworks of green and gold, adding fishponds that flash like sheets of silver as the sun reflects off their surface. It was a remarkable achievement, and they gloried in it by claiming that they had made the desert bloom. But I have seen the desert in bloom this year, in colors no crops can reproduce, and it was only the rain and the sun and the soil, by themselves, that brought out that riotous profusion of beauty. Sometimes I think that this land is mocking our vanity and visions of lordship. We may shed one another's blood and delude ourselves that if we bash, smash, shatter, and ultimately stamp out a competing dream, we can by sheer dint of force overcome this land as well; we can have this soil, this sunshine, these showers exclusively to ourselves. But when a spring comes like this year's, I wonder if the land isn't mocking us by glutting our senses with its outburst of raw, irrepressible life while we go on spreading death and destruction in its name.

I am not a romantic by nature, and I'm not sure why the spring has affected me so deeply this year. Perhaps it's because I have witnessed so many ugly brushes with death lately. Or perhaps it's because this spring I have a new son, whose arrival has touched off a rush of unaccustomed musings in me. We give our children life, and then we raise them to be ready to die for their country. I want my children to be eager to live for the betterment and to the credit of their country. I want them to love it, to enjoy it, and to share it—just as they share a multitude of traditions and identities, as Israelis, Arabs, and Druse, and are all the richer for it. I have no pat answers for them or for anyone else. There is no moral to this tale—except, perhaps, the tentative hint that, having seen our mistakes and failures, our children may value peace over the illusion of possession and may learn the secret of sharing without losing. I hope so for their sakes. I hope so for ours. And I hope it doesn't take too much longer.

Dalyat el-Carmel–Jerusalem
April 1981

INDEX

PLO. *See* Palestine Liberation
    Organization
Popular Front for the Liberation
    of Palestine, 61, 79, 122, 195
Porat, Hanen, 205–7
Prison Service, 240
Protocols of the Elders of Zion, 283
Purim caper of 1981, 222–25

Rabat Conference of Arab
    Nations (1974), 99–100, 181,
    194
Rabin, Yitzhak, 98, 114, 128, 211,
    229
Radio Cairo, 19
Rafiah salient, 203, 204, 228; use
    of child labor in, 266, 267–68
Rakah. *See* New Communist List
Ramadan (holy month), 7
Ramallah, 55, 90, 91, 104–5, 110,
    119, 121, 122, 124, 125, 171,
    172, 176, 177, 181, 184, 195,
    197, 207, 220, 221, 250, 277,
    278, 286; mayoral elections
    of 1976, 116, 117; reaction to
    Sadat's visit to Israel, 124;
    reaction to tensions in
    Hebron, 139, 151, 156, 165
Ramallah Chamber of Commerce,
    71
Ramle prison, 133, 134
Rayes, Zuheir, 122
Red Crescent, 122, 189
Red Cross, 281
Red Sea, 99
Refugee camps (in Gaza), 78–79,
    80, 82, 86, 87, 88–89. *See also*
    names of camps
Regularization Ordinance No. 1
    of 1967, 35
Rentisi, Odeh, 286
Rifai, Abdul Munem, 92–93
Rivol Hotel (East Jerusalem), 47
Rockefeller Museum, 44
Rogers, William, 22
Rogers plan, 92
Rohan, Dennis Michael, 47
Roman Empire, 206
Rujeib village, 128, 129, 211,
    214

Sa'adeh, Osama, 183

Sabru, Sheikh Sa'id, 30
Sabuba, Atzam, 198
Sadat, Anwar, 96, 98, 168, 174;
    visit to Jerusalem, 123–24,
    179, 285
Safed, city of, 24, 38, 246
Safiye, Anton, 31–32
Sahnein vineyards, 246, 247, 248,
    249
Sa'ih, Sheikh Abdul Hamid, 36,
    38–39, 65; deported, 39
Sajour village, 17
Saleh, Abdul Jawad, 90, 91, 107,
    108, 162
Saloma, Yahoshua, 151–52, 153
Samaria, 51, 99, 119, 181, 191,
    198, 204, 209, 210, 218, 280
Samua village, 190
Sarid, Yossi, 266, 267
Saudi Arabia, 271
Sebastia, ancient site of, 210
Self-determination, 4, 244
Settlements. *See* Jewish
    settlements
"Settlers' Buffet" (Cave of the
    Patriarchs), 142
Shafi, Dr. Haydar Abdul, 122,
    174, 175
Shahshir, Maryam, 273
Shaka, Bassam, 115, 117, 128–34,
    135, 144, 156, 182, 195, 218,
    251; Amman conference
    (1980), 171; arrested, 132,
    133, 168, 272; Beit Hanina
    meeting (1978), 122; Elon
    Moreh affair, 128–29, 134;
    General Matt meeting, 120,
    129–30, 131, 134, 148;
    mayoral election of, 111–13;
    protest rally against Camp
    David agreements, 125–26;
    wounded, 135, 136, 286
Shaka, Mrs. Inaya, 273
Shaka, Walid, 170
Shari'a Court, 36
Sharm a-Sheikh, 96
Sharon, Ariel, 84, 150, 159, 210;
    Knesset scene, 212–13
Shati refugee camp, 78–79, 82,
    86, 87
Shavei Hebron, yeshiva of, 222
Shayukh village, 218